The Germans and the Holocaust

Vermont Studies on Nazi Germany and the Holocaust

General Editor:
Alan E. Steinweis, Miller Distinguished Professor of Holocaust Studies and Director of the Carolyn and Leonard Miller Center for Holocaust Studies, University of Vermont

Editorial Committee:
Jonathan D. Huener, University of Vermont
Francis R. Nicosia, University of Vermont
Susanna Schrafstetter, University of Vermont

The University of Vermont has been an important venue for research on the Holocaust since Raul Hilberg began his work there in 1956. These volumes reflect the scholarly activity of UVM's Miller Center for Holocaust Studies. They combine original research with interpretive synthesis, and address research questions of interdisciplinary and international interest.

Medicine and Medical Ethics in Nazi Germany: Origins, Practices, Legacies
Edited by Francis R. Nicosia and Jonathan Huener

Business and Industry in Nazi Germany
Edited by Francis R. Nicosia and Jonathan Huener

The Arts in Nazi Germany: Continuity, Conformity, Change
Edited by Jonathan Huener and Francis R. Nicosia

Jewish Life in Nazi Germany: Dilemmas and Responses
Edited by Francis R. Nicosia and David Scrase

The Law in Nazi Germany: Ideology, Opportunism, and the Perversion of Justice
Edited by Alan E. Steinweis and Robert D. Rachlin

The Germans and the Holocaust: Popular Responses to the Persecution and Murder of the Jews
Edited by Susanna Schrafstetter and Alan E. Steinweis

Nazism, the Holocaust, and the Middle East: Arab and Turkish Responses
Edited by Francis R. Nicosia and Boğaç Ergene

THE GERMANS AND
THE HOLOCAUST

Popular Responses to the Persecution and Murder of the Jews

Edited by
Susanna Schrafstetter
and
Alan E. Steinweis

berghahn
NEW YORK · OXFORD
www.berghahnbooks.com

First published in 2016 by

Berghahn Books

www.berghahnbooks.com

©2016, 2017 The Miller Center for Holocaust Studies at the University of Vermont
First paperback edition published in 2017

Library of Congress Cataloging-in-Publication Data

The Germans and the Holocaust : popular responses to the persecution and
  murder of the Jews / edited by Susanna Schrafstetter and Alan E. Steinweis.
    pages cm
  "The contributions to this volume are based on lectures delivered at a sympo-
sium on The German People and the Persecution of the Jews, which took place
at the University of Vermont on April 22, 2012."—Preface.
  Includes index.
  ISBN 978-1-78238-952-1 (hardback : alk. paper) — ISBN 978-1-78533-
  736-9 (paperback) — ISBN 978-1-78238-953-8 (ebook)
    1. Jews—Persecutions—Germany—History—Congresses. 2. Antisemitism—
Germany—History—19th century—Congresses. 3. Antisemitism—Germany—
History—20th century—Congresses. 4. Germany—Jews—Public opinion.—
Congresses. 5. Public opinion—Germany—Congresses. 6. Germany—Ethnic
relations—History—Congresses. I. Schrafstetter, Susanna, editor. II. Steinweis,
Alan E., editor.
  DS134.25.G46 2015
  940.53'18—dc23

British Library Cataloguing in Publication Data

A catalogue record for this book is available from the British Library

ISBN: 978-1-78238-952-1 (hardback)
ISBN: 978-1-78533-736-9 (paperback)
ISBN: 978-1-78238-953-8 (ebook)

CONTENTS

Contents

Appendixes

PREFACE

THIS VOLUME GREW OUT OF a symposium titled "The German People and the Persecution of the Jews," which took place at the University of Vermont on 22 April 2012. Organized by the Carolyn and Leonard Miller Center for Holocaust Studies at the University of Vermont, this was the sixth symposium bearing the name of Carolyn and Leonard Miller, generous supporters of the center's work and great friends of the university.

Established to honor the legacy of Raul Hilberg, who served on the faculty of the University of Vermont for more than three decades, the Miller Center for Holocaust Studies is committed to furthering research and education about the Holocaust and to serving as a forum for the presentation and discussion of new perspectives on the subject. Hilberg's pioneering scholarship remains a model and a standard for scholars and is an inspiration for the center's programming and for publications such as this book. The Miller Symposia have contributed significantly to the center's efforts to explore insufficiently charted areas in the history of the Third Reich and the Holocaust. Our goal in organizing them has been to address topical, or even controversial, themes in that history, relying on the expertise of some of the most accomplished scholars and other authorities in the field.

The first Miller Symposium, held in April 2000, convened some of the world's leading scholars in the history of eugenics and the German medical establishment during the Third Reich. It resulted in the anthology *Medicine and Medical Ethics in Nazi Germany: Origins, Practices, Legacies*, published by Berghahn Books in 2002. The second Miller Symposium, with its focus on German business and industry under Nazism, took place in April 2002. It brought together scholars who are among the most respected and innovative analysts of German business, industry, and finance in the years of the Third Reich. The resulting volume, *Business and Industry in Nazi Germany*, was published by Berghahn

Books in 2004. The third Miller Symposium in 2004 featured some of the most important scholars in the history of the arts in Nazi Germany. Their contributions to the volume *The Arts in Nazi Germany: Continuity, Conformity, Change,* published by Berghahn Books in 2006, address, among other subjects, the activities of artists, writers, musicians, filmmakers, and Jewish cultural institutions during the Nazi era. The fourth Miller Symposium brought some of the world's leading scholars of the history of German Jewry to the University of Vermont in 2006. Their papers addressed research and controversies in the tragic history of German Jews from Hitler's appointment as chancellor in January 1933 to the initiation of the "Final Solution" in 1941. The volume was published by Berghahn Books in 2010 under the title *Jewish Life in Nazi Germany: Dilemmas and Responses.* The fifth Miller Symposium, held in April 2009, was devoted to "The Law in Nazi Germany." The volume with the identical title was published by Berghahn Books in 2013, representing a collaboration between historians and practitioners of the law.

The present volume deals with one of the most important and emotionally charged questions to have arisen out of the Nazi years: the responses of the German people to the persecution and mass murder of the Jews. It addresses this subject in a manner that is at once scholarly and accessible to students and non-expert readers. In this respect, the volume fulfills one of the key elements of the mission of the Miller Center, namely to promote "public awareness about the events that brought about, comprise, and continue to issue from the Holocaust."

ABBREVIATIONS

DAF	Deutsche Arbeitsfront (German Labor Front)
DP	Displaced person
Gestapo	Geheime Staatspolizei (Secret State Police)
HJ	Hitlerjugend (Hitler Youth)
JDC	Joint Distribution Committee
NS	National Socialist
NSKK	Nationalsozialistisches Kraftfahrkorps (National Socialist Motor Corps)
NSDAP	Nationalsozialistische Deutsche Arbeiterpartei (National Socialist German Workers Party—the Nazi Party)
SA	Sturmabteilung (Storm Detachment—the Nazi Brownshirts)
SD	Sicherheitsdienst (Security Service)
SPD/Sopade	Sozialdemokratische Partei Deutschlands (Social Democratic Party of Germany)
SS	Schutzstaffel (Protection Squadron—the Nazi Blackshirts)
UNRRA	United Nations Relief and Rehabilitation Administration

FIGURES

Figure 1. Members of the Hitler Youth building a snowman with features based on anti-Semitic stereotypes.

Introduction

THE GERMAN PEOPLE
AND THE HOLOCAUST

————&&&————

Susanna Schrafstetter and Alan E. Steinweis

ON 14 NOVEMBER 1938, FOUR days after the nationwide "Kristallnacht" pogrom had wrought devastation on the Jews of Germany, the chief of the Gestapo office of the northwest city of Bielefeld circulated a memorandum to the local secret police offices in the region. He was interested in collecting keys pieces of information about the pogrom and its consequences.[1] Which synagogues had been destroyed by fire? Which had suffered severe damage? Which Jewish-owned businesses had been destroyed or damaged, and what was the financial extent of the damages? Which homes of Jews had been vandalized? Which Jews had been killed or injured? What property had been plundered from Jews? In all, the inquiry listed fourteen sets of questions. The last of these related to "responses to the action in the population." The Gestapo wanted to know who had uttered criticism of the pogrom, where they lived, and precisely what it was that they had said. Scientific surveys of popular opinion of the sort that we take for granted today did not exist in Germany in 1938. But this did not mean that the Nazi regime made no effort to keep track of what the population was thinking about a wide variety of questions, including the persecution of the Jews.

One of the responses to the inquiry from the Bielefeld Gestapo office came from the mayor of Amt Borgentreich, an administrative district consisting of several communities located in the triangle between Paderborn, Kassel, and Göttingen.[2] Writing on 17 November, the mayor summarized the situation in the following way:

Large segments of the population did not understand the operation, or rather, they did not want to understand it. Some people felt sorry for the Jews. In particular, they felt sorry for them because their property was damaged and because male Jews were sent to concentration camps. To be sure, these sentiments were not shared by the entire population, but I would estimate that around here at least 60 percent of the population thought in this way. [See Appendix E.]

On its surface, this document provides a useful piece of information in a fairly straightforward way. But there are several respects in which the document points up the difficulty of assessing the responses of "ordinary Germans" to the persecution of the Jews. First, it is probably impossible to ascertain whether the mayor's quantitative estimate rested on shoot-from-the-hip speculation or from a more serious consideration of the facts. Second, it is extremely difficult to adjust for the possible biases that lay behind the mayor's estimate. Was he understating the extent of popular criticism of the pogrom to avoid creating the impression that he had failed to instill sufficient enthusiasm for Nazism in his population? Or was he exaggerating the extent of the criticism because he had considered the pogrom a foolish mistake by the regime's leadership? If we were to presume that his estimate was accurate, then what are we to make of it? Do we emphasize the 60 percent majority of the population that reacted to the pogrom disapprovingly, or do we focus on the very sizable 40 percent minority that did not respond negatively? Then there is the question of whether and to what extent Borgentreich may be considered typical, and, if not, what peculiarities of the community may account for the actions and attitudes of its citizens? Even when we have a detailed, contemporary document purporting to report systematically on public opinion, historians remain confronted by perplexing questions of interpretation.

At the time of the Kristallnacht, Lore Walb was a nineteen-year-old woman living in Alzey, a town located about thirty-five miles southwest of Frankfurt. Walb, who possessed literary and journalist ambitions, kept a diary in which she recorded her impressions of the major events of her day. She was an admirer of the Nazi regime. Decades later she would observe that she had been convinced that "everything the Nazis did is correct, the National Socialist behaves honorably, is a good person, righteous, reliable, truthful." She had embraced the truth of the Nazi slogan "The Jews are our misfortune" and had acknowledged the necessity of marginalizing and persecuting them.

After World War II, Walb became a journalist, retiring in 1979 after twenty years as director of the Women and Family Department of Bavarian State Radio. She published her diary in 1997.[3] Rather than let the document speak for itself, Walb engaged critically with her own record of events from the Nazi era. One question she put to herself almost sixty years after the event was why her diary for 1938 ended with an entry for 6 November. In retrospect she recognized what had been her inability at the time to confront the "the terror against the German Jews." She had possessed full knowledge of what had taken place during the Kristallnacht and sensed that a great crime had been committed, but she could not process the information lest it undermine her "entire orientation system," which had been based on a positive attitude toward Nazism.[4] The dissonance between her ideology and her instinctive grasp of the wrongness of the pogrom generated feelings of shame, and the shame, in turn, resulted in silence. The momentous events of November 1938 simply remained absent from her diary.

The Walb diary offers important lessons for historians. Even such a so-called ego document, which was not intended for publication at the time it was created, can contain significant discrepancies between what was witnessed and what was recorded. People withhold the truth not only from others, but also from themselves. And when they report on events in their diaries, correspondence, or memoirs, they can do so in ways that are distorting, self-serving, or based on faulty memory.

The reliability and biases of source materials will arise time and again in the following chapters. Scholars and students of all historical events should, of course, remain conscious of the strengths and limitations of their sources. But special vigilance is in order when examining the questions at the heart of this volume: How did ordinary Germans respond to the persecution and mass murder of the Jews between 1933 and 1945? What did they know, when did they know it, and how did they react? From the time of the Holocaust into the present day, these questions have generated intense and often emotional disagreements. When carried out in the public arena, such disagreements have often been based more on emotion and the received wisdom of collective memory than on a sober examination of the historical evidence.[5] Communities of memory in many countries and across several generations have had a strong emotional stake in the question, and their perceptions have often been shaped by anger, guilt, and shame. As the Nazi period recedes into the past, however, the passing of generations offers the opportunity for a more sober and nuanced appreciation of this difficult history.

The discrepancy between the historical significance of the topic, on the one hand, and the fragmentary nature of the evidence that is available to analyze it, on the other, has posed a continual challenge to scholars. Fortunately, historians have persisted in their efforts to find new and previously overlooked sources. Serious scholarship in this area has accelerated, rather than slowed, in the past few years.[6] The aim of this volume is to encapsulate some of these recent findings and to present some new, original work that is still in progress. The chapters that follow reflect the enormous sophistication with which contemporary scholars have been approaching a controversial subject.

When considering German responses to the persecution and mass murder of the Jews, it is important to remain very cognizant of the chronology and geography of the Holocaust. Between January 1933 and September 1939, Nazi measures directly affected only German Jews as well as those who lived in areas annexed by the Reich in 1938—Austria and the Sudetenland region of Czechoslovakia—and in the Reich "Protectorate" established over the Czech lands of Bohemia and Moravia in 1939. Accounting both for the emigration of German Jews as well as for the acquisition of these new territories, the number of Jews subjected to direct Nazi control hovered at around half a million throughout the prewar period. It was only with the advent of World War II in Europe in September 1939 that the number of Jews under German control grew from the hundreds of thousands into the millions.

During the prewar period, Nazi Jewish policy radicalized over time. After the Nazi takeover of the German government in 1933, Jews were subjected to economic boycotts, expelled from a variety of professions, deprived of their citizenship, and placed under pressure to have their property Aryanized, that is, transferred to non-Jewish Germans. This process of marginalization was carried out in a legal and bureaucratic fashion, although it was accompanied by a good deal of humiliation, intimidation, and waves of genuine violence.[7] The Kristallnacht pogrom saw violence on an unprecedented level, with the mass destruction of synagogues and Jewish-owned businesses, widespread physical attacks on Jews in their homes and on the streets, and the arrest of about thirty thousand Jewish men, who were transferred to concentration camps.

After the outbreak of war in September 1939, the Jews who remained in Germany were removed from their homes and compelled to live in segregated apartment buildings or other facilities. They were also subjected to forced labor. Beginning in 1941 and extending into the following year, the majority of German Jews were deported to ghettos and camps in Poland and the Baltic region, where most of them died or were murdered. German Jews who survived the Holocaust fell mainly into several categories: those who lived in mixed-marriages with their so-called Aryan spouses and could thereby avoid deportation; those who managed to go underground and escape deportation; those who were deported initially to the Theresienstadt (Terezin) ghetto but managed to avoid subsequent deportation to Auschwitz; and those who were selected for forced labor in the east and remained fortunate enough to escape the gas chambers. The deportation of most of Germany's Jews was common knowledge throughout the German population.

The measures targeted at German Jews after the onset of the war unfolded roughly in parallel with the persecution of Jews in countries occupied by or allied with Germany. By the early summer of 1941, about two million Jews were subjected to compulsory ghettoization and forced labor in German-occupied Poland. Policies of persecution were implemented across German-dominated Europe. Information about these developments was by no means kept secret from the German population.

The Nazi regime initiated the systematic mass murder of Jews upon its invasion of the Soviet Union in June 1941. These killings took the form of mass shootings carried out by mobile killing units across a large swath of territory in eastern Poland, the western Soviet Union (Ukraine and White Russia), and the Baltic States. In this first phase of the Final Solution, German special task forces organized and carried out the killings, often receiving significant assistance from local militias whose members were motivated by a combination of anti-Semitism and an eagerness to ingratiate themselves with their new German overlords. These killings were officially carried out in secret, but it has been well documented that information about them leaked back into Germany. This was recently confirmed again dramatically by the publication of the wartime diary of Friedrich Kellner,[8] a court civil servant in the small Hessian town of Laubach. On 28 October 1941, Kellner made the following entry in his diary:

A soldier on leave reports to have been an eyewitness to horrible atrocities in the occupied region of Poland. He watched as naked Jewish men and women, who were lined up in front of a long, deep ditch, were shot at the base of their skulls by Ukranians at the order of the SS and fell into the ditch. The ditch was then shoveled closed. Screams still came out of the ditch!

Kellner was convinced that "99 percent of the German population bears indirect or direct guilt for the present situation. One may only conclude: 'it will serve us right' [*mitgegangen – mitgefangen*]."

The information about the massacres that was available to Kellner, who lived in a small, provincial town, was also available to millions of other Germans. So the debate revolves not around whether German *could* have known, but more around other questions: How widespread was such knowledge? Did the information suffice for Germans to understand that the massacres were part of a systematic program of mass murder? To what extent were Germans distracted by other war-related issues? Through what kinds of psychological mechanisms did Germans avoid, repress, or deny such information?

In 1942 the mass murder program expanded to include all of the Jews of Europe. In this new phase of the Final Solution, the killing was shifted from mass shooting by mobile task forces to a more centralized, industrialized process, based at extermination camps in German-occupied Poland. A team of German officials, coordinated by Adolf Eichmann, organized the deportations of Jews from their home countries to the killing sites. Deportations on such a scale could hardly be carried out in secret, and knowledge about them was widespread across Europe. The key question for historians is not whether ordinary Germans knew of these deportations—they obviously did—but rather whether they comprehended the ultimate fate of the deported Jews and, to the extent that they did, how they reacted. In Germany after World War II the refrain "*Davon haben wir nichts gewusst*"—"We didn't know about that"—was often invoked when the subject of the mass murder of the Jews was raised. This assertion can be assessed on the basis of concrete historical evidence.

Four of the six essays in this volume focus on the period from 1933 to 1945, while the other two essays frame the Nazi period within the broader context of modern German history. Chapter 1, written by Richard S. Levy, is titled "Anti-Semitism in Germany, 1890–1933: How Popular Was It?" Levy's definition of anti-Semitism will strike some readers as unconventional. Levy distinguishes between anti-Jewish prejudice, on the one hand, and anti-Semitism, on the other—the latter, in his opinion, being an actual willingness to act on the basis of anti-Jewish animus, politically or even through acts of violence. According to Levy, from the 1890s through about the midpoint of World War I, anti-Semitism—as he defines it—was not especially widespread in Germany. To be sure, "most Germans did not like Jews," but few Germans were prepared to act on that sentiment. German Jews enjoyed legal equality and prospered economically and professionally, even though they suffered under various forms of social exclusion.

World War I, Levy argues, and especially the German defeat in 1918 constituted the turning point. After November 1918 there was a significant increase in the number of Germans willing to join or support political movements that advocated concrete anti-Jewish measures. Levy cites evidence for this transformation in a variety of places, including growing membership in the Nazi Party and other right-wing political associations as well as a dramatic rise in the desecrations of synagogues and Jewish cemeteries. There was also a notable intensification of rhetorical attacks against Jews in public, which must be considered as part and parcel of the coarsening of Germany's political culture during the Weimar Republic. As Levy points out, when fourteen million Germans voted Nazi in July 1932, they lent their support to a political party that had quite openly advocated anti-Semitic positions since 1919. While not all of these voters were anti-Semites, they were also not willing to defend the rights or the dignity of Germany's Jewish citizens. By the time of the Nazi takeover in January 1933, a large number of Germans had abandoned any commitment to the equality of Jews.

The first of the volume's four contributions on the Nazi era is Frank Bajohr's analysis of "German Responses to the Persecution of the Jews as Reflected in Three Collections of Secret Reports." Bajohr compares and contrasts three published collections of documents that are indispensable to historians working in this area. The first, which Bajohr refers to as the "regime-internal reports," is a set of slightly under four thousand documents collected from a large number of German archives as part of a joint German-Israeli project and made available in 2003.[9] The second collection consists of reports on the persecution of the Jews filed by foreign diplomats stationed in Germany. Bajohr himself led the project that collected and published these consular reports in 2011.[10] The third collection, published in 1980, is composed of reports produced during the Nazi era by the German Social Democratic Party (SPD) in exile.[11]

The regime-internal reports, according to Bajohr, distinguish mainly between Germans and Jews, while the diplomatic and SPD reports "present a more complex structure" of German society, differentiating among Jews, Germans, and Nazis. Bajohr also contends that the diplomatic reports tended to offer a "functionalistic" rather than ideological interpretation of Nazi anti-Jewish measures. The diplomats often pointed to the use of anti-Semitism as a nationalistic mobilization strategy, believing that it had to be understood within the context of the regime's other priorities. Despite such differences, all three sets of reports converged with respect to the prewar period. They agreed on the existence of "a general anti-Semitic consensus" in German society and at the same time agreed that there was widespread rejection of anti-Jewish violence.

For the war years, Bajohr explains, the comparison among the three sets of documents is more difficult. The SPD collection ends in 1940, and the number of consular reports dwindled as countries broke diplomatic relations with Germany. Only the regime-internal reports offer a substantial body of relevant documentation. From there it emerges, as Bajohr observes, that "many Germans were speaking about the treatment of the Jews in a kind of mélange of bad conscience, fears of future retribution, and projection of guilt." Many interpreted the bombardment of their cities by the Allies as punishment for the persecution of the Jews. Bajohr concludes his essay by noting that the Nazi regime did not require a popular consensus in favor of mass murder. The general anti-Semitic consensus in German society provided the regime with the room for maneuver it needed in order to plan and carry out the Final Solution.

Chapter 3, by Wolf Gruner, is also focused on documentation, although in this case on a single, unpublished archival source. Titled "Indifference? Participation and Protest as Individual Responses to the Persecution of the Jews as Revealed in Berlin Police Logs and Trial Records, 1933–45," Gruner's contribution offers a detailed, richly textured portrait of how non-Jewish Berliners interacted with their Jewish neighbors during the Nazi era. The article is based on research in the log books of almost three hundred police precincts in Berlin, which was both Germany's largest city and the site of the country's largest Jewish population. The chapter is also based on an analysis of a large number of cases of *Heimtücke* (literally: malice), the term used by the Nazi regime to designate the crime of maligning the national leadership and its policies. In view of Berlin's status as the national capital, the country's largest city, the focal point of Germany's Jewish community, and the center of progressive politics and culture, Berlin was, it must be emphasized, by no means a typical German community.

Gruner examines two waves of organized attacks against Jewish-owned businesses in Berlin in 1933 and 1935. These attacks, he contends, created social space and legitimacy for further anti-Jewish violence and contributed to the gradual marginalization of Jews in German society. But, as Gruner emphasizes, the attacks were greeted with disapproval and disgust by a great many Berliners. The Berlin police recorded numerous instances in which residents of the city expressed compassion for the Jews and outrage over their treatment. This was true not only in 1933 and 1935, but also applied to reactions to the Kristallnacht pogrom in November 1938. Negative reactions to the pogrom within the German population have been well documented, but often with an emphasis on popular objections to the destruction of property.[12] In contrast, Gruner argues that the condemnations recorded by the Berlin police did not focus on property, but rather on moral outrage and humanitarian concerns for the Jewish victims of the pogrom. At the same time, Gruner explains, a significant number of Berliners profited from the misfortune of their Jewish neighbors and did what they could to exploit the situation to their own advantage.

Gruner provides a detailed analysis of the Berliners' reactions to the deportation of the city's Jews in 1941 and 1942. "No one in Berlin could overlook the deportation of tens of thousands of Jews." Here again, the response was complex. On the one hand, some Berliners were happy to take possession of property and dwellings left behind by the deported Jews. Others denounced Jews who had tried to escape deportation by going underground. On the other hand, many expressed concern about the fate of the Jews and responded very negatively to information about mass murder that had leaked back to Berlin. It is precisely this last issue that lies at the heart of Peter Fritzsche's contribution, "Babi Yar, but not Auschwitz: What Did Germans Know about the Final Solution?" Through a careful reading of the diaries kept by Germans during the Nazi era,[13] Fritzsche offers a detailed analysis of popular responses to Nazi Jewish policy against the chronologies of deportation, mass murder, and the Allied bombing of German cities.

Fritzsche grounds his argument in an analysis of the complex interrelationship among four distinct categories of knowledge. The first of these was the widespread knowledge within Germany of the massacres of Jews that took place in Eastern Europe in the second half of 1941. The second was the even more widespread knowledge of the mass deportation of German Jews to that region in late 1941 and 1942. The third was the experience of the Allied bombing of Germany, which over time "eroded knowledge of the Final Solution" and fueled Germans' fantasies of Jewish revenge. And the fourth was the official propaganda campaign of 1943, in which the mass murder of the Jews was tacitly acknowledged in the regime's warnings about the potential catastrophic consequences of a German defeat.

Fritzsche arrives at the conclusion that ordinary Germans possessed extensive knowledge of the Final Solution but that this knowledge was incomplete and "deformed" by the convergence of factors described above. Germans, he argues, knew more about the mass executions of Jews by the Einsatzgruppen in 1941 and 1942 than they would learn about the subsequent killings in the extermination camps.

In the volume's final contribution devoted to the Nazi period, "Submergence into Illegality: Hidden Jews in Munich, 1941–45," Susanna Schrafstetter shifts the focus to *Rettungswiderstand,* or resistance through rescue. This term originated from the impulse to recognize those few Germans who came to the aid of Jews as resisters against Nazism. But the term is also problematic inasmuch as it obscures the actions of the hidden Jews as active agents who helped determine their own destinies. The concept of *Rettungswiderstand* also deflects attention away from the fact that hidden Jews also encountered ordinary Germans as traitors, blackmailers, or robbers.

While stories of hidden Jews have been well documented in Berlin, other regions in Germany have received far less attention. Chapter 5 examines several cases in which Jews from the Bavarian capital of Munich survived the Holocaust in hiding with support from non-Jews. For her sources, Schrafstetter relies on memoirs, compensation claims by Jewish survivors, de-Nazification files, and applications to Yad Vashem for inclusion of rescuers as "Righteous among the Nations." Individual compensation claims, in particular, form a hitherto underused set of sources for the study of German-Jewish experiences, as survivors had to account for their whereabouts during the war in their applications.

Schrafstetter explains the peculiarities of Munich that determined the patterns of underground life and prospects for its success. When the deportations of German Jews began in the fall of 1941, there were about thirty-four hundred Jews still living in Munich, amounting to only a small fraction of the remaining Jewish population in Berlin. Of these thirty-four hundred, about one hundred survived in hiding inside the city of Munich, in the city's rural hinterland, or on an odyssey through the entire country. For each of these Jews to remain in hiding successfully, the active support of several non-Jews was necessary. Some of these acted out of altruism, others acted out of greed, while still others acted out of a complex combination of these motivations. Even though the absolute number of Jews who survived underground was relatively small, the cases do underscore the existence of non-Jewish Germans who were prepared to run the considerable risk of lending assistance. Unlike in Berlin, the overall number of Jews left in Munich in 1941 was small, and therefore organized structures designed both to aid and to exploit fleeing Jews did not develop to the same degree as in Berlin.

The volume concludes with Atina Grossmann's chapter "Where Did All 'Our' Jews Go? Germans and Jews in Post-Nazi Germany." Any assessment of German popular responses to the Holocaust must also consider the extent to which anti-Semitism persisted in German society after the defeat of the Nazi regime. Grossmann's contribution examines German attitudes toward Jewish Holocaust survivors, mainly from Eastern Europe, who lived as displaced persons (DPs) in postwar Germany. Most, although not all, lived in camps administered by the United Nations Relief and Rehabilitation Administration (UNRRA), concentrated primarily in the American and British zones of occupation. Despite their status as refugees whose presence in Germany was intended to remain temporary, the Jewish DPs came into close contact with the German population. They interacted on a variety of levels: economic, personal, and even sexual.

Grossmann describes how these interactions were influenced by "lingering stereotypes and renovated traditional prejudices against *Ostjuden*" in German society. Given the nature of their situation, many of the DPs were compelled to engage in black-market commerce, which reinforced anti-Semitic stereotypes about Jewish dishonesty and lack of respect for honest labor. When the American military government extended a protective hand over the DPs, some Germans took this as a validation of their suspicion that the Allies had been in the hands of the Jews.

Resentment toward the perceived alliance between Americans and Jews intensified as a result of American support of Jewish reparations claims. Many Germans regarded such claims as further evidence of Jewish "moneygrubbing," which in this case they saw as threatening the normalization of postwar German society and undermining the nation's economic recovery. To be sure, Grossmann points out, most postwar Germans denied harboring anti-Semitic prejudice. But, she concludes, "there should be no doubt that the philo-Semitism or shamed silence that tabooized anti-Jewish acts or utterances often attributed to postwar Germany not only coexisted with, but was often overwhelmed by, a strong and entirely acceptable anti-Semitism."

Taken together, the contributions to this volume convey a broad picture of how anti-Semitism functioned in German society during the first half of the twentieth century. A broadly based set of prejudices was endowed with political potency by the trauma of war and defeat between 1914 and 1918. Anti-Semitism became a central tenet of the German right during the Weimar Republic, and a large segment of German society, even if not actively anti-Semitic, was not repelled by the Nazi movement's obsession with Jews. Between 1933 and 1939, the Nazi regime consolidated an anti-Semitic consensus in German society. The consensus did not extend to include anti-Jewish violence, but it did provide the hard-core anti-Semites who governed Germany with the room for maneuver that they needed to pursue their maximalist agenda. Once that regime had been destroyed through external intervention, politically organized anti-Semitism ceased to be a factor, but many of the foundational prejudices persisted in the German population.

More than twice as much time has elapsed between the end of World War II and today than between World War I and 1945. How German attitudes toward Jews have developed since the immediate postwar period is a question that lies beyond the scope of this volume. But we should note that Germany today is a far different—and better—place today than it was in 1945.

Susanna Schrafstetter is associate professor of history at the University of Vermont. Her publications include *Die dritte Atommacht. Britische Nichtverbreitungspolitik im Dienst von Statussicherung und Deutschlandpolitik, 1952–1968* (Munich, 1999) and (with Stephen Twigge) *Avoiding Armageddon: The United States, Western Europe and the Struggle for Nuclear Non-Proliferation, 1945–1970* (New York, 2004). She has published a number of articles on German compensation to the victims of Nazism and on the post-1945 careers of Nazi-era officials. She has recently completed a book-length study about Jews who avoided deportation and went underground in Munich and the surrounding region during the early 1940s.

Alan E. Steinweis is the L & C Miller Distinguished Professor of Holocaust Studies at the University of Vermont, where he also serves as director of the Miller Center for Holocaust Studies. His books include *Art, Ideology, and Economics in Nazi Germany* (Chapel Hill, 1993); *Studying the Jew: Scholarly Antisemitism in Nazi Germany* (Cambridge, MA, 2006); and *Kristallnacht 1938* (Cambridge, MA, 2009). He has been a guest professor at the Universities of Heidelberg, Frankfurt, and Munich.

Notes

1. Stapostelle Bielefeld, Rundverfügung, 14 November 1938, in *Die Juden in den geheimen NS-Stimmungsberichten, 1933–1945*, ed. Otto Dov Kulka and Eberhard Jäckel (Düsseldorf, 2004), document 357 (document 2558 on the accompanying CD-ROM). A translation of the printed collection is *The Jews in the Secret Nazi Reports on Popular Opinion in Germany, 1933–1945*, eds Otto Dov Kulka and Eberhard Jäckel, trans. William Templer (New Haven, 2010). It should be noted that both editions are accompanied by a CD-ROM containing a much more extensive collection of documents only in German.
2. Bürgermeister Amt Borgentreich, "Betrifft: Aktion gegen die Juden am 10.11.1938," 17 November 1938, in Kulka und Jäckel, *Stimmungsberichte*, document 357 (2624 on the CD-ROM).
3. Lore Walb, *Ich, die Alte—ich, die Junge: Konfrontation mit meinen Tagebüchern 1933–1945* (Berlin, 1997).
4. Ibid., 118–21.
5. Geoff Eley, ed., *The "Goldhagen Effect": History, Memory, Nazism; Facing the German Past* (Ann Arbor, 2000).
6. Key works have included (listed in order of publication): Otto Dov Kulka, "'Public Opinion' in National Socialist Germany and the 'Jewish Question,'" in *Zion: Quarterly for Research in Jewish History* 40 (1975): 186–290 (in Hebrew, with English summary and German-language documents); a condensed version of the Kulka article published entirely in English can be found in *Jerusalem Quarterly* (1982), Nr. 25, 121–44, and Nr. 26, 34–45; Ian Kershaw, *Popular Opinion and Political Dissent in the Third Reich, Bavaria 1933–1945* (Oxford, 1983); Sarah Gordon, *Hitler, Germans, and the "Jewish Question"* (Princeton, 1984); David Bankier, *The Germans and the Final Solution: Public Opinion under Nazism* (Oxford, 1992); Peter Longerich, *"Davon haben wir nichts gewusst!" Die Deutschen und die Judenverfolgung 1933–45* (Munich, 2006); Frank Bajohr and Dieter Pohl, *Der Holocaust als offenes Geheimnis. Die Deutschen, die NS-Führung und die Alliierten* (Munich, 2006); Bernward Dörner, *Die Deutschen und der Holocaust. Was niemand wissen wollte, aber jeder wissen konnte* (Berlin, 2007).
7. Michael Wildt, *Hitler's Volksgemeinschaft and the Dynamics of Racial Exclusion: Violence against Jews in Provincial Germany, 1919-1939* (New York, 2012).
8. Friedrich Kellner, *"Vernebelt, verdunkelt sind alle Hirne." Tagebücher 1939–1945*, 2 vols, eds Sascha Feuchert et al. (Göttingen, 2011).
9. See note 1 above.
10. Frank Bajohr and Christoph Strupp, eds, *Fremde Blicke auf das "Dritte Reich." Berichte ausländischer Diplomaten über Herrschaft und Gesellschaft in Deutschland 1933–1945* (Göttingen, 2011).
11. *Deutschland-Berichte der Sozialdemokratischen Partei Deutschlands (Sopade), 1934–1940*, 7 vols (Frankfurt, 1980).
12. For example, Bankier, *Germans and the Final Solution*, and Kershaw, *Popular Opinion*. Gruner's argument in this volume supports the assertion in Longerich, *"Davon haben wir nichts gewusst,"* that the moral outrage of the German population at the pogrom has probably been underestimated.

13. See also Peter Fritzsche, *Life and Death in the Third Reich* (Cambridge, MA, 2008), which relies mainly on memoirs and published diaries.

Selected Bibliography

Bajohr, Frank, and Dieter Pohl. *Der Holocaust als offenes Geheimnis. Die Deutschen, die NS-Führung und die Alliierten.* Munich, 2006.

Bajohr, Frank, and Christoph Strupp, eds, *Fremde Blicke auf das "Dritte Reich." Berichte ausländischer Diplomaten über Herrschaft und Gesellschaft in Deutschland 1933–1945.* Göttingen, 2011.

Bankier, David. *The Germans and the Final Solution: Public Opinion under Nazism.* Oxford, 1992.

Deutschland-Berichte der Sozialdemokratischen Partei Deutschlands (Sopade), 1934–1940. 7 vols. Frankfurt, 1980.

Dörner, Bernward. *Die Deutschen und der Holocaust. Was niemand wissen wollte, aber jeder wissen konnte.* Berlin, 2007.

Fritzsche, Peter. *Life and Death in the Third Reich.* Cambridge, MA, 2008.

Gordon, Sarah. *Hitler, Germans, and the "Jewish Question."* Princeton, 1984.

Kershaw, Ian. *Popular Opinion and Political Dissent in the Third Reich, Bavaria 1933–1945.* Oxford, 1983.

Kulka, Otto Dov, and Eberhard Jäckel, eds. *Die Juden in den geheimen NS-Stimmungsberichten, 1933-1945.* Düsseldorf, 2004. English translation: *The Jews in the Secret Nazi Reports on Popular Opinion in Germany, 1933–1945.* Translated by William Templer. New Haven, 2010.

Longerich, Peter. *"Davon haben wir nichts gewusst!" Die Deutschen und die Judenverfolgung 1933–45.* Munich, 2006.

Wildt, Michael. *Hitler's Volksgemeinschaft and the Dynamics of Racial Exclusion, Violence against Jews in Provincial Germany, 1919-1939.* New York, 2012.

Figure 2. Anti-Semitic caricature adorning the cover of a German satire magazine, early 1920s.

Chapter 1

ANTI-SEMITISM IN GERMANY, 1890–1933

How Popular Was It?

---◌◌◌---

Richard S. Levy

IT IS GIVEN ONLY TO anti-Semites to find the simplest answers to the thorniest questions regarding Jews. For the rest of us, even the most straightforward of matters, such as the one that provides this essay with its title and topic, defy easy solutions. What follows will, at certain crucial junctures, be speculative and tentative, rather than conclusive and unambiguous. Fine distinctions and guarded judgments—such as anti-Semites cannot abide—characterize the findings presented here.

Beyond doubt, however, is the crucial importance of the question. Any serious student of the murder of European Jewry in the twentieth century must sooner or later recognize that the Holocaust cannot be properly understood as just the doing of the decision makers of the Third Reich and their high-level subordinates, that all lesser accomplices and bystanders were dragged along against their wills or that they were indifferent to the "Jewish Question" and its possible solutions. What was the role of the mass of other Germans in the genocide of the Jews? What did anti-Semitism have to do with their behavior, and to what degree did anti-Semitism in the general public contribute to the Jewish catastrophe? Such questions give this topic its significance.

The Evidence and Its Limitations

Several difficulties get in the way of arriving at satisfactory answers to these questions. First among them is our inclination toward the teleological. We know how this tragic story ends, and it is only natural to see that end foreshadowed in the beginning. In the case of the history of German anti-Semitism, this knowledge has produced a well-worn scenario. It usually begins with the medieval conceptions of Jews as religious deviants and economic tormentors and then describes the eruptions of violence produced by the resultant animosities. With the passage of time, old and new grievances, imagined and real, come to dominate the culture and mold the population's attitudes toward Jews. Potent stereotypes and negative images, sometimes actively deployed, sometimes lying deceptively dormant, build in intensity and momentum, until Hitler arrives to orchestrate the dreadful, but predictable climax that Germans in their heart of hearts had wanted for so long. The trajectory is linear, the outcome inevitable. Tempting in its simplicity, but reductionist in all its essentials, the scenario ought to be jettisoned. It looks for and finds only the evidence it needs. Where the evidence is nonexistent, it is nonetheless assumed. Where it is open to multiple interpretations, only one is found appropriate.[1]

That this approach still appeals to both scholars and thoughtful laymen derives in part from a second problem, the definition of anti-Semitism, a term that has become so all-inclusive, so imprecise that it effortlessly supports the scenario just outlined or any other one might wish to hang on it. This essay understands anti-Semitism much more narrowly. Like the word coined to describe it, anti-Semitism is a late nineteenth-century phenomenon. It was a response to the terribly exaggerated perception of the Jews' highly visible successes in all aspects of modern life, usually tied to their achievement of legal equality in Europe and, more commonly, to their phenomenal rise in the world during the course of the nineteenth century. The movement produced by this perception was predicated on *taking action against Jews,* putting a stop to their advance and, at the very least, abolishing their rights as equal citizens and driving them back into marginality. It is this action component that distinguishes anti-Semites from traditional Jew-haters, be they casually or even pathologically prejudiced. Anti-Semitism prided itself on going beyond feeling to embrace and then institutionalize a desperate activism. Anti-Semites, according to this conception, are all those who take action against Jewish power or are willing to have others do so on their behalf; anti-Semitism is the ideology that justifies such action and the action itself. Distinguishing between a great range of anti-Jewish feelings—neither unimportant nor inconsequential—and goal-oriented actions to disempower the Jews is essential to arrive at meaningful conclusions about the popularity of anti-Semitism in Germany between 1890 and 1933. Emotions and their consequences vary too greatly to be accurately measured. They are too widely present to tell us anything useful. Actions leave clearer footprints.

A third set of problems has to do with the evidence. Both the victims and victimizers in the history of German anti-Semitism have left abundant records of their views and experiences of each other. While one would think that such evidence would be extremely valuable in assessing the level of the popularity of anti-Semitism in Germany at given moments and over long duration, many complications become immediately apparent when the attempt is made. Of course, the lack of objectivity on both sides of the equation is only to be expected, but the reluctance to confront the realities, apparent in both Jewish and anti-Semitic witnesses, goes well beyond this and requires some explication.

As an example of the limited usefulness of Jewish sources, the diaries of Victor Klemperer, one of the great observers of the terrible history of the twentieth century, illustrate the point. Looking back from 1938, Klemperer declares that his childhood was without anti-Semitism, a minor irritant he recognizes as having become serious only after finding himself in Munich in 1919. What had been merely "historical" had now turned personal.[2] This is more than a bit puzzling. He was born in 1881, making him a teenager when Hermann Ahlwardt, the most flamboyant political anti-Semite of the day, campaigned for and won the district in which Klemperer lived. The family had moved to Berlin by then, but Berlin in the early 1890s was bristling with anti-Semitic politics. Moreover, Klemperer went to school back in his hometown, still represented in the Reichstag by the headline-grabbing Ahlwardt—represented, that is, when he was not off trying to establish an anti-Semitic party in Brooklyn or selling cigars for the "anti-Semitic smoker" on the Reichstag grounds. As Klemperer grew to adulthood, he certainly had to know that there were anti-Semitic political parties and lobbying groups, some with highly educated memberships, that there were university student associations pursuing vigorous anti-Semitic agendas, which he could not join. Is he being disingenuous when he says there was no problem back then, this acute observer who unflinchingly faced the harshest truths during the Third Reich?

I believe that Klemperer and any number of other Jewish witnesses who could be cited were unable to face this particular truth—that anti-Semitism from its earliest appearance was a serious threat to Jewish well-being—because of the total identification with Germandom they had negotiated. Klemperer, the son of a rabbi, had converted to Christianity, married a Christian, immersed himself in German (and European) culture, and fought bravely during the war. He opted completely for Germandom, wholly abandoning his Jewish identity. He, and others like him, could not bring themselves to admit that many of their fellow Germans despised them—not, that is, until it became inescapably obvious. For Klemperer, even the triumph of Hitler could not fully convince him that the Nazis spoke for all his countrymen. His diary for the Nazi years asks the question being discussed in this essay, again and again. How popular was anti-Semitism with the Germans? How representative was Nazi fanaticism?

The historian has access to numerous collections of Jewish memoirs and letters reporting on experiences from the imperial and Weimar eras. One of the most useful of them assembles forty testimonies from a wide variety of Jewish eyewitnesses, making a largely successful attempt at capturing the diversity of German Jewry. They make for fascinating reading, but most suffer from a common flaw. Very few are contemporary to the events they describe; most, composed after the Holocaust, bear the marks of those horrors. The clearest effect of this timing is to relativize the importance of happenings during the period of the kaisers and the republic, diminishing, one suspects, the real impact of anti-Semitism on the writers. They make few connections between the anti-Jewish social slights they experienced in their youths and the utter inhumanity they suffered at the hands of the Nazis. Like Klemperer, they mark the sea change in their lives by the rise of the Hitler movement to national prominence, in most cases the end phase of the republic (1930–32), by which time it was impossible to ignore the danger.[3] This renders their accounts of earlier times relatively useless—it is evidence simply too subjective to be evaluated, too overwhelmed by the realities of Nazism.

There is, however, a body of evidence that satisfies the need for contemporaneity, although it too falls short of the (even relative) objectivity that would help achieve an accurate reading of anti-Semitism's popularity before 1914. In 1906, Julius Moses (1868–1942), a physician and journalist, sent out a survey to approximately three thousand prominent Jews and non-Jews, including some known anti-Semites, asking for their views on the "Jewish Question" and its possible solutions. The responses appeared in his newspaper, and a selection of about one hundred of them were later published in a separate book.[4] Several shortcomings in the results become immediately clear, at least from the historian's perspective. Confining the survey to the Jewish (and non-Jewish) elite in the arts, politics, and religious/institutional life does not give a candid rendering of the experiences or outlook of ordinary Jews, who were probably a good deal less insulated from the more egregious forms of anti-Semitism. Further, the survey was conducted in the shadow of the second wave of pogroms in the Russian Empire (1905–6), far more lethal than the first (1881–84). Respondents tended to see anti-Semitism as a Russian, rather than a German, problem and for the most part do not talk about German manifestations. Despite these drawbacks, a few limited insights concerning the way some Jews saw the problem of anti-Semitism in the decade before the war can be extracted from the survey. Although scant on detail, few denied that there was a "Jewish problem," even in Germany. Almost unanimously, Jewish contributors believed that the solution to the problem lay in ongoing and more complete assimilation. This required both greater effort on the part of Jews and a spirit of accommodation on the part of the state and the non-Jewish majority. It was anti-Semitism—a vague set of prejudices among the uneducated who were easy prey to a few demagogues—that impeded the process by which Jews would become ever less objectionable to their neighbors, at least to those of good will. Organized political anti-Semitism, surely visible in the Reichstag, the press, and associational life of the empire, is completely absent as a worrisome factor. Another indication of optimism among the Jewish elite was the near-unanimous rejection of the Zionist solution—a separate Jewish state to which Jews could emigrate. (This was vastly more acceptable to the non-Jewish respondents, some of whom were clearly "anti-Semitic Zionists.") Few Jewish witnesses saw the Jewish problem as insoluble; fewer yet betrayed fear of an immediate or future threat to their well-being.

Evidence that could have countered this rosy view or at least have dampened its inherent optimism was plentiful.[5] But it does not seem to have registered. For whatever reason so many Jews were unable to assess their situation accurately, an interpretation of the popularity of anti-Semitism in Germany between 1890 and 1933 ought not rest too heavily on personal assessments of their circumstances. This is equally true of other sorts of evidence: deeds rather than words meant for publication. Intermarriage, conversion, and emigration have long been interpreted, at least in part, as reactions to perceived anti-Semitic threats to Jewish well-being. While Jewish community spokesmen and independent observers had much to say about these acts, seeing them usually in a negative way and almost always as a (wrong) response to anti-Semitism, the motives of the actual actors remain mostly obscure and therefore difficult to evaluate as perceptions of anti-Semitism's strength in German society. Victor Klemperer, for example, may well have thought he was acknowledging the Christian essence of German culture and his identification with it when he converted in 1912. Or he may have simply ceased being an indifferent Jew, becoming an indifferent Christian, in the hope of overcoming the obstacles to his academic career posed by Jewishness. Similarly, rates of intermarriage, legal only since 1875, rose and fell throughout the period under consideration; it may be understood as an escape attempt from anti-Semitism into the larger society, but it can also be seen as evidence that Jewishness was not an insuperable obstacle to acceptance by non-Jewish society.[6] Emigration from the countryside to the metropolis or overseas might have been a flight from discrimination or an intolerant environment, but it might also have been something completely different, a pursuit of better educational or economic opportunities that had little to do with anti-Semitic oppression. Deeds, such as these, may speak more loudly than words, but they do not always speak more clearly.

Anti-Semites, like Jews, produced a wealth of important evidence that must be addressed when studying the history of anti-Semitism. But when it comes to the question of the general popularity of their movement and ideology, they are no more helpful or reliable than their Jewish targets. They were generally a pessimistic lot, and little could move them to foresee a rosy future for their cause. Not even the rise of Hitler altered their stance—the Jews, they were certain, would be victorious. This was perhaps the disappointed reaction to foolishly exaggerated hopes, hatched at the birth of their political parties in the late 1870s. Anti-Semitism then drew from every political direction—disappointed democrats, Christian conservatives, radical nationalists, agrarians, culture critics, "life reformers"—confident that they had found the key to national salvation, true community, and, just possibly, a brilliant new career for themselves. All the anti-Semitic parties backed universal suffrage, feeling convinced that since almost all Germans hated Jews to one degree or another, it was only a matter of time before they could be herded into a mighty mass movement that would enable its representatives to legislate a solution to the Jewish Question. They made the mistake that many who write about anti-Semitism continue to make. They confused the majority's inherited anti-Jewish prejudices, lingering medieval stereotypes, resentments, and contempt with the activists' own commitment to solve the Jewish Question, disempower the Jews, and cleanse German life of all Jewish influence—a much more ambitious project. Mere prejudice was only a starting point. What anti-Semites had in mind was a long and methodical process. The masses had to be educated and steered into understanding that it was a question of survival, an absolute life-and-death struggle, not "a mere soap-bubble to be popped with a cheap 'Hep-Hep' pogrom.[7] Jews had become too powerful to be dealt with by the customary methods. Anti-Semites came only slowly to the recognition that the kind of sustained, disciplined, and focused action required for a solution to the Jewish Question was beyond the capacity of the German masses. The raw Jew-hatred was there, but most of their feckless countrymen did not see a solution to the Jewish Question as something that would solve their problems or bring them happiness. They just did not care enough to do the hard work that was necessary over the long haul, and there seemed to be no way to change them, their character, or their IQs. Hence the pessimism of committed anti-Semites and their unreliability as witnesses concerning the popularity of anti-Semitism. For their purposes, it was never "popular" enough. Too many Germans never felt called upon to *act* on their prejudices.

Wilhelm Marr, often credited with coining the word *anti-Semite* and the first to organize a specifically anti-Semitic political party in 1879, grandiosely termed his stance "heroic pessimism." His dire prediction of the "Victory of the Jews over the Germans" was, at least in part, designed to anger his audience and spur it to action, but it also accurately reflected his shipwreck of a life, one that justified genuine rather than "heroic" pessimism. For Theodor Fritsch, a key transitional figure between the founders of the anti-Semitic movement and the Nazis, it was no pose, however. Fritsch was one of the few anti-Semites who made anti-Semitism pay, a successful publisher who sold or gave away millions of pamphlets, mostly to other anti-Semites. In 1926, recalling nearly fifty years of dedicated fighting against Jewish power (including his thirty-three convictions in court cases), that is, well after the rise of the Hitler movement and the establishment of other powerful racist-nationalist groups, Fritsch was still filled with gloom. The movement, he pronounced, had not progressed beyond its promising takeoff in the 1890s. He blamed warring leaders. He heaped scorn especially on "blowhard orators" who indulged in foolhardy political adventures—a clear allusion to Hitler and his putsch attempt of 1923. They could occasionally seduce the masses but lacked the "deep knowledge" of Jewry necessary to educate them in anti-Semitism. Without those masses becoming enlightened as to the true existential significance of the Jewish Question, the outlook was hopeless. He had wasted his life.[8]

The tears we might be inclined to shed for Fritsch should not keep us from wondering about the quality of the guidance he, and the many others like him, can offer in the assessment of anti-Semitism's popularity in the empire or the republic. Perhaps, their standards for what constituted "authentic" anti-Semitism were too lofty. It is more than a bit ironic that many Jews and anti-Semites before the Great War were in essential agreement: anti-Semitism was not much of a problem. But irony aside, their evidence is not very serviceable for the purposes of this essay. For dramatically different reasons, they were unable to see the situation objectively.

This raises a final problem of interpretation. What can be ascertained about the great German public, all those who stood between the Jews and their most active adversaries? Before the age of scientific polling, even getting at popular attitudes toward Jews is well-nigh impossible.[9] In the absence of hard data, I will here advance a hypothesis: most Germans did not like Jews, value their difference, respect their achievements, or believe in their professed allegiance to Germany. Even those willing to defend their rights against the anti-Semites hoped that they would give up their Jewish identity and become wholly German. Those few who rose above the centuries of negative thinking about Jews, the countless expressions of contempt in art, architecture, literature high and low, and even in music, were the remarkable exceptions. It is this very ubiquity of anti-Jewish feeling that makes the distinction between thinking and acting imperative. What Germans thought about Jews, while far from insignificant, cannot be the main issue, not, that is, if the more circumscribed definition of anti-Semitism put forward at the beginning of this essay is adhered to.

By 1890, if Germans wanted to take *action* against their fellow Jewish citizens, they could do so in many ways, within or outside the law: cast a vote for an anti-Semitic political party, sign a petition calling for an end to Jewish immigration and the curtailment of occupational freedom, boycott Jewish businesses, join lobbying groups, professional associations, or one of the many societies that made anti-Semitism a part of their programs. One could subscribe to anti-Semitic newspapers or periodicals, ban Jews from privately owned hotels, or—rarely during the imperial era—commit acts of violence or vandalism against their persons, religious institutions, or property. All these sorts of acts have left evidence of Germans' orientation toward anti-Semitism. That evidence, like all evidence, is not without its ambiguities. Nonetheless, it is time to evaluate, as far as possible, what it says about the popularity of anti-Semitism between 1890 and 1933.

Anti-Semitism's Ineffectiveness in the German Empire

The obvious place to start is with the organized political movement. Beginning in 1879, a number of parties dedicated to the disenfranchisement of Jews but with otherwise varying programs, regional strengths, and special constituencies took root all over Germany.[10] They were supported by 140 grassroots "reform clubs," numerous newspapers, and auxiliary organizations. They contested national, state, and municipal elections, catering to the economic interests of the Protestant lower middle class in the countryside, small towns, and a few larger cities. They might well have drawn votes from people whose first commitment was not necessarily fighting Jewish power but rather the saving of their threatened livelihoods and social status. But even allowing for mixed motives, the number of Germans who voted for the anti-Semites because of or in spite of their anti-Jewish agenda was not impressive. The high point of their effectiveness came in 1893 when three parties elected sixteen deputies to the Reichstag, winning 263,861 votes out of a total 7.7 million cast. Another seven candidates who ran anti-Semitic campaigns but chose to sit with the Conservative Party raised the total anti-Semitic vote to 342,425, or 4.4 percent.[11] The parties, unable to penetrate the Catholic or working-class masses, could not get beyond this percentage of the vote. They probably never had more than thirty to thirty-five thousand members.[12] Their near-total ineffectiveness as legislators—they passed no anti-Semitic laws, although not for want of trying—led to their virtual disappearance during the course of World War I, by which time they held only six seats in the Reichstag (but still could not manage to form a united party). Other parties and occupational interest groups that had shown varying degrees of interest in using anti-Semitism as a mobilizing tool were edging away in the years just before the war. Anti-Semitism had not demonstrated its indispensability as a vote-getter and, in its parliamentary political form, never escaped its somewhat tawdry public image. Measured by these standards, it would be reasonable to declare that conventional political anti-Semitism did not appeal strongly to the German public. By 1914, many Jews could realistically look forward to its withering away.

The stark failure of conventional parliamentary anti-Semitism is a powerful indication of the limited popularity of anti-Semitism in the German public before World War I, but it cannot suffice as the only measurement. For example, running parallel to the formation of the anti-Semitic parties in 1880 and 1881 was an extra-parliamentary petition drive that called upon Otto von Bismarck's government to enact four measures that would have amounted to the rescinding of Jewish emancipation. The petition demands were rejected even before the text was formally delivered, but they lived on as the essential minimum program of all the anti-Semitic political parties. Crucial to the circulation of the petition was the participation of university students, who gathered the signatures of 265,000 adult males. Once again, this was not all that imposing a number (several activists cautioned against trying the strategy again for fear of it showing the weakness rather than the strength of the movement). There's no telling for sure who signed, but it was generally believed that a great many students, the sons of the elite of property and education, the future decision makers and opinion leaders of the German state and society, were prominent among those ready to disenfranchise Jews.[13] The petition effort spilled directly into the formation of the Verein Deutscher Studenten (Association of German Students), whose supporters, although they rejected party politics, championed a racist-nationalist outlook, banned Jews and the sons of Jewish converts from membership, and later held positions of leadership in many of Germany's important patriotic societies and rightist organizations. Although the conventional political anti-Semites commanded the most attention during the German Empire, there were several individuals and nonparty groups, in addition to the Association of German Students, that contributed directly to the vocabulary of radical anti-Semitism. (See Appendix A.) When the Nazis and other rightists appeared in the 1920s, they were able to step into an ideology that was almost fully formed. In particular, they had very little need to invent new conceptions of the "Jewish Peril."

Yet, notwithstanding these extra-parliamentary developments, 1914 marked the end of one phase and the beginning of another in the history of German anti-Semitism. Between 1890 and the outbreak of war, anti-Semitism fluctuated in popularity, gradually losing its appeal; it is at least arguable that the organized movement was drifting toward the fringe of German politics and that anti-Semitism as an issue had already reached the limits of its modest usefulness as a tool of mobilization.

The underlying reasons for this general failure are worth examining. Neither the ineffective politicians and their incompetent parties, nor the racist-nationalist students, nor the numerous and active propaganda societies—their "learned" journals, shabby newspapers, or multitudinous pamphlets—had been able to stop the "rise of the Jews." Jews continued on their path of upward social mobility, enjoyed not all, but most of the prizes of public life, and lived secure in their rights and property.[14] To be sure, they were also subjected to insulting and psychologically wounding accusations, not just from the rabble, but from well-educated and successful individuals. Yet in the last analysis anti-Semites of all varieties had failed to achieve a single one of their goals (which went much further than making Jews feel bad). The best explanation for that failure was their inability to awaken sufficient interest in the general population. Jew-haters had not been converted into anti-Semites. An insufficient number of Germans (Hungarians, Frenchmen, and Austrians) cared deeply enough about the Jewish Question to commit to it as one of their political priorities. Anti-Semitism was not popular enough. The war changed this.

War, the Radicalization of Anti-Semitism, and the Decline of Jewish Security

Whether the turmoil of the war years and their aftermath increased the sum total of anti-Jewish feeling among Germans and prompted more people to act on those feelings is probably not ascertainable, although it seems likely. What is certain is that Jews felt more vulnerable. Many, especially those who had served in the war, were now willing to write about their unpleasant interactions with non-Jews, much more so than about their prewar experiences; these more recent experiences tended to trivialize prewar slights and insults.[15] That more Jews recognized a greater threat to their safety in the rise of anti-Jewish activities explains the spurt in membership in the major Jewish anti-defamation organization, the Central Association of German Citizens of Jewish Faith (Centralverein deutscher Staatsbürger jüdischen Glaubens). Since its founding in 1893, the Centralverein had compiled a fairly successful record of prosecuting slanderers and winning convictions against most of the major anti-Semitic politicians and publicists. During the Weimar years, its legal bureau continued tried-and-true tactics, combing the anti-Semitic press looking for libels of the Jewish community and religion. Its larger purpose was to criminalize anti-Semitic activities wherever and whenever possible, relying on the courts to achieve this goal. Already the largest Jewish voluntary association in prewar Germany, its membership spiked in the early 1920s before tailing off.[16]

Further evidence that the war experience contributed to a general worsening of relations between Jews and non-Jews is not hard to find. Germans who served on the Eastern Front came into contact with large concentrations of *Ostjuden,* those unearthly, unkempt, and devious eastern European Jews they had probably known about only from hearsay and frightening newspaper stories. In most cases their preconceptions were corroborated, and it is at least possible that this led them to support postwar efforts by various anti-Semitic organizations calling for the expulsion of foreign Jews.[17] As the war turned against Germany, notions concerning the Jewish character, already common currency, gathered new force. Talk of profiteering and black marketeering, suspicions about international connections, and accusations concerning lack of true patriotism made the rounds on the home front. At first, military censors exercised strict control over what could be published in the popular press. The common view today is that the censors were "blind in the right eye," but in the name of unity and maintaining morale, a number of anti-Semitic newspapers and articles were suppressed, at least in the early months of the war. This even-handedness disappeared in 1916.

In October and November 1916, the War Ministry undertook a census to determine how many Jews were serving at the front, as opposed to the rear echelons. Whoever thought up the measure—there is no historical agreement regarding its precise origins—it was clearly anti-Semitic in purpose, meant to demonstrate that Jews were slackers and savvy players of the system. Also clear, and setting an ominous precedent, was the unapologetically official nature of the act. For years, left-liberal and socialist Reichstag deputies had chastised government for violating the constitutional rights of Jews by excluding them from positions in the civil service or holding up their promotions when they were allowed to serve. The authorities had always denied anti-Semitic motives. In the case of the "Jew Census" of 1916, even the usual hollow assurances of government neutrality on the Jewish Question were conspicuously absent.[18] The results of the census were never published, thus giving added government sanction to the suspicions of non-Jews that Jews were shirkers. (In fact, one hundred thousand served, approximately eighty thousand at the front; they volunteered, fought, won medals, and died in very much the same proportions as non-Jews.)[19]

As the war was being lost, anti-Semites became reinvigorated—and less restrained. In June 1917, the Pan-German League, with a small but elite membership, declared war on Jewry (*Alljudentum*) and took the lead in rallying those still active in the struggle against Jewish power.[20] In the context of war-weariness and then shocking defeat, anti-Semitic discourse became ever more radical. The charges escalated. No longer just shady dealers, exploiters of family farmers, intruders into German cultural life, or pushy strivers, Jews had engaged in gigantic and bloody crimes. They had unleashed the world war and the Russian and German revolutions, pitted classes against each other, corrupted the young, undermined the Christian faith, and were seeking to install a Jewish despot to rule over all nations. The Weimar Republic was declared to be their crowning victory. The *Protocols of the Elders of Zion* made its timely appearance in Germany in 1920, melding variations of these and other accusations into an arcane historical conspiracy that revealed the relentless drive toward Jewish world domination.

A few stalwart survivors from the prewar anti-Semitic movement began new careers in the aftermath of the war. They were joined by a host of newcomers who had no ties to the tamer, mostly law-abiding anti-Semitism of those days. In this new era, very few could be found who still advocated a conventional, legislative solution of the Jewish Question. In a republic where "Jews made the laws" such timorous remedies met with contempt. The debate among these radicals went well beyond the need to disenfranchise Jews. Undoing emancipation, even segregation, would no longer save the nation. Now the talk was of expulsion and—in contrast to the imperial era—openly and earnestly about the need for physical violence. What "dignified" anti-Semites used to call *Radauantisemitismus* (rowdy anti-Semitism) was now referred to as *Pogromantisemitismus* (pogrom anti-Semitism). And it was not just talk. A brutalization of political life took effect with stunning swiftness. In this environment many criminal acts on the persons of Jews were recorded in the early years of the republic. The murders of Jewish revolutionary leaders Kurt Eisner, Rosa Luxemburg, Hugo Haase, and Gustav Landauer in 1919 were seen by some as the radical right's response to the revolutionary left. However, the assassination in 1922 of the Jewish foreign minister Walther Rathenau, a key figure in the German war effort, and certainly no radical leftist, removed all reasonable doubts about the anti-Semitic motives for all these killings.[21]

These were the acts of emboldened political extremists. But lesser crimes were also rife. At least partly responsible for the general audacity in breaking the law was the knowledge that, if caught, most criminals would be punished by a republic whose courts were much more lenient than the kaiser's, and generally much less respected. Convictions before the war that had once stigmatized such lawbreakers and occasionally ended their careers were now often celebrated as badges of honor bestowed by the "Jew Republic." A sorry state of affairs, but what did the deeds of these activists and their consequences, or lack of consequences, prove about the growth of anti-Semitism's popularity among the bulk of the population? The evidence strongly suggests that the absolute number of individuals willing to act against Jews far surpassed the levels of the imperial era. They flocked to a welter of organizations, some of which received financial support from the respectable right and many of which employed a rhetoric of unabashed violence.[22] It is likely that this new, more radical activism helped desensitize the public to politically inspired violence, extending the boundaries of what now had "only to be expected" from zealots and fanatics in the chaotic conditions of postwar Germany. But this was still a long way from popular approval or ironclad proof of a general readiness to join in the mayhem. Lawless acts were roundly condemned across the political spectrum (except those committed against the extreme left). The funeral rites for Walther Rathenau, for example, took on the character of a national act of contrition.[23] Even after the Nazis came to power in 1933 and quickly cowed the general population into obedience, actual violence against Jews continued to arouse unease (in ways that "legal" discrimination, expropriation, and gradual disenfranchisement did not). There is some compelling evidence that this restraining sense of the permissible reasserted itself after the chaos of the early 1920s subsided; it should be weighed against the clear markers of the growing popularity of anti-Semitism.

Dirk Walter, one of the few historians of this era who takes its anti-Semitic violence seriously, is quick to point out that the experts in brutal intimidation, the Nazi storm troopers, operated within what they perceived to be socially imposed limits. Truth to tell, there were not a great number of Jewish fatalities, and many of these resulted when Jews defended themselves or intervened against anti-Semitic demonstrations—a not infrequent response. Nazi brutality produced many physical injuries, but attacks on Jews had something of a ritual, exclusionary character, designed to let them know who controlled the streets and who ought to disappear, but not necessarily who deserved to die. Even when political violence reached new heights during the end-phase of the republic, the Nazis were reluctant to use deadly weapons against Jews (as opposed to Communists), fearing the social consequences.[24]

There were other sorts of violence directed against Jews that also proved objectionable to the general public. Rare before the 1920s, the desecrations of Jewish cemeteries and synagogues now became commonplace. Between 1923 and 1932, 189 such events took place. In forty-three instances, the police were able to identify the malefactors; half of them had clear affiliations with radical rightist groups. Who were the other known perpetrators, and what were their motives? Fully 25 percent were children. Their vandalism ought not be attributed simply to high spirits. Somewhere—at home, at school, in the streets?—they had formed the notion that while thrillingly naughty, such actions were okay when practiced against Jewish targets. Desecraters of all ages seemed quite able to distinguish between Christian and Jewish cemeteries, churches and synagogues. Whatever the motives at work, public response was uniformly negative, and penalties for those convicted were stiff fines and almost always time in jail.[25] Paradoxically, the judicial punishments for insulting dead Jews were generally harsher than for menacing and maligning live ones.

Notwithstanding the public disapproval for such actions and other evidence that anti-Semitism had not wholly poisoned relations between Jews and non-Jews or spread to every nook and cranny of Germany by 1933, a realistic judgment is that the Weimar Republic was becoming more anti-Semitic, a more dangerous place for Jews than in the prewar era. In terms of the definition of anti-Semitism framed at the outset of this essay, a key criterion had been met: there were more people more willing to act against Jews. The startling growth of Nazism in the last years of the Weimar democracy ought to be sufficient evidence for this conclusion. Of the more people more willing to act, a good number of them found their way to the Nazi Party and its paramilitary arm, the SA. But even this seemingly unassailable evidence of the growth of popular anti-Semitism requires qualification.

Just how anti-Semitic were rank-and-file Nazis? The scholarly literature dealing with this question suggests that anti-Semitism exerted a much stronger appeal for the earliest recruits (1919–23) than for the mass of newer members who joined after 1930. Among these late joiners, the number who could be regarded as fanatical anti-Semites or who exhibited strongly ideological views that required action on the Jewish Question has been estimated at about 20 percent.[26] Leaving aside all sorts of personal motives that prompt people to join political movements, the admittedly anecdotal evidence on which this estimate rests prioritizes other ideological concerns: anti-Communism, national recovery, "social justice," the restoration of German power, among others. Even Hitler, whose personal commitment to anti-Semitism seems beyond all doubt, saw relatively early on the need to broaden his recruitment efforts, having recognized that anti-Semitism had probably exhausted its mobilizing potential for his movement. Anti-Marxism, sometimes connected to the Jewish Question and sometimes not, supplanted his earlier focus on the evils of Jewry and the need to combat Jewish power. After 1928, anti-Semitism played a diminishing role in Nazi Party election campaigning for the Reichstag or in Hitler's speeches and newspaper writing.[27] The party represented itself as the best hope to stave off the Communist threat and to restore the failing economy rather than to save Germany from the Jews. The growth of the Nazi movement, therefore, ought not be seen as the simple equivalent of a growth in anti-Semitism or its popularity.

The Abandonment of the Jews

However ambiguous the evidence concerning the popularity of anti-Semitism in Germany between 1890 and 1933, at least two provisional conclusions can be drawn from this survey. The first of them argues in favor of acknowledging the ambiguity and giving it greater importance than it usually gets when passing judgment on the responses of German Jewry to its growing peril. This discussion has stressed the multiple meanings to be derived from the experience of anti-Semitism before Hitler took power. The Jews who lived this history had good cause to be confused and generally ambivalent. Few of them would have thought that things were getting better rather than worse, but how much worse could they get? They were not irrational to see Nazism as a response to awful economic conditions brought on by the Depression. Nor were they unreasonable to think that Hitler's movement would lose its appeal once the crisis began to ebb, as surely it would.

Of course not everyone was prone to such confidence. The leaders of the Centralverein read the evidence differently than did most of their members. They took a much dimmer view of the present and future. Even in the so-called good years of the Weimar Republic (usually defined as 1924–30), they never ceased urging vigilance against anti-Semitism or trying to develop better strategies against its hate campaigns. As the Nazi movement gathered force in the early 1930s, they continued publishing apologetic literature, pursued anti-Semites with nearly a hundred lawsuits a year, and supported anti-anti-Semitic candidates for the Reichstag and state parliaments. However, as hardheaded as they were, even the Centralverein leaders were subject to moments of hopefulness, based on a belief that anti-Semitism, although a present danger, was essentially alien to the German people and that, even if not wholly conquerable, it could be driven to the fringes of politics and public life. As the republic was crumbling, neither the leaders of the Centralverein nor those of the much smaller Zionist movement counseled flight.

In the eyes of posterity, there is something desperate about this optimism. But was it, as many still insist, willful self-delusion? Despite alarming evidence to the contrary, few Jews could have predicted Germany's descent into barbarism. Much more probable, given the prior history of organized anti-Semitism, was that the forces of order and the legal authorities would continue to protect the lives and rights of Jewish citizens and that the majority of Germans would stand behind these efforts.[28]

The second tentative conclusion calls this last statement into question. Germany's Jews were slowly but surely being abandoned by other Germans. The isolation that would render them ever more vulnerable to Nazi persecution was already in evidence before 1933. Not only were substantially more people more willing to act against them during the final years of the republic, there were also fewer willing to act on behalf of the rights of Jews. This represented a marked change in their relationship to German society. From the earliest days of anti-Semitic organizing in the 1880s, Jews had always found important and numerous allies among non-Jews. The Hohenzollern heir to the throne, Friedrich III, condemned anti-Semitism as the "shame of the century." Thirty eminent men of science and letters put their names to the "Declaration of Notables" that was widely published in the mass circulation press; they called upon all Germans of conscience to resist the attempt to curtail Jewish equality. In 1891, 535 prominent Germans called upon Christians of both churches to join the Association for the Defense against Anti-Semitism (Abwehr-Verein).[29] It was not the number of such individuals or the loftiness of their status that mattered, but the fact that they were willing to take a public stand against anti-Semitic defamation. Such willingness, while never altogether absent in the Weimar Republic, became less and less visible, especially after the Nazi movement achieved a size and a reputation for ruthlessness that a great many Germans found intimidating.

Several telling examples of this chilling effect on German-Jewish relations were apparent during Weimar's last years. The monthly publication of the Centralverein, always aimed at a non-Jewish readership and to involve them in the struggle against anti-Semitism, had had a circulation of fifty to sixty thousand in its heyday; by 1932, many subscribers, leery of receiving a journal with so obvious a Jewish identity, requested it not be sent. At about the same time, the Abwehr-Verein newspaper, with a readership of twenty-five thousand in the late 1920s, experienced a sharp drop-off in circulation, despite its being sent out in a plain brown wrapper.[30] The organization, after many years of valiant struggle, grew more cautious in its interventions and began a process of withdrawal that ended with its voluntary dissolution. The Nazis reinforced this sort of squeamishness in dramatic fashion. In Berlin on the eve of the Jewish New Year in September 1931, five hundred SA men, in a well-organized action, waylaid those they presumed to be Jews (many mistakes were made), hurling anti-Semitic insults and beating up several. This took place in the heart of the capital's main shopping district, the Kurfürstendamm. Many perpetrators were arrested, tried, and convicted; the usual outrage over lawlessness, the rebelliousness of youth, and the damage done to Berlin's reputation made the rounds of the daily press. But few wanted to discuss the anti-Semitic motivation for the riot, although the choice of targets and locale made this absolutely transparent. The Centralverein called for the formation of a "front of the decent people" (*Front der Anständigen*), certainly mindful that there had been a time when it would not have been necessary to make such a plea. In any case, no such public gesture to defend the Jews against Nazi hooliganism materialized.[31]

That their abandonment was in full progress by this time must have been depressingly clear to contemporary Jews, even for those who clung to the hope that the storm would pass and things would return to normal. This attempt to keep the faith became ever more grueling as the signs of Jewish isolation mounted. An emphatic reminder of this was the Reichstag election of 30 July 1932, when 13,779,111 Germans voted Nazi. They were surely not all anti-Semites, not as defined in this essay at any rate. But if they were not people who were willing to act *against* Jews or even anxious to have others act in their name, they were also not people who were willing to act *for* them, to protect their rights as citizens and human beings, at a moment when it still would have cost them nothing to do so.

Richard S. Levy has taught German history and the history of the Holocaust at the University of Illinois at Chicago since 1971. His writing has gradually expanded from analysis of German anti-Semitism before World War I to the study of anti-Semitism worldwide, treating the subject in its cultural context and examining its function in politics and society. He is author of *The Downfall of the Anti-Semitic Political Parties in Imperial Germany* (New Haven, 1975), editor of *Antisemitism in the Modern World: An Anthology of Texts* (Lexington, MA, 1991), *Antisemitism: Historical Encyclopedia of Prejudice and Persecution,* 2 vols (Santa Barbara, 2005), and (with Albert Lindemann) *Antisemitism: A History* (Oxford, 2010). He cofounded and edited H-Antisemitism, an Internet electronic discussion forum, from 1993 to 2004.

Notes

1. Two examples of this non-nuanced approach are Daniel J. Goldhagen, *Hitler's Willing Executioners: Ordinary Germans and the Holocaust* (New York, 1996), and John Weiss, *Ideology of Death: Why the Holocaust Happened in Germany* (Chicago, 1996).

2. Victor Klemperer, *Ich will Zeugnis ablegen bis zum letzten: Tagebücher 1933– 1945,* 2 vols, ed. Walter Nowojski (Berlin, 1995), 1:372–73, 379, 383, 430. Klemperer's diaries, running over 1,700 pages for the Nazi years, provide an incomparable record of the steady decline of German Jewry.

3. For some other reasons why Jews did not fully acknowledge anti-Semitism in the empire period, see Monika Richarz, ed., *Jüdisches Leben in Deutschland: Selbstzeugnisse zur Sozialgeschichte im Kaiserreich,* 3 vols (Stuttgart, 1979), 2:35–37. Of the seven memoirs by Berliners she reproduces, only one mentions specific events—the Konitz ritual murder case of 1900 and the anti-Semitic parties' attempts to ban kosher butchering. The other six show an awareness of anti-Jewish prejudice without going into particulars. Jews living outside the capital were certainly more sensitive to anti-Semitism. Of the eight memoirs gathered from those who lived in small towns or the countryside, all but one recount anti-Semitic experiences; some go into detail about Otto Böckel's anti-Semitic peasant movement in Hesse; others talk about more ancient prejudices that troubled their childhoods, such as having the accusation of Christ-killer thrown at them by fellow students. Every account, however, insists that relations with Christian neighbors were generally good, respectful, and peaceful. A condensed English-language version is *Jewish Life in Germany: Memoirs from Three Centuries,* trans. Stella and Sidney Rosenfeld (Bloomington, 1991).

4. Astrid Blome, Holger Böning and Michael Nagel, eds, *Die Lösung der Judenfrage: Eine Rundfrage von Julius Moses im Jahre 1907* (Bremen, 2010). The book contained some contributions not published in the newspaper, *General-Anzeiger für die gesamten Interessen des Judentums;* non-Jewish respondents were nearly twice as well-represented as Jewish ones.

5. Not all Jews were so confident about the future. The activists in various antidefamation organizations, in contrast to the rank and file membership, vigorously engaged political anti-Semitism and were, by and large, realistic about the dangers it posed to German Jewry, at least insofar as these could be imagined before 1914. See Ismar Schorsch, *Jewish Reactions to German Anti-Semitism, 1870–1914* (New York and Philadelphia, 1972).

6. Milton L. Barron, "The Incidence of Jewish Intermarriage in Europe and America," *American Sociological Review* 11, no.1 (February 1946): 6–13. Barron notes that mixed marriages were more frequent in times of prosperity than crisis (9). For a different interpretation, see Steven M. Lowenstein, "Jewish Intermarriage and Conversion in Germany and Austria," *Modern Judaism* 25, no. 1 (2005): 23–61.

7. See Wilhelm Marr, *Der Sieg des Judenthums über das Germanenthum*, translated in *Anti-Semitism in the Modern World: An Anthology of Texts*, ed. Richard S. Levy (Lexington, MA, 1991), 76–93; quotation from 82. "Hep-Hep," a catchphrase of indeterminate origin and meaning, traditionally signaled the beginning of anti-Jewish riots.

8. Fritsch in *Hammer: Zeitschrift für nationales Leben* 25, no. 571 (April 1926): 137–43.

9. For some thoughts on how to deal with "historical" public opinion, see Lee Benson, "An Approach to the Scientific Study of Past Public Opinion," *Public Opinion Quarterly* 31, no. 4 (1967–68): 522–67.

10. On the laughably differentiated agendas of the anti-Semitic parties, see Margaret Lavinia Anderson, *Practicing Democracy: Elections and Political Culture in Imperial Germany* (Princeton, 2000), 186 n116, which points out that the standard source on Reichstag electioneering required nineteen pages for the individual programs of the anti-Semitic parties, six times as much space as was devoted to the much larger and far more important Center Party.

11. See Richard S. Levy, *The Downfall of the Anti-Semitic Political Parties in Imperial Germany* (New Haven, 1975), 85–90; for the statistical decline of the anti-Semitic parties in national elections, see Max Schwarz, *MdR: Biographisches Handbuch der Reichstage* (Hannover, 1965), 806–8.

12. The grounds for this rough estimate can be found in Levy, *Downfall*, 118. On the difficulty of approximating party membership numbers, see Ludwig Bergsträsser, *Geschichte der politischen Parteien in Deutschland*, 10th edn (Munich, 1960), 32.

13. Nearly half the student body of the University of Berlin signed; Halle and Leipzig universities were also strongly represented. See Richard S. Levy, ed., *Anti-Semitism: Historical Encyclopedia of Prejudice and Persecution*, 2 vols (Santa Barbara, CA, 2005), 1:20–21.

14. This did not go unnoticed by Jews outside Germany. Starting in the 1880s, and despite the existence of popular anti-Semitism, Germany remained a desirable place to settle for a sizable minority of the eastern European Jewish immigrants (*Ostjuden*) who chose not to continue on to North or South America. By 1914, nearly 20 percent of the Jewish population was foreign born, this despite the many obstacles put in the way of immigrants becoming citizens. See Richarz,

Jüdisches Leben, 17. For the hostile response of government to this influx, see Jack Wertheimer, *Unwelcome Strangers: East European Jews in Imperial Germany* (New York, 1987), 24.

15. For accounts of wartime experiences, not at the front, but while on leave, see Richarz, *Jüdisches Leben*, 104–5; also Sabine Hank and Hermann Simon, eds, *Feldpostbriefe Jüdischer Soldaten 1914–1918*, 2 vols (Teetz, 2002), 2:400–1. A brief but informative survey of the effects of war service on Jewish identity, often disillusioning, is Michael Brenner, "The German army orders a census of Jewish soldiers, and Jews defend German Culture," in *Yale Companion to Jewish Writing and Thought in German Culture, 1096–1996*, eds Sander Gilman and Jack Zipes (New Haven, 1997), 348–54.

16. This is not the place to go into the intense debate concerning the effectiveness of the Centralverein's tactics. For a largely positive view, see Arnold Paucker, *Der jüdische Abwehrkampf gegen Antisemitismus und Nationalsozialismus in den letzten Jahren der Weimarer Republik*, 2nd rev. edn (Hamburg, 1969); an at times hostile evaluation, written as the destruction of the German Jewish community was being carried out, is Ambrose Doskow and Sidney B. Jacoby, "Anti-Semitism and the Law in Pre-Nazi Germany," *Contemporary Jewish Record* 3 (1940): 498–509. A balanced, not uncritical, view is Donald Niewyk, *The Jews in Weimar Germany* (Baton Rouge, 1980), chap. 4.

17. Vejas Liulevicius, *War Land on the Eastern Front: Culture, National Identity, and German Occupation in World War I* (Cambridge, 2000), 58, 120, 132, records the mostly negative impressions among the upper ranks, from Ludendorff on down. Even before the war, Hitler claims to have experienced an epiphany regarding the "Jewish Question" upon seeing an eastern European Jew in central Vienna. See Adolf Hitler, *Mein Kampf*, trans. Ralph Manheim (Boston, 1943), 56ff. On the history of *Ostjuden* and their central role in anti-Semitic discourse, see Trude Maurer, *Ostjuden in Deutschland 1918–1933* (Hamburg, 1986). Dirk Walter, *Antisemitische Kriminalität und Gewalt: Judenfeindschaft in der Weimarer Republik* (Bonn, 1999), 60–65, sees agitation against eastern European Jews as an attempt at consensus building on the right.

18. The Prussian government denied that anti-Semitism prompted its expulsion in 1885–86 of approximately thirty thousand Polish-Russian subjects, although fully a third were Jews. Similarly, military officials refused to acknowledge discrimination against Jews, even though there were none on the Prussian Army General Staff from the 1870s until the early years of World War I and there were no Jews or Jewish converts to be found among the prestigious reserve officer corps. On the "Jew Census" of 1916, see Brian Crim, in *Anti-Semitism: Historical Encyclopedia*, 1:371–72.

19. Tim Grady, *The German-Jewish Soldiers of the First World War in History and Memory* (Liverpool, 2011), 32–34, denies that the "Jew Census" was a watershed for German Jews, because their reaction to it was so diverse, much more disillusioned on the home front than in the trenches. David J. Fine, *Jewish Integration in the German Army in the First World War* (Berlin and Boston, 2012) also sees little significance in the "Jew Census," and for similar reasons. For the consensus view, see Trude Maurer, "Die Juden in der Weimarer Republik," in

Richard S. Levy

Zerbrochene Geschichte: Leben und Selbstverständnis der Juden in Deutschland, eds Dirk Blasius and Dan Diner (Frankfurt/M, 1991), 106–7.

20. Otto Bonhard, *Geschichte des Alldeutschen Verbandes* (Leipzig, 1920), 6–7, 98–99. This "authorized" history of the Pan-German League sounds an almost apologetic note because of the length of time it took for the organization to "achieve clarity" on the "Jewish Question," Jewish membership, and the validity of anti-Semitism. The war finally convinced members that the time for equivocation was past. On its adoption of overt anti-Semitism, creation of the Deutschvölkischer Schutz- und Trutzbund, a mass propaganda organization with terroristic inclinations, and Pan-German influence on Hitler, see Helmut Berding, *Moderner Antisemitismus in Deutschland* (Stuttgart, 1988), 179–87; more cautiously, Roger Chickering, *We Men Who Feel Most German: A Cultural Study of the Pan-German League* (Boston, 1984), 299.

21. For example, Victor Klemperer, *Leben sammeln, nicht fragen wozu und warum. Tagebücher 1918-1924,* 2 vols, ed. Walter Nowojski (Berlin, 1996), 1:51, 245, 598.

22. Berding, *Moderner Antisemitismus,* 178, claims over 100 racist-nationalist "circles, associations, orders, and unions" were operative after 1918. Maurer, "Juden in der Weimarer Republik," 107, counts a considerably greater "400 völkisch organizations and 700 anti-Semitic periodicals." Whichever set of numbers is closer to the truth, they dwarfed those of the prewar movement.

23. But certainly not on the right. See Theodor Fritsch, "The Desperate Act of a Desperate People," translated in Levy, *Anti-Semitism in the Modern World,* 192–99. Because of this article, Fritsch was tried, convicted, and fined heavily, escaping jail only because of his age. Public and private reactions may also have diverged. Some supposedly reputable elements of society expressed pleasure at Rathenau's death. See Carole Fink, "The Murder of Wather Rathenau," *Judaism* 44, no. 3 (1995): 259–69.

24. Walter, *Antisemitische Kriminalität,* 24–25, 35–37, 81–86, and especially 221. For the historical roots of symbolic violence exercised against Jews and the disparity between lethal threats and lethal realities, see Christhard Hoffmann, Werner Bergmann and Helmut Walser Smith, eds, *Exclusionary Violence: Anti-Semitic Riots in Modern German History* (Ann Arbor, 2002).

25. Walter, *Antisemitische Kriminalität,* 164–66, 176, 298n30.

26. The best discussion of the strength of anti-Semitism within the party is in Ian Kershaw, *The "Hitler Myth": Image and Reality in the Third Reich* (Oxford, 1989), chap. 9. Kershaw downplays its importance in the Weimar era and doubts the primary role of anti-Semitism in Hitler's achievement of massive popularity during the Third Reich (250). See also Sarah Gordon, *Hitler, Germans, and the Jewish Question* (Princeton, 1984), 56–65; Peter H. Merkl, *Political Violence Under the Swastika: 581 Early Nazis* (Princeton, 1975), 33, 453, 566–67, an analysis of life stories submitted by Nazi Party members for a contest staged by the Columbia University sociologist Theodore Abel in 1934. Merkl estimates that nearly half of these stories showed little or no anti-Semitism. Although neither scholar defined this term, both apparently worked from a much broader conception than mine.

27. Gordon, *Hitler, Germans, and the Jewish Question,* 67–71.

28. On the hectic activity of the Centralverein, the difficulty in mobilizing their own members, and fluctuating levels of confidence about the future, see Paucker, *Der jüdische Abwehrkampf,* 17–22.
29. Levy, *Downfall,* 136, 145–46. During the empire period, the Abwehr-Verein remained largely non-Jewish, numbering nearly thirteen thousand members by 1893.
30. On the Centralverein, see Paucker, *Der jüdische Abwehrkampf,* 51. On the Abwehr-Verein, see Barbara Suchy, "The Verein zur Abwehr des Antisemitismus (2): From the First World War to Its Dissolution in 1933," *Leo Baeck Institute Year Book* 30 (1985): 98–99.
31. Walter, *Antisemitische Kriminalität,* 211–22. On the gradual isolation of Jews, see Cornelia Hecht, *Deutsche Juden und Antisemitismus in der Weimarer Republik* (Bonn, 2003), 400–3.

Selected Bibliography

Berding, Helmut. *Moderner Antisemitismus in Deutschland.* Stuttgart, 1988.

Chickering, Roger. *We Men Who Feel Most German: A Cultural Study of the Pan-German League.* Boston, 1984.

Fine, David. J. *Jewish Integration in the German Army in the First World War.* Berlin and Boston, 2012.

Grady, Tim. *The German-Jewish Soldiers of the First World War in History and Memory.* Liverpool, 2011.

Hecht, Cornelia. *Deutsche Juden und Antisemitismus in der Weimarer Republik.* Bonn, 2003.

Hoffmann, Christhard, Werner Bergmann and Helmut Walser Smith, eds. *Exclusionary Violence: Anti-Semitic Riots in Modern German History.* Ann Arbor, 2002.

Levy, Richard S., ed. *Antisemitism in the Modern World: An Anthology of Texts.* Lexington, MA, 1991.

Levy, Richard S. *The Downfall of the Anti-Semitic Political Parties in Imperial Germany.* New Haven, 1975.

Niewyk, Donald. *The Jews in Weimar Germany.* Baton Rouge, 1980.

Paucker, Arnold. *Der jüdische Abwehrkampf gegen Antisemitismus und Nationalsozialismus in den letzten Jahren der Weimarer Republik.* 2nd rev. ed. Hamburg, 1969.

Richarz, Monika, ed. *Jüdisches Leben in Deutschland: Selbstzeugnisse zur Sozialgeschichte im Kaiserreich.* 3 vols. Stuttgart, 1979.

Schorsch, Ismar. *Jewish Reactions to German Anti-Semitism, 1870–1914.* New York and Philadelphia, 1972.

Walter, Dirk. *Antisemitische Kriminalität und Gewalt: Judenfeindschaft in der Weimarer Republik.* Bonn, 1999.

Wertheimer, Jack. *Unwelcome Strangers: East European Jews in Imperial Germany.* New York, 1987.

Figure 3. Jewish men who had been placed under arrest after the Kristallnacht pogrom being marched through the streets of Baden-Baden, 10 November 1938.

Chapter 2

German Responses to the Persecution of the Jews as Reflected in Three Collections of Secret Reports

Frank Bajohr

If we wish to get some idea about public opinion in democratic states, there are a variety of sources available, most notably reporting by a pluralistic media, opinion surveys, and voting behavior. None of these sources are available for the National Socialist dictatorship in Germany, and the state-controlled media of that regime yielded little useful data. The Nazi state lacked a key element of democratic societies, namely an autonomous public sphere. Especially in the media, which were run and shaped by state and Nazi Party (NSDAP) propaganda, the broad spectrum of public opinion in Nazi Germany was reflected only in a highly rudimentary form.

Precisely for this reason, the Nazi regime had a very keen interest in finding out something about popular opinion in the country—for example, regarding the persecution of the Jews. Therefore it ordered numerous institutions to assemble so-called situation reports (*Lageberichte*) to that end. Most of these reports stem from the Gestapo, the Security Service (Sicherheitsdienst—SD) of the SS, the judicial authorities, and organs of the local and regional bureaucracy.[1] All of these were required from 1933 onward to keep Jewish organizations under surveillance. But they had the additional task, under the heading of "Jews" or "Judaism," to report confidentially on measures against Jews, on problems that had arisen in implementing anti-Jewish policy, on reactions to individual events, and on the prevailing attitude and behavior of the broad population. These topics were of abiding central importance in the situation reports, so that beginning in 1933, we have an almost unbroken dense chain of such reports and messages.

According to official instructions, the Nazi regime expected to obtain "unvarnished reports." Nevertheless, many of those who did the reporting were convinced Nazis whose language was regulated by regime-internal provisions on what was acceptable in political discourse, so-called *Sprachregelungen.* For this reason, they tended to embellish, cover over, and veil certain facts. Thus, violent actions against Jews carried out by individuals, so-called *Einzelaktionen,* which as a rule were forbidden, represented a special problem for those reporting. As a result, they often did not specifically name the persons who were involved. Functionaries of the Hitler Youth, for example, were innocuously referred to as "young people." And very often the authors of the reports employed expressions like the "anti-Semitic wave,"[2] as though the anti-Jewish persecution were some sort of natural phenomenon. The Holocaust was not named as such, nor were internal expressions such as "Final Solution" used, but instead the reports contained cryptic paraphrases like "resettlement" or "evacuation of the Jews."[3] However, this strategy of euphemistic embellishment had its limits. It is striking that almost no reporter characterized the November 1938 pogrom (Kristallnacht) as "spontaneous popular anger," the expression in the official propaganda version, but reports rather openly referred to the highly organized character of these pogroms by utilizing the word *Judenaktion,* literally "operation against the Jews."[4]

A second characteristic feature clearly limits the analytical value of the regime-internal situation reports in regard to understanding popular reactions to Jewish policy. These reports were largely situational, focused usually on local incidents that happened at a particular time. The authors of the reports were not allowed to offer general observations on anti-Jewish policy, the significance of anti-Semitism, or the role of Hitler in the Nazi persecution of the Jews. Nor could they speculate on future developments or give advice to their superiors.

This lack of reflection distinguished the regime-internal situation reports from two other groups of sources that likewise shed light on the practice of National Socialist rule in general and on the persecution of the Jews in particular. First there were the very numerous—more than one hundred thousand—reports that foreign consuls and diplomats composed in Nazi Germany and then sent on to their respective embassies or foreign ministries.[5] These reports were a routine duty of diplomats and were meant to inform their superiors in an open and unbiased way about important internal developments within the National Socialist state. In contrast to the regime-internal situation reports, the diplomatic reports were written by observers who were not National Socialists and who in addition were looking at events in Germany with foreign eyes, as outsiders. While the reports from within the Nazi regime contained no general reflections on the situation or prognoses about the persecution of the Jews, this was precisely what foreign governments expected from the reports by their diplomats. The diplomats devoted substantial space in their reports to the persecution of the Jews, because they were directly confronted with the consequences of this policy in connection with the issuing of visas. The diplomats also speculated about possible future developments and already in 1933 pointed to the particularly radical character of National Socialist anti-Jewish policy. Most of the diplomats quickly realized that this policy was not designed simply to accord the Jews a reduced legal status inside German society. In March 1933, the American consul general in Berlin, George Messersmith, spoke of "instances of a brutality and a directness of action which have not been excelled in the history of modern times."[6] (See Appendix B). The Nazis were aiming at the "practically unrestricted persecution of a race." In 1935, Messersmith's French counterpart in Munich stated that with respect to the Jews, National Socialism's goal was none other than their "simple naked elimination."[7] The French observer did not predict a Holocaust in 1935, but referred to the policy of economic destruction and the expulsion of the Jewish minority. Nevertheless a murderous solution to the "Jewish Question" could not be ruled out, as the French ambassador indicated, quoting radical anti-Semites: "The Jews must 'croak' or disappear."[8] The considerable abilities to forecast what might transpire did not often result in any concrete practical action on behalf of the persecuted Jews. Although the persecution generated feelings of sympathy and compassion for the Jews among most diplomatic observers, there were also fears of an imminent large number of immigrants landing on their doorstep. The result was that most, though not all, consuls tended to be restrictive in dealing with the issuing of visas. In this regard their actions were, of course, consistent with the expectations and regulations of their respective governments.

Comparable reflections on the persecution of the Jews were also contained in a third group of sources, the so-called "Germany Reports," which from 1934 to 1940 were published by the party executive in exile of the German Social Democratic Party (SPD), initially in Prague, and from 1938 onward in London.[9] The Social Democratic reports were based on messages and observations on developments in Nazi Germany by anti-Nazi former members of the now-prohibited SPD. The reports were then clandestinely smuggled abroad via so-called border secretariats. Some of these reports were written by Jewish members of the SPD, in which they reported about their own personal situation in vivid terms. However, in contrast to the regime-internal situation reports and the reports by diplomats, the persecution of the Jews initially played only a minor role in these Social Democratic reports. This changed gradually from 1935 on, but reports on persecution of the Jews were still always placed under the general heading of "Terror." Not until 1939 did they appear for the first time in a separate new column titled "Persecution of the Jews."

This was due in part to the fact that at the beginning of the Third Reich, the Social Democrats had clearly been more persecuted than the German Jews. When the SPD was officially banned in June 1933, many thousands of its members were already under arrest in concentration camps. Another reason for treating the persecution of the Jews more marginally was the Social Democratic analysis of Nazism. It viewed the Nazi regime as a dictatorship by capitalist power elites aiming in particular at the suppression of the working class. Accordingly, Social Democrats saw the persecution of the Jews as a secondary phenomenon with functionalist aims.[10] The Social Democratic analysis was that the Jews had been singled out to serve largely as a scapegoat. In addition, it held that the persecution of the Jews had been engineered to deflect interest from the internal difficulties of the Nazi regime. The Social Democrats did not revise this position until 1938, when it became clear to them that the Nazis were pursuing the total expulsion and even annihilation of the German Jews and were not intending to keep them in the country as some sort of scapegoat community. Now the Social Democrats appealed to their European partners, especially the sister parties in Scandinavia, to become active in a more generous policy of admitting Jewish refugees to their countries. In early 1939, the Social Democratic reports stated very clearly:

> In Germany at the moment, what is taking place is the complete extermination of a minority using the brutal means of murder, torture to the point of lunacy, theft, attack and starvation. What the Armenians suffered during the war in Turkey is being carried out against the Jews in the Third Reich, more slowly and according to plan.[11]

Comparative Analysis of the Three Kinds of Secret Reports

A comparison of the dominant narrative structure in the regime-internal, diplomatic, and Social Democratic reports reveals a striking difference. The regime-internal reports distinguish mainly between Germans and Jews, while the diplomatic and Social Democratic reports present a more complex structure, differentiating between Germans, National Socialists, and Jews. Interestingly, however, the dominant narrative repeatedly had to be set aside, or at least modified, in all three kinds of reports. The result is that the reports, which were written by authors who clearly differed in terms of political convictions, origin, and motivation, in the final analysis frequently display an astonishing convergence.

With their fundamental distinction between Germans and Jews, the regime-internal reports excluded the Jews from the so-called *Volksgemeinschaft* (national community), while endeavoring at the same time to maintain the fiction of a unity between the German people and National Socialism. However, especially in local reports, this narrative was repeatedly breached when the practice of anti-Jewish persecution led to local conflict and a majority of the local residents objected to specific anti-Jewish measures. To take one example, the Hitler Youth in Hechingen, a small town south of Stuttgart, on 26 June 1935, disrupted an event of the Jewish community by assembling in front of the synagogue with noisy fanfare and the chanting of slogans. The local Gestapo reported:

> This operation displeased large segments of the local population of Hechingen, especially the workers employed in the Jewish workshops and factories ... and who fear the loss of their jobs should these firms close. The workers have threatened to resign from the German Labor Front if their [Jewish] employers are not given satisfaction. That naturally is impossible. Now the workers are being given an oral explanation by the director of the German Labor Front, emphasizing that such incidents should in future be eliminated.[12]

The report indicated that the non-Jewish population in particular was opposed to such anti-Jewish operations lest they come into conflict with their own interests—in this case, the protection of their own jobs. For the same reasons, boycott actions against Jewish firms and shops at which the customers were often photographed and later denounced in public were unpopular because they clashed with the interest of the population as consumers. Ordinary Germans appreciated the often lower

prices offered by the Jewish shops and the possibility of buying on installment, while in the countryside many farmers preferred dealing with Jewish cattle merchants because they paid more than the market price.

According to the regime's own situation reports, the population also rejected anti-Jewish measures when they had a negative impact on public order or were associated with the use of violence. In June 1935, the district president in Trier noted that the majority of the population was "quite uncomprehending" when it came to violent attacks on Jews or desecration of synagogues and cemeteries. He stressed that people had little understanding for, and were especially outraged by, the conspicuous involvement of youth and teenagers in these actions. The district president openly stated, "I also think the manner in which children are taking part in anti-Semitic propaganda was regrettable."[13] Some in the population were even circulating jokes about the anti-Jewish propaganda, in which they caricatured the propaganda rather than the Jews. A situation report from the Minden District for September 1935 included a typical joke:

> A lion has broken out of his cage in some city. Everyone runs away when he appears in the street. But one small Jew goes right up to the lion, grabs the creature by the mane, and hauls him back to his cage. The next morning the newspaper carries the story: "Jewish Insolence—a Jewish lout had the gall to pull so hard at the mane of a poor defenseless lion in the street that the lion was forced to follow him. It is high time that some limit be set to the outrageous brazenness of the pack of Jews."[14]

The regime-internal secret reports saw the adversaries of the persecution of the Jews as situated principally in the ranks of political opponents and in Christian circles. Yet caution is required in interpreting this feature of the reports because both groups were counted among the ideological adversaries about whom the authors of the situation reports had to report regularly. Thus, for example, the routine surveillance of sermons and church gatherings indicated that Roman Catholics criticized the methods of persecuting the Jews but did not criticize the anti-Jewish policy as such. In the stenographically recorded statements of Catholic clergy, criticism of the persecution of the Jews and anti-Semitic stereotypes were often blended together. Thus, a chaplain at a meeting of the Catholic Men's Association St. Matthew in Berlin remarked in October 1935, "The Jewish Question must be regulated using permitted means and must not be allowed to decline into acts of persecution."[15]

Yet it was equally unacceptable, he added, "that Jews should dominate everything," and the chaplain described their persecution at the same time as a form of divine retribution: "Only because they crucified Christ is His blood upon them and their children." Although the clergyman expressed his pity for the persecuted Jews, he nonetheless classified them as "Christ murderers" and was convinced that a "Jewish Question" certainly existed.

Only very rarely, therefore, did the regime's own situation reports note a total rejection of all anti-Jewish policies, and they pointed repeatedly to the fact that legal measures aimed at the Jews met with broad popular acceptance. According to the reports, the anti-Semitic Nuremberg Laws were viewed with "substantial satisfaction" and enjoyed "full recognition."[16] In addition, they were "perceived as a very clever solution by Adolf Hitler"[17] and had thus enhanced Hitler's positive image among the population. On the one hand, the regime-internal situation reports had to repeatedly modify the narrative of a dichotomy between Germans and Jews, emphasizing the special role played by National Socialist activists in the persecution of the Jews as well as criticisms of elements of that policy inside German society. On the other hand, the narrative of a fundamental dichotomy was never totally repudiated, as legal measures against the Jews enjoyed a quite broad basis of social consensus within the non-Jewish population.

This ambivalence was also evident in the reports on the November 1938 pogrom, which a majority of the population strongly rejected. The regime's secret situation reports certainly did not try to conceal the widespread objections in the population. A mayor in eastern Westphalia estimated that "at least 60 percent" of the population was clearly against the pogrom.[18] (See Appendix E.) According to reports, Christian circles had particularly criticized the destruction of synagogues, while workers had objected to the destruction of material assets and property. Violent attacks, acts of looting, and the participation of youths younger than eighteen in the pogrom were likewise criticized, and there was an expression of pity after the mass arrest of Jewish men. However, there was little mention of openly voiced criticism. What was noted instead was an "embarrassed silence"—"People are ashamed."[19]

Yet most authors of the secret situation reports stressed at the same time that the majority of the population raised no fundamental objections against anti-Jewish measures and accepted even a stringent approach—though without open violence. The majority was certainly in agreement with "less drastic means,"[20] as a report formulated it. For that reason, the ordinances for the Aryanization of the German economy that were issued in the wake of the pogrom were not rejected at all. To the contrary, they were welcomed with "satisfaction," as the district president of Upper Bavaria noted in a report in December 1938. [21]

Were these tendencies that marked the regime-internal secret reports also present in the diplomatic and Social Democratic reports? As already mentioned, their basic narrative was grounded on the distinction between National Socialists, Germans, and Jews. Foreign diplomats as well as German Social Democrats saw the initiative for anti-Jewish measures as always clearly stemming from the Nazi government, the Nazi Party, and other National Socialist organizations, according only a reactive role to the German population as a whole. The U.S. consul general Douglas Jenkins remarked in November 1935 that anti-Semitism was "deeprooted in the National Socialist Party." [22] A few days later, his counterpart in Berlin, Raymond Geist, presented a noteworthy analysis of the forces driving Nazi anti-Jewish policy. Geist stressed the function of anti-Semitism for the internal integration of the Nazi Party and its place in the overall system of rule. He wrote:

> In the Party itself anti-Semitism is the common tie which unites the various groups and factions which manifest otherwise entirely different political tendencies, and binds them strongly because they all know that on this point Adolf Hitler will not compromise. Anti-Semitism provides a channel for all the explosive forces in the Party— an exhaust which continues to function successfully. ... The Party as the determining living factor must be in a constant state of aggression and must endeavor to maintain the offensive and consequently must have an ever present object of attack. [23]

Like the Social Democrats, many diplomats preferred a more functionalistic interpretation of anti-Jewish policy. This view interpreted that policy not primarily as a product of ideology, but rather emphasized its function in mobilizing the Nazi movement. This view always tried to integrate anti-Jewish measures into a more comprehensive framework of Nazi politics and policy. Seen from this perspective, the Third Reich was not an ideologically grounded dictatorship, but rather a dictatorship of mobilization. Anti-Semitic ideology first took on a fundamental importance in the memoirs published by some of the diplomats after 1945. In these memoirs, anti-Semitic ideology was described as an integrating factor that extended from Hitler's *Mein Kampf* to the gas chambers of

Auschwitz.[24] But there was little of this in the contemporary reports authored by diplomats before 1945. Thus, it was on the whole quite significant when the American consul general Leon Dominian, who presented the Department of State with an analysis of *Mein Kampf* in May 1933, chose to interpret the book as a blueprint for a German grab for world power. In his view, the book articulated a "German intention to dominate Europe by violence," which was only the "prelude to plans of world control."[25] The anti-Semitism was clearly evident to Dominian, but at the time he believed that it possessed a mainly nationalistic mobilizing function.

In the diplomatic reports, the German population appeared principally as observers to events, who on occasion became outraged. In September 1935, a British consul reported, "There are great numbers of Germans of all classes to whom this Jewish persecution is abhorrent."[26] The open use of violence was disgusting to many Germans, as reactions to the November 1938 pogrom showed. Far more than in the regime's situation reports, the consular reports stressed that many Germans were displeased with the progrom, indeed openly indignant. "Many people, in fact, are banging their heads with shame,"[27] the U.S. consul general Honacker reported from Stuttgart. The Italian diplomat Guido Romano, who represented a country allied with Berlin, called the mood in the population "deeply enraged."[28] His colleague Francesco Pittalis reported on voices of rejection even from among the ranks of Nazi Party members. He noted that the "idea of personal violence" was generally perceived "as inappropriate" for solving the so-called "Jewish Problem."[29]

A closer look, however, reveals that many diplomatic reports contain references that contradict a strict antagonism between party and population in regard to the persecution of the Jews. Consul Honacker in Stuttgart estimated that at least 20 percent of the population had been explicitly satisfied with the November 1938 pogrom. This is very much in keeping with the regime's situation reports, which had reported a rejection rate of "at least 60 percent." In the university town of Heidelberg, for example, students had also participated in the searches of Jewish homes after the November pogrom. The Argentine ambassador Edouardo Labougle commented that "many persons" had made use of the situation in order to help loot the destroyed Jewish businesses.[30]

In addition, the diplomats noticed that the rejection of open violence was by no means the same as rejection of the anti-Jewish policy as such. A memo by the British consulate general in Hamburg, commenting on the attitude of the younger generation, stated in the spring of 1939:

> The attitude of the German youth to the Jewish Question is not much different from that of the nation as a whole. They regret the recent excesses and the barbarous methods of carrying out anti-Semitic principles, but are nonetheless firmly convinced of the necessity for ridding Germany of the last Jew. The women are perhaps even more intolerant on this last point.[31]

In other words, although the Germans criticized the violent practices employed in the persecution of the Jews, the diplomats also noted the presence of an anti-Jewish consensus that had crystallized after six years of National Socialist rule. This consensus meant that Jews were no longer viewed as Germans, and in keeping with this, no objections were raised to their expulsion. Despite differing starting conditions, diplomatic and regime-internal situation reports were in agreement on this point in an astonishing way.

This combination of a general anti-Jewish consensus and a specific rejection of the use of violence was reflected even more pointedly in the Social Democratic reports. In the beginning, the SPD reports had assumed that the population totally rejected anti-Semitic measures. In a 1935 report that reflected this tendency, the author claimed that the anti-Jewish actions of the Nazis "found no favor among the population."[32] A report from the city of Lübeck stated that anti-Semitism had not sunk "deeper roots," but at the same time it referred, almost unwittingly, to certain anti-Jewish tendencies in the population: "The general expression in Lübeck is: 'The Jews are not the bad ones, it's the white Jews who are!'"[33] The concept of the "white Jew" referred to non-Jews whose behavior was considered problematic. The term was quite widespread at the time in the German population. The National Socialists used the expression to refer especially to so-called friends of Jews, while among Social Democratic workers it was employed as a synonym for a non-Jewish capitalist exploiter. Generally speaking, the concept of "white Jew" points up an underlying anti-Semitism in the German population, since it implicitly attributed presumed "typically Jewish" problematic characteristics to Jews, even though it was not used to refer to Jews themselves.

There was a clear change in the tenor of Social Democratic reporting on the behavior of the Germans in 1936. It stated that although a majority in the population still rejected "Streicher's methods" (a reference to the virulently anti-Semitic Julius Streicher, the Nazi gauleiter of Franconia), anti-Jewish propaganda was exerting an ever greater impact. A report noted, "It is now a generally held view that a 'Jewish Question' exists."[34] A Social Democrat from Saxony even espoused the view that a "substantial proportion of the population today is already convinced of the correctness of the National Socialist racial doctrines."[35] He emphasized that anti-Semitism had "taken root in broad circles of the people." Moreover, he stressed that many Germans "no longer wanted to have anything to do with the Jews" and that even their own former SPD party members were by no means totally immune to anti-Semitic influences:

> There are quite a few who, although not National Socialists, nonetheless within certain limits endorse the view that civil rights for the German Jews should be curtailed and they should be separated from the German people. Many socialists also espouse this standpoint. It is true that they don't agree with the harsh methods the Nazis employ, but they nonetheless say: "It doesn't harm the greater majority of the Jews!"[36]

Such statements also gave clear expression to the social distance separating the Social Democratic largely blue-collar workers from the German Jews, the majority of whom were more prosperous and middle class.

The reports in subsequent years precisely followed the ambivalence that has already been described. On the one hand, the population clearly criticized certain anti-Jewish practices, such as the violent events of the November 1938 pogrom, which according to the Social Democrats had triggered feelings of shame "that such things were at all possible in Germany." At the end of 1938 the Social Democratic Executive in exile in London tried to build on this sense of outrage in developing an anti-Nazi propaganda campaign. At the very same time, however, many reports noted that the National Socialists had actually succeeded in "deepening the chasm between the German people and the Jews."[37] (See Appendix D.)

On the whole, in 1938–39 the regime-internal, diplomatic, and Social Democratic reports arrived at a very similar conclusion—this despite the different views of their authors and the likewise divergent narratives of their reports. They referred to the continuing criticism of violent anti-Jewish practices, but at the same time discerned an anti-Jewish consensus that raised no objections to the exclusion of the German Jews.

The War Years

A comparative perspective is no longer possible when it comes to the war years and the events of the Final Solution. This is because the Social Democratic reports largely ceased publication in 1940, while diplomatic reporting diminished after the outbreak of the war, as most countries no longer maintained a diplomatic representation in Germany. Down to the beginning of the war, however, it was clear to all those reporting that the German population raised no objections to the systematic exclusion and expulsion of the Jews. At the same time, the aversion of many Germans to the use of open violence suggested that there was no social consensus for the systematic mass murder of the Jews. This is implied not just by the diplomatic reports of the early war years, such as those by American diplomats, but also by the numerous critical voices raised when the wearing of the "yellow star" was introduced for all Jews in September 1941 and at the beginning of deportations in October the same year.[38] It was not anti-Jewish policy as such that marked a rupture in the social consensus, but rather the mass murder.

In 1941, at the time of the deportations, the regime-internal secret reports reflected at least in part the presence of objections and compassion for the victims. According to internal situation reports compiled by the regime, "the politically educated segment of the population" endorsed the deportations—along with "national comrades [*Volksgenossen*] who are firm in their National Socialist outlook" and "national comrades who are well informed about the Jewish Question."[39] Objections were raised primarily by older Germans as well as by conscious Christians and individuals from the middle class. In July 1942, the Security Service office in Lemgo commented on statements regarding the deportation that "many of the older national comrades criticized":

> Some said the Jews were doomed to die out in Germany anyhow, and that this measure, which was for the Jews especially severe, was thus superfluous. Even those national comrades who earlier on every occasion, suitable and nonsuitable, had emphasized their National Socialist Outlook, in this respect expressed their support for the interest of the Jews, or national comrades who are connected with the church. Within the circles connected with the church, people said: "We only hope that one day the German people will not have to face the punishment of the Lord."[40]

Particularly in the reports in 1943 and 1944, it became clear that many Germans were speaking about the treatment of the Jews in a kind of melange of bad conscience, fears of future retribution, and projections of guilt. The Allied bombing war was interpreted specifically as punishment for the persecution of the Jews, and people were making a direct association between the destruction of churches in the bombing raids and the burning of the synagogues in the November 1938 pogrom. (See Appendix F.) For example, after the air raids of Operation Gomorrah against Hamburg in July and August 1943, pastors noted that a "sense of guilt" was spreading in the population. The East Asian import-export merchant in Hamburg, Lothar de la Camp, wrote in this regard to his friends:

> Despite all the anger against the British and the Americans for the inhuman way they are conducting the war, you have to note very objectively that the common people, the middle class and the other circles repeatedly make statements privately among themselves, and even in a larger group, to the effect that the attacks are a reprisal for the way we treated the Jews.[41]

Other Security Service (SD) offices reported on numerous statements by people who had been bombed out of their homes, noting, for example, as asserted in Würzburg, that "this was the retaliation for our action in November 1938 against the Jews."[42] The SD in Schweinfurt reported a comment that "if we had not treated the Jews so badly, we would not have to suffer so much from terror attacks,"[43] while the SD in Halle noted the opinion that "it was irresponsible on the part of the government and the NSDAP to engage in such measures toward the Jews."[44]

The Holocaust, then, cannot simplistically be attributed to a general German consensus in favor of the murder of the Jews in the population, as Goldhagen suggested with his thesis of "eliminationist anti-Semitism" as a pervasive attitude in German society.[45] Instead, among the unsettling findings of the situation reports was that there was no need whatsoever for such a consensus in favor of murder. The anti-Jewish consensus described above proved sufficient for the purpose.

Frank Bajohr is head of the Center for Holocaust Studies at the Institute for Contemporary History (Institut für Zeitgeschichte) in Munich and

teaches at the Universities of Hamburg and Munich. His many publications include *Aryanization in Hamburg* (New York, 2002); *"Unser
Hotel ist judenfrei"*: *Bäder-Antisemitismus im 19. und 20. Jahrhundert*
(Frankfurt, 2003); *Der Holocaust als offenes Geheimnis. Die Deutschen,
die NS-Führung und die Allierten* (with Dieter Pohl) (Munich, 2006);
and *Fremde Blicke auf das "Dritte Reich.*" *Berichte ausländischer Diplomaten über Herrschaft und Gesellschaft in Deutschland 1933–1945* (Göttingen 2011). He is presently coediting the diaries of the Nazi chief
ideologue Alfred Rosenberg.

Notes

1. Otto Dov Kulka and Eberhard Jäckel, eds, *The Jews in the Secret Nazi Reports on Popular Opinion in Germany, 1933–1945* (New Haven, 2010).
2. See, for example, Stapostelle Police District Berlin, "General Overview," Berlin, 13 June 1935, in Kulka and Jäckel, *Jews in the Secret Nazi Reports,* 123.
3. Compare District Governor Lower and Central Franconia, Report for April 1942, Ansbach 5 May 1942, or District Governor Swabia, Report for April 1942, Augsburg 9 May 1942, in Kulka and Jäckel, *Jews in the Secret Nazi Reports,* 584.
4. County Commissioner Höxter, "Operation against the Jews," Höxter, 18 November 1938, in Kulka and Jäckel, *Jews in the Secret Nazi Reports,* 352.
5. Frank Bajohr and Christoph Strupp, eds, *Fremde Blicke auf das "Dritte Reich." Berichte ausländischer Diplomaten über Herrschaft und Gesellschaft in Deutschland 1933–1945* (Göttingen, 2011).
6. George S. Messersmith, Consul General, "With Further Reference to the Manifold Aspects of the Anti-Jewish Movement in Germany," Berlin, 31 March 1933, in Bajohr and Strupp, *Fremde Blicke,* 363.
7. Bourdeille, French Vice Consul, "Report from Munich," 8 October 1935, in Bajohr and Strupp, *Fremde Blicke,* 437–38.
8. André François-Poncet, French Ambassador, "Campaign against the Jews," Report No. 1566, 30 October 1935, in Bajohr and Strupp, *Fremde Blicke,* 438.
9. *Deutschland-Berichte der Sozialdemokratischen Partei Deutschlands (Sopade), 1934–1940,* 7 vols (reprint, Frankfurt am Main, 1980).
10. See also David Bankier, "German Social Democrats and the Jewish Question," in *Probing the Depths of German Antisemitism: German Society and the Persecution of the Jews, 1933–1941,* ed. David Bankier (New York and Oxford, 2000), 511–32.
11. *Deutschland-Berichte,* 1939, 201–2.
12. Stapostelle Government District Sigmaringen, Report for June 1935, Sigmaringen, 12 July 1935, in Kulka and Jäckel, *Jews in the Secret Nazi Reports,* 135.

13. District Governor Trier, Report for April and May 1935, Trier 6 June 1935, in Kulka and Jäckel, *Jews in the Secret Nazi Reports,* 128.
14. Government District Minden, State Lippe and District Hameln-Pyrmont, Report for September 1935, in Kulka and Jäckel, *Jews in the Secret Nazi Reports,* 159.
15. For this and the following quotations, see Stapostelle State Police District Berlin, Report for October 1935, Berlin, in Kulka and Jäckel, *Jews in the Secret Nazi Reports,* 165.
16. Stapostelle Government District Arnsberg, Report for September 1935, Dortmund, in Kulka and Jäckel, *Jews in the Secret Nazi Reports,* 154.
17. Government District Minden, State Lippe and District Hameln-Pyrmont, Report for September 1935, in Kulka and Jäckel, *Jews in the Secret Nazi Reports,* 159.
18. Mayor of Amt Borgentreich, Operation against the Jews on 10 November 1938, Amt Borgentreich, 17 November 1938, in Kulka and Jäckel, *Jews in the Secret Nazi Reports,* 358.
19. District Governor Minden, Secret Order of 28 November 1938, Minden 5 December 1938, in Kulka and Jäckel, *Jews in the Secret Nazi Reports,* 365.
20. District Governor Upper Bavaria, Report for December 1938, Munich, 9 January 1939, in Kulka and Jäckel, *Jews in the Secret Nazi Reports,* 389.
21. Ibid.
22. Douglas Jenkins, U.S. Consul General, Political and Economic Trends in Germany during the Past Twelve Months, Berlin, 4 November 1935, in Bajohr and Strupp, *Fremde Blicke,* 440.
23. Raymond H. Geist, U.S. Consul, The German Economic Situation with Particular Reference to the Political Outlook, Berlin, 12 November 1935, in Bajohr and Strupp, *Fremde Blicke,* 441.
24. See, for example, the memoirs of the French ambassador André François-Poncet, *Als Botschafter in Berlin, 1931–1938* (Mainz, 1947).
25. Leon Dominian, "Evidences of German Preparation of Aggression," Stuttgart, 19 May 1933, National Archives, College Park, MD, Record Group 59: United States Department of State, Central Decimal File 1930-39, 862.20/611 (microfilm edn, roll 17).
26. Robert Smallbones, British Consul General, to B.C. Newton, British Embassy, Frankfurt, 4 September 1935, in Bajohr and Strupp, *Fremde Blicke,* 432.
27. Samuel W. Honaker, U.S. Consul General, "Anti-Semitic Persecution in the Stuttgart Consular District," Stuttgart, 12 November 1938, in Bajohr and Strupp, *Fremde Blicke,* 505.
28. Guido Romano, Italian Consul General, Political Situation, Innsbruck, 12 November 1938, in Bajohr and Strupp, *Fremde Blicke,* 509.
29. Francesco Pittalis, Italian Consul General, "Further Effects of the Recent Anti-Semitic Manifestations," Munich, 19 November 1938, in Bajohr and Strupp, *Fremde Blicke,* 518.
30. Edouardo Labougle, Envoy of Argentina, to Foreign Minister José Maria Cantilo, Berlin, 14 November 1938, in Bajohr and Strupp, *Fremde Blicke,* 514.
31. British Consulate General in Hamburg to Nevile M. Henderson, "Memo-

randum on the General Attitude of the Young Generation," Hamburg, 5 July 1939, in Bajohr and Strupp, *Fremde Blicke,* 534.

32. *Deutschland-Berichte,* 1935, 812.
33. Ibid., 814.
34. Ibid., 1936, 24.
35. Ibid.
36. Ibid., 26.
37. Ibid., 24.
38. See, for example, Leland B. Morris, U.S. Embassy, Telegram, Berlin, 30 September 1941, in Bajohr and Strupp, *Fremde Blicke,* 562.
39. Stapostelle Bremen, Report, Bremen, 11 November 1941; SD District Office Detmold, Deportation of the Jews, Detmold, 31 July 1942; SD District Office Minden, "Attitude of the Population to the Evacuation of the Jews," Minden, 6 December 1941, in Kulka and Jäckel, *Jews in the Secret Nazi Reports,* 557, 599, 563.
40. SD District Office Detmold, Deportation of the Jews, Detmold, 31 July 1942, in Kulka and Jäckel, *Jews in the Secret Nazi Reports,* 599.
41. Quotation from *Die Hamburger Katastrophe vom Sommer 1943 in Augenzeugenberichten,* ed. Renate Hauschild-Thiessen (Hamburg, 1993), 230.
42. SD District Main Office Würzburg III A4, General Mood and Situation, Würzburg, 7 September 1943, in Kulka and Jäckel, *Jews in the Secret Nazi Reports,* 635.
43. SD District Office Schweinfurt, Report, n.d. (1944), in Kulka and Jäckel, *Jews in the Secret Nazi Reports,* 643.
44. SD Regional Division Halle/S. III C4, General Guidance of the Press, Halle, 22 May 1943, in Kulka and Jäckel, *Jews in the Secret Nazi Reports,* 622.
45. Daniel Jonah Goldhagen, *Hitler's Willing Executioners: Ordinary Germans and the Holocaust* (New York, 1996).

Selected Bibliography

Bajohr, Frank, and Dieter Pohl. *Der Holocaust als offenes Geheimnis. Die Deutschen, die NS-Führung und die Alliierten.* Munich, 2006.

Bajohr, Frank, and Christoph Strupp, eds, *Fremde Blicke auf das "Dritte Reich." Berichte ausländischer Diplomaten über Herrschaft und Gesellschaft in Deutschland 1933–1945.* Göttingen, 2011.

Bankier, David. *The Germans and the Final Solution: Public Opinion under Nazism.* Oxford, 1992.

Deutschland-Berichte der Sozialdemokratischen Partei Deutschlands (Sopade), 1934–1940. 7 vols. Frankfurt, 1980.

Dörner, Bernward. *"Heimtücke": Das Gesetz als Waffe. Kontrolle, Abschreckung und Verfolgung in Deutschland 1933–1945.* Paderborn, 1998.

Kulka, Otto Dov, and Eberhard Jäckel, eds. *Die Juden in den geheimen NS-Stim-mungsberichten, 1933–1945.* Düsseldorf, 2004. English translation: *The Jews in the Secret Nazi Reports on Popular Opinion in Germany, 1933–1945.* Translated by William Templer. New Haven, 2010.

Longerich, Peter. *"Davon haben wir nichts gewusst!" Die Deutschen und die Judenver-folgung 1933–45.* Munich, 2006.

Figure 4. Policemen on patrol in Berlin after the Kristallnacht pogrom, November 1938.

Chapter 3

INDIFFERENCE?

Participation and Protest as Individual Responses
to the Persecution of the Jews as Revealed in
Berlin Police Logs and Trial Records, 1933–45

———— ⌾ ————

Wolf Gruner

THE NOVEL *ALONE IN BERLIN* recently enjoyed great success in the English-speaking world after being translated from the German. The well-known German author, Hans Fallada, had published the book originally in 1946. One of the causes for the belated success of the translation may be that the story, based on Fallada's intimate knowledge of Berlin during the Third Reich, confronts the reader with a set of complex characters. They include both Nazi activists as well as opponents of the regime's anti-Jewish persecution, and therefore challenge the still prevalent view of a widespread indifference among the German people.[1]

Historians have characterized the reactions of Germans to anti-Jewish policy mainly on the basis of three categories of sources: the serial reports of the Security Service (Sicherheitsdienst—SD), Gestapo, or state institutions, which are strongly shaped by National Socialist perspectives; the secret reports of the Social Democrats, which are often regarded as not sufficiently critical of the anti-Semitic attitudes of the population (see Appendix D); and the diaries or testimonies of individual Jewish and non-Jewish Germans and of foreigners, which can hardly be generalized.[2] Reliance on these sources has served to reinforce the German postwar construction of a triad of perpetrators, victims, and an overwhelming majority of silent bystanders.

But perpetrator studies of the last decade have offered a much more complex picture, emphasizing the heterogeneity of biographies as well

as the variety of social, political, and cultural factors that shaped individual actions in a fluid environment. Moreover, research on formerly
overlooked institutions, such as city governments, tax authorities,
and labor offices, has shown that many so-called bystanders had been
actively involved in the persecution of the Jews. The following micro-
historical approach focusing on the Berliners and their reactions allows
us to explore this question in a more systematic way.

The Berlin State Archives house key collections of documents that
historians have never consulted in this context. The first is a collection
of reports on political incidents prepared by the Berlin police precincts.
The second is a collection of logbooks for the period 1933–45, which
have survived for about forty of the roughly three hundred police precincts. The third collection contains approximately two thousand case
files of the Berlin special court materials regarding the Law against Malicious Attacks on the State and Party of 1934, the so-called *Heimtücke*
(malice) law.[3] The police reports and logbook entries are very brief,
often just half a page, sometimes even less, and offer only the basic
information about each incident and the reason for arrests. They rarely
contain biographical details or information about what happened to
the arrested persons subsequently. In their brevity they are less biased
than the *Heimtücke* law indictments produced by procecutors at the
newly established Special Courts (*Sondergerichte*). This is especially true
for the 1930s, when police officers who had been appointed during
the Weimar Republic still worked in the precincts. The Special Court
indictments, usually comprising one to three pages, provide somewhat
more information about the incident and the prosecuted person. In
most cases, however, no data about the actual trial or the sentence survived in Berlin.

These collections of documents challenge the widespread assumption that non-Jewish Germans were indifferent to the persecution of
the Jews. Many cases demonstrate that critique of anti-Jewish measures
was more widespread than we have previously assumed,[4] thus placing
in question the assertion that solidarity with the persecuted Jews was
minimal.[5] On the other hand, the documents also contain strong evidence that perpetrators did not necessarily belong to Nazi organizations.
While the evidence that will be presented here is not representative of
the majority of Berliners, it nonetheless demonstrates that choices existed for every individual, including police officers. It also offers insights
into the spectrum of possible reactions of Berliners against and in favor
of the persecution of the Jews.

Berlin and the Jews

Berlin was by far the largest city in Germany as well as its political center. Its municipal government had traditionally been powerful, which remained the case during the Nazi era. An industrial center, the city housed a strong working-class element, a fact that shaped the local politics, commerce, and culture. While Berlin provided a haven for political extremes, it also offered, more than any other German city, tolerance and anonymity for artists, immigrants, social outsiders, and religious minorities.[6]

In 1933, a third of German Jews lived in the capital city. Of 4.2 million Berliners, 3.8 percent, that is, 160,000 people, identified with the Jewish religion. In districts such as Wilmersdorf, where 13.5 percent of the inhabitants were Jews, or Mitte, with a Jewish segment of 9.2 percent, the Jewish population was a good deal more visible than in districts such as Spandau, where they accounted for only 0.5 percent of the total.[7] Although Berlin's Jews represented different political, social, and cultural strands, Jewish immigrants from Russia and Poland were concentrated in the centrally situated district of Mitte, especially the so-called Scheunenviertel, where their Orthodox way of life made them easy targets for anti-Jewish violence even before 1933. In the capital of the Third Reich, Jewish Germans lived at the intersection of three processes of persecution: the policies of the national government, the restrictions introduced by the Nazi-dominated city government, and the frequent incidents of organized violence committed by local Nazi organizations.[8]

On 1 April 1933, the Nazi Party organized a nationwide anti-Jewish boycott. Gangs of storm troopers and SS men roamed through the city, posting guards at Jewish shops, law firms, and medical practices to prevent customers, clients, and patients from visiting them. While some courageous Berliners, under the eyes of countless onlookers, would enter stores nonetheless, many shops closed at noon. As the London *Times* reported, the Berlin population remained mostly passive. While only a few Berliners demonstrated active anti-Semitism, according to the *Times*, many nevertheless felt uncomfortable about the Jews.[9]

Following the boycott, organized attacks were suspended and replaced by "legal" methods for almost two years. Municipal anti-Jewish measures complemented national laws as well as restrictions introduced by private organizations and clubs at all levels.[10] Only after Germany won back the Saarland in January 1935 did the Nazi Party reactivate violence as a political method against Jews.[11] As in other regions, followers of the party attacked Jewish stores in Berlin in the spring of 1935. Anti-Jewish demonstrations began in outlying districts such as Spandau and Pankow and then spread. Storm troopers, members of the Hitler Youth, and increasingly Berliners who were not members of party formations stood in front of shops chanting, "Don't buy from Jews." Police dissolved the demontrations yet also closed Jewish shops. Despite the fact that the SA Berlin-Brandenburg and the local Hitler Youth both prohibited their members from participating in demonstrations on 25 June 1935, the attacks extended to the entire city during the end of June and continued into July.[12]

On 14 July 1935, Berliners found flyers at buildings, trees, and lampposts with the following content: "Volk comrade, do you know that the Jew is raping your daughter, abusing your wife, that the Jew is lying to you and betraying you, and Jewish doctors are killing you?"[13] Fueled also by the screening of the Swedish anti-Semitic movie *Petterson und Bendel* and incitement contained in the Nazi newspaper *Völkischer Beobachter,* riots took place over the next days on the Kurfürstendamm, the main commercial boulevard in the western half of the city.[14] On 19 July, SA leader Count Helldorff was appointed the new head of the Berlin police. Only a week after his appointment, he put a stop to the so-called anti-Jewish "individual actions." This was twelve days after the beginning of the riots and almost two months after the first anti-Jewish incidents.[15]

The late reaction of the authorities may have reinforced the belief of members of party formations that such actions by individuals would be tolerated. During the night of 21 July 1935, the SS man Kurt Lamprecht had, for example, marked shops in Friedenau with the slogan "I am a Jew."[16] The same night, a gang of teenagers smeared red oil paint on the windows of "Jewish stores" throughout the Kreuzberg district. Police caught the instigator, Hitler Youth member Horst Forschmann, and brought him to the Gestapo. Although the nature of these new sources do not reveal what happened to him subsequently, Forschmann's arrest, and especially the deliberate involvement of the Gestapo, speaks to the fact that the police perceived such individual actions as against the law and as potentially harmful politically.[17] While a violent socialization of the SS and SA members has been well established by research, we know less about the tendency for violence among members of the Hitler Youth, although the signs point in the same direction.[18]

Opportunities for Individual Violence

The attacks in 1933 and 1935 led many Germans to assume that violence against Jews, be it property damage or physical assault, was legitimate.[19] Even punishment for murder, which was committed during the first months of the "Nazi revolution," was blocked by authorities at the highest level.[20] As police precincts documented, some Berliners exploited the presumed liberty to act on their personal prejudices, to take revenge, or to enrich themselves. One night in May 1934, the twenty-year-old SA man Heinz Lucas, who still lived with his parents, ran into his fifty-year-old neighbor Luise Mehnert at the front door of their apartment building in Tempelhof. Unprovoked, he yelled at her, "You mean and dirty old Jewess," and punched her in the face, head, and back. While the attacker may have felt empowered by the general anti-Jewish atmosphere, Luise Mehnert still thought that justice could be achievable and filed charges at the nearest police station. The policemen took the complaint seriously and referred to it as an attack with a "political context."[21]

SA men randomly molested "Jewish" guests at restaurants[22] or so-called Aryan visitors to "Jewish" shops and department stores.[23] When the victims approached the police, the latter would file a report and refer the suspects to the local party organizations for disciplinary action. Some police officers openly supported the illegal activities, such as one Captain Zadow, who in 1935, despite an official complaint, released two SA men who had threatened non-Jewish clients in the store of Leo Gottlieb.[24]

Not only members of Nazi Party formations felt empowered to attack Jews.[25] In the same Gottlieb furniture store in 1936, following a dispute over prices, Otto Handge threatened the shop owner's wife: "I had never anything against the Jews, but the Jews are our misfortune. During the next action, we'll get them too." When she nevertheless stood firm, the attacker Handge suddenly felt libeled and turned to the police; this time Captain Zadow informed the Gestapo about the impudent Jewish woman.[26] Such complaints about Jews were themselves a form of violence. Ten days before the enactment of the notorious Nuremberg Laws in September 1935, the student Hans Thomas denounced the Jew Gerhard Panke to the police for having behaved strangely with a "German girl" in public.[27] Here, obviously a recent propaganda effort of the SS leadership to criminalize the Jews had borne fruit. On 7 August, the SS newspaper *Das schwarze Korps* had pronounced that henceforth every *Volksgenosse* (Volk comrade) could arrest Jews, even by force, if the latter were to "abuse their guest status and would appear with a German woman in public."[28]

In some cases even foreigners came under attack. In the autumn of 1935, the owner of the bar Bajadere in Charlottenburg called the riot squad for help after Dr Karl Theuerkauf, a functionary of the National Socialist Motor Corps (NSKK), and Paul Bergmann, a low-level official at the Nazi Party regional (*Gau*) office in Düsseldorf, had both threatened to vandalize the establishment unless the Jews (in reality Italians and Americans) left within fifteen minutes.[29] Some weeks later, the engineer Stephan Luther called a high-ranking diplomat from the Egyptian embassy "Jew and annoying foreigner" and then struck him in the face as the result of a conflict over a parking space on the Kurfürstendamm. The diplomat filed a complaint, and because of potential foreign repercussions, the police officer immediately informed the Gestapo and the criminal police.[30]

Berliners who deeply believed in anti-Semitism felt libeled when someone would call them a Jew. On 15 August 1934, the waiter Paul Landowski filed a complaint at the criminal police station in Prenzlauer Berg after the tailor Max Schydronski and the worker Walter Köpsel had both castigated him with "*Du Judenjunge*" (Jew boy) and similar epithets.[31] When Berliners felt offended by being called "*Judenlümmel*" (Jewish lout),[32] "*alte Judenschickse*" (old Jewish hag),[33] or "Jew," the police registered the identities of persons but did not file complaints automatically.[34]

Some Berliners viewed Jews as fair game. In 1934, the unemployed bank clerk Rudolf Gehrke and the tailor Richard Börner met in a restaurant and allegedly agreed upon their mutual anti-Semitic feelings. During the riots of summer 1935, Gehrke and Börner, pretending to be Gestapo officers, assaulted and robbed, together with three confederates, a total of nine Jewish families in their homes. Gehrke had proposed to target Jews on the assumption that they would be so frightened by the prospect of a "Gestapo" raid that they would not dare to ask for any legitimization. For organized gang robbery, document forgery, and especially the wearing of false party insignia, which was perceived by the court as a severe offense, Gehrke and one of the others later received five years in penitentiary, and Börner two years, while one member of the gang was punished less severely, with nine months in jail. The court claimed that the instigators had used anti-Jewish sentiment as a mere pretext for personal enrichment.[35]

During and after the organized attacks of summer 1935, the police logbooks documented an increase in individual actions against Jews. The same is true for the organized riots of summer 1938. In May and June of that year, Jewish shopkeepers filed more and more complaints after SA and Hitler Youth had started a new campaign. Everywhere in Berlin, SA men and members of the Hitler Youth orchestrated demonstrations, marked storefronts with "Jew," and even resorted to the vandalism and plunder of shops.[36] During the third week of June 1938, the attacks reached a new high. Meanwhile, the police had ordered Jewish owners to close their businesses to prevent further rallies.[37]

In comparison to 1935, individual attacks on Jewish property intensified significantly in 1938. On 18 June, an alert neighbor in Prenzlauer Berg denounced to the police the SA man Fritz Behrendt, who had destroyed a shop window in her building.[38] In Spandau, the drunken Franz Kaletztko, who was not a member of any party formation, threw a bottle with red paint into a shop window, damaging all the fabrics on display.[39]

During the same week, the police organized mass arrests after Hitler had ordered the incarceration of "asocial and criminal Jews." A total of 824 Jewish Berliners were sent to the concentration camp Sachsenhausen on account of previous minor convictions.[40] Propaganda minister and gauleiter of Berlin Joseph Goebbels declared in front of an audience of three hundred police officers that harassment was the preferred means to drive the Jews out of the capital city.[41] Later, on 20 July 1938, police chief Count Helldorf ordered that the officers needed to enforce all existing regulations serverely against Jews, imposing higher fines and intensified controls.[42] The chief of the Grolmann Street police station quickly made a name for himself by organizing recurring raids and traffic traps. After a decree was issued in the fall that Jews had to hand over all weapons in their possession, one police station in the northeast of Berlin ordered Jews to appear several times during the Jewish High Holidays, while another station forced hundreds of Jewish men to wait for hours while their weapons were processed.[43]

Debates and Protest

Not all Berliners thought or acted in an anti-Semitic way. The terror of the first weeks of Nazi rule led to a circulation of news and rumors about physical abuse of Jews in the city and in concentration camps.[44] The increasing discrimination against the Jews by both the German state and the Berlin municipality triggered public and private debates among Berliners to a much larger degree than we have assumed, as police precinct reports indicate. In November 1933, a woman called the police in Friedenau to demand the arrest of her landlady Elsa Lucas, who had supposedly stated, "Goering is a brutal and virulent man. He is full of hatred against the poor Jews, who are equally children of God and more respectable than most Christians."[45] The anti-Jewish furor produced compassion even among some Nazis. In March 1934, the SA man Walter Betlin exclaimed in the waiting area of the Zoo railroad station, "The Jews are also fellow Germans." The police denounced his behavior to his local SA group.[46]

The organized attacks of 1935 and 1938 in particular provoked public discussion. When in 1935 officials of the German Workers Front (DAF) posted flyers on the Kurfürstendamm warning "Aryans" against having relationships with Jews, the police removed them because people had gathered in large groups to discuss them, hindering traffic.[47] Heated debates, fueled by the consumption of alcohol, took place at night, as police files reveal. On 4 September 1935, the very drunk Berlin visitor Karl Korff ended up in a police cell after he had exclaimed in a bar on the Kurfürstendamm, "What, you want to expel the Jews? The Jews stay, even if you call the Gestapo, SS, and SA. The Jews are equally respectable people as everybody else." After sobering up, he was released the next morning. The police officer informed the Gestapo about the incident.[48]

The Berlin police logbooks of summer 1935 mostly document police interventions against organized anti-Semitic demonstrations and attacks and provide only scarce traces of critique.[49] In contrast, the logs for 1938 contain evidence of more widespread spontaneous street discussions about anti-Jewish measures. Times had changed. Although Nazi Germany could celebrate foreign policy successes, such as the annexation of Austria, many Germans worried about a war with Czechoslovakia. During the organized attacks of summer 1938, Berliners gathered in numbers in front of vandalized Jewish shops. On 17 June 1938, Nazi Party members felt challenged by a crowd to defend the devastation at the Strausberger Platz in the Friedrichshain district.[50] Three days later, at a rug store in Charlottenburg, fifty-two-year-old Franziska Warnholz criticized the smearing of slogans on Jewish shops, demanding that those responsible should be made to wipe it off with their own noses.[51]

Debates continued at night in the bars of Berlin. In the morning of 21 June, the SA man Richard Frödl brought Walter Apelt to the Kreuzberg police, claiming that he had said, "This is all bullshit. Only fools go around defacing things. Yesterday, I punched a Hitler Youth guy, who was besmearing Jewish shops, right in the face. Nowadays, we have only slavery and exploitation." Police officer Trepschuh nevertheless released Apelt, with the argument that he had been drunk.[52] On the same day, Hitler personally intervened to stop the Berlin attacks, because of international concerns.[53] This did not stop the critique among Berliners, however. On the evening of 28 June 1938, the printer Alfred Epstaedt was denounced to the police for berating the government in a public park and expressing sympathy with the "poor Jews."[54]

Only two months later, the day-and-a-half-long "Kristallnacht" pogrom of November 1938 managed to eclipse even the weeklong attacks of the summer. On orders of Nazi leaders, SA, SS, and Hitler Youth systematically destroyed countless private homes and flats, shops and businesses, and Jewish institutions and synagogues throughout the Reich. Many people died during the pogrom.[55] Shaken by what had happened on Wednesday night and Thursday, Sabine Alenfeld summarized her state of mind in her diary in just two words: "Black Friday."[56]

Some historians have underlined the widespread support of the German population for the violence, while others have emphasized that some people did not welcome the attacks,[57] but only because of the pointless destruction of property, an argument that official Nazi reports had emphasized.[58] Many Berliners, as we can learn from police logbooks, precinct reports, and trial material, reacted with critique, protest, and even resistance, but, interestingly, never for economic reasons.[59] After the violent night, quite a few Berliners were denounced for raising critical voices.[60] The eighteen-year-old Hans Neumann had claimed in front of an "Etam" store on Potsdamer Street, "The same people who smashed the store windows also stole. They drank the stolen liquor and sorted the Persian rugs in the Grunewald, which they had taken away at the Kurfürstendamm." The police arrested him under paragraph 2 of the so-called *Heimtücke* law and handed him over to the local Gestapo.[61] At the cigar store of Chaim Leinert at Blücherplatz, a large number of passersby were still discussing on the afternoon of 10 November how "members of the party smashed the windows and plundered the displays."[62] To identify Nazi Party members as the perpetrators and looters contradicted the official view of a spontaneous outburst of people's anger after the shooting of a German diplomat in Paris. It was tantamount to accusing the party of criminal activities.

Disgusted by the violence, several Berliners documented the devastation, for which they were arrested. One was Rudolf Neubauer, who photographed the demolished facade of the department store Joseph in Schöneberg.[63] Other people denounced perpetrators to the police—for example, an apprentice who reported observing how the passengers of the car with the license plate IA 312577 demolished the textile store of Margarete Danziger in Prenzlauer Berg and then drove away.[64] Some Berliners even resisted the organized mob. The 72-year-old Julius Braun, for example, stood in the entrance of the Savoy and called a waiter to close the pub to prevent the attackers from intruding and smashing everything inside.[65] (See Appendix C.)

Days later, Berliners still disputed the traumatic events.[66] The material reminders of the destruction could be seen for weeks,[67] and the emotional impact lasted at least as long. On 27 November 1938, inscriptions were found in a telephone book in a public phone booth with an open critique of Goebbels and the Nazi propaganda: "Jos. lies. XI/9 Germany's big day of shame."[68] This may have referred not only to the attacks on synagogues, shops, and people, but also to the massive plunder that ensued thereafter.

Theft and Robbery

Many Berliners tried to take advantage of the violent events. Based on their experiences with previous local attacks and with Nazi policy in general, these people probably assumed that the robbing of Jews would be tolerated. The plundering began during the night of the pogrom, even as the police tried to prevent it.[69] In the morning, Berliners discovered countless destroyed shop windows. More than a hundred people gathered in front of the Kurt Levy shoe store at the Frankfurter Allee at 6:00 AM and searched for their sizes until a riot squad arrived and arrested fourteen of them, who were caught red-handed. Interrogated by the criminal police, the individuals claimed that they had no plan to plunder and were released with a warning. Criminal proceedings stemming from the case in the spring of 1939 ended in vain.[70]

Children also took their turn at plundering. In Rüdersdorf, teenage intruders took coats, jackets, money, and other valuables from a department store and a weekend home.[71] In Mitte, fifth graders brought films, shoes, a comb, a watch, and other bounty from the "Jew action" to school.[72] Because of the scale of children's participation in the looting, the Nazi leadership debated the unwelcomed issue during the first high-ranking meeting two days after the pogrom.[73]

News about the plundering spread quick as lightning. Margarete Grundmann revealed in her boarding house that these "pigs drove around all night in the car of Minister Rust" and stole bracelets, rings, and furs. Her acquaintance Gerda Rust had received "forty pairs of stockings and eight or ten pairs of shoes." Most plunderers were never punished, as the Reich Ministry of Justice instructed against the prosecution of criminal acts commited during the pogrom. Thus property damage, robbery, plunder, and blackmailing were all treated as misdemeanors.[74] For her part, Margarete Grundmann was sentenced to four months in jail for violating the *Heimtücke* law by sharing the story about the robbery and maligning education minister Bernhard Rust.[75]

Since not all shop owners could replace their windows fast enough, the police established special patrols to prevent people from looting.[76] Officers of the 108th Police Precinct in Kreuzberg arrested three men during the first night after the pogrom alone for stealing clothing from two stores.[77] Many Berliners now looked for property of Jews. The SS-Storm 3/6 requested the keys of the synagogue in Schulstraße from the nearby police station in order to use it as a future SS base, which the police declined to permit.[78] Following the decree for the "de-Judaization of the economy,"[79] issued immediately after the pogrom, hundreds of Berliners stormed the city hall to acquire one of the 3,000 or so remaining businesses, which was half of the number that had existed in 1933. Within weeks, 535 stores were sold to "Aryans." Berliners also profited from the liquidation of 2,570 businesses by acquiring real estate and goods or renting the newly available spaces.[80]

Business Contacts and Private Relationships

After six years of Nazi rule, some Berliners still did not acquiesce to anti-Jewish rules. One was Erich Majewski from Kreuzberg. When a new law of April 1939 abolished protection for Jewish tenants,[81] Majewski did not cancel his contract with a subtenant who had lived with him for four years. He defended Edith Britz even to the police, after she had been denounced for allegedly receiving blond male visitors at night. He did this at enormous risk to himself, after having been previously accused of defending Jews and having engaged in politically controversial conversations.[82]

By contrast, some Berliners exploited the possibility of denunciation as a method for gaining advantage in their personal and business conflicts. In early summer 1939, Ludwig Lenz, a metalsmith in Prenzlauer Berg, filed a complaint against his neighbor Dora Salz, claiming that she would do everything to harm his business. According to Lenz, the impudent Jewess, now living in the basement of the building, had already in 1937 resisted handing her shop over to him and would now collect signatures against him in their apartment building, even from Nazis. Lenz, who had previously filed charges against Salz to no avail, now accused her of committing the crime of race defilement and of carrying sexual diseases. As a response, the Jewish woman filed charges for false accusation. Astonishingly, the neighbors defended Dora Salz before the police. One retiree, Friedrich Soller, explained that tight relationships still existed between Jewish and non-Jewish neighbors in an atmosphere of mutual assistance in the building. That a whole community of tenants, including Nazi Party members, would speak in favor of a Jewish neighbor convinced the police to drop the case.[83]

After Germany invaded Poland in September 1939, Jews had to forfeit their radios, and a curfew was enacted for them after 8:00 PM. Despite the increased segregation, Berliners would find opportunities for frequent contacts, whether in shops, at work, or during visits of friends or acquaintances. The Neukölln family Zadek could count on their neighborhood bakery to provide bread at any time, despite a decree of July 1940 that limited shopping time for Jews in Berlin to one hour in the afternoon.[84] While all Jews had to perform forced labor in separate groups commissioned by the Labor Office, a few continued to work illegally on an individual basis for non-Jews.[85] In addition to such "business" relationships, personal relationships also continued to exist. In June 1940, the merchant Hugo Mannheimer, a convert to Protestantism who lived in what Nazi racial laws defined as a mixed marriage, visited his friend's office, who worked as a landlord. Both discussed the situation after the German invasion of France, a possible final victory for England, and the fact that the newspapers were not trustworthy. Landlord Schütz disclosed to Mannheimer that his daughter had gotten in trouble with the Nazi Party because she had shaken hands with a Jewish tenant.[86] Since in Berlin the authorities never managed to segregate all Jews in so-called Jew houses, neighborly contacts often survived until late in the war,[87] yet at ever increasing risk of denunciation.[88]

In October 1941, the Reich Security Main Office threatened all Germans who still "would cultivate friendly relationships to Jews in public" with three months in a concentration camp.[89] Since Jews were at this point easily indentifiable by the yellow star, this measure opened the gate for a wave of denunciations. The order was designed in particular to prevent the spontaneous emergence of solidarity with Jews during the upcoming deportations.

Participation in the Deportations versus Rescue

When the mass deportations started in October 1941, the Gestapo selected the deportees and organized the transports in close contact with the labor offices, private firms, the German railway, the army, and the Jewish community. The Order Police helped to escort the deportees from their apartments to collection points and camps and arrested Jews designated for transport on the street, at offices, or at the police station.[90]

While some have seen indifference as the dominant attitude of Germans toward the mass transports, documents demonstrate that many in Berlin had close knowledge of the deportation of tens of thousands Jews and that some of them became really upset.[91] In May 1942, the non-Jewish fifty-year-old Gertrud Roensch wrote to her niece, whom she perceived as anti-Jewish, about the expulsion of Jews from their homes, about the drastic persecution, and about how the Jews were subjected to torments from German officials who were like so many small Hitlers. As for the deportations, she stated that the roundups that took place at night were even more horrible than those that occurred during the daytime. Just imagine, she explained, how the bell rings like crazy in the middle of the night, you awake drowsy and scared, you dress quickly, pack the necessary belongings, and depart, leaving most of your things behind as if you would come back in a minute, but you don't come back, ever.[92]

The deportations wrecked all hope for many Jews.[93] Even though only a few tens of thousands of Jews were left in Berlin, in 1942 up to a thousand of them committed suicide,[94] most because they feared "evacuation," as police officers noted in their logbooks.[95] These documents also reveal that not only neighbors knew about the suicides. Locksmiths opened doors, physicians issued death certificates, policemen organized the transfer of bodies and sealed apartments, sheriffs secured the estates. The custodians of the buildings kept the keys of all abandoned apartments in sealed envelopes. These included apartments of the tenants who had committed suicide as well as of those who had been deported. Some even stole from the belongings of the dead or deported Jews, as did two women in Prenzlauer Berg, who took clothes and marmalade jars out of the apartment of their neighbor Himmelweit.[96]

Since the flats often stayed empty for months or years, city employees came to read meters so that gas and electric accounts could be closed, and handymen came to repair windows or broken pipes.[97] The municipality was in charge of selling the belongings and finding new tenants.[98] Many Berliners could now acquire cheap furniture in this way.[99] Army officers, wounded soldiers, higher civil servants, and Germans who had been rendered homeless by Allied bombing could all obtain city permits to rent a "Jew flat," as the police logbooks frequently called them. An appointment to view such a flat was anything but normal, as a police officer had to officially unseal the flat, which often still contained private belongings.[100] Occasionally, the visitors discovered broken seals, as fleeing Jews had returned to pick up clothes and food.[101]

The police logbooks contain plenty of information about Jewish Berliners who tried to flee from the deportations. Some janitors would denounce hiding Jews to the police, as occurred in the case of Golda Wisen and her seven-year-old son when they returned to their home on Fehrbelliner Street in April 1943.[102] During the so-called *Fabrikaktion* (factory raid) at the end of February 1943, around four thousand Jews had gone into hiding, after being warned by neighbors, company employees, even policemen.[103]

In total, between five thousand and seven thousand Jews tried to survive in hiding in Berlin. They needed shelter, food, forged papers, and trustworthy contacts. To save one Jew, many Berliners were necessary.[104] Their motives could not have been more diverse, as the police logbooks reveal. Kurt Jacobson was hidden by a non-Jew because he managed his firm for the incapable owner.[105] Thus economic interest or humanitarian ideas, friendship, love, and even sex motivated people to help Jews, though at high risk. In November 1943, the fifteen-year-old Margot Glazik informed a welfare worker that the fugitive and former neighbor Max Marcus had stayed with her mother overnight for weeks. The City Welfare Department denounced Glazik and Marcus to the police and seized the three children.[106]

That Berliners cared about the persecuted and their fate can be also confirmed by the wide circulation of rumors about mass deportations and murder. In a barbershop on the outskirts of the city, a woman told the other clients, "During the big air attack on Berlin, the Jews have been evacuated from their flats. They were driven into the burning houses, where they died; others had been driven into homes and the gas taps had been opened; after a time a new group of Jews had been pushed in there."[107] This last story conflated facts of a massive Allied bombing campaign on 1 March 1943, the deportation of thousands of Berlin Jews during the factory raid on 27 February, and the available information about the mass extermination in the occupied east.

Conclusion

After 1933, Berliners were confronted countless times with anti-Jewish laws or local restrictions and their effects, as well as with organized collective and spontaneous individual violence against Jews. Since almost everybody frequently needed to position him- or herself vis-à-vis the anti-Jewish measures, indifference is not an adequate description for individual German reactions toward the persecution during the Nazi period. The examples presented in this chapter illuminate especially the extremes of human behavior in Berlin, as unauthorized violence, protest, and solidarity with the persecuted all left their traces in police files and court materials.

Berliners witnessed violence against Jews whether in the form of willful damage of property, verbal threats, or physical attacks. Organized collective riots involving the SA and the Hitler Youth lasted for months in 1935 and 1938 and were understood by some individuals, and not just Nazis, as a license to use violence to solve their personal conflicts and by others, even children, to take possession of Jewish property. This new micro-historical research on Berlin challenges previous assumptions that violence against Jews occurred predominantly during the early years of the Third Reich and more in rural areas with strong anti-Semitic traditions than Berlin.

All aspects of the persecution were frequently discussed by Berliners in the streets, in shops, in bars, and with their neighbors. Surprisingly, as the new sources show, many people did express criticism in public, and some even protested against persecution, violence, and looting, facing enormous risks. Foreign newspapers and radio broadcasts as well as personal experience and rumors confirmed and nourished the existence of a public sphere of limited size in which the regime could be critized.[108] The fact that the majority of critical voices were raised not during the early years of the regime, but in reaction to the events of 1938, contradicts the common assumption of an increasing conformity among the non-Jewish population after 1933.

Like many Berliners who were involved in the persecution, Berlin police officers possessed room for maneuver, which is demonstrated by the varying individual treatment of anti-Semitic extremists or opponents of persecution. However, after 1933 the police had to enforce anti-Jewish restrictions in close contact with the Gestapo and in 1938 were specifically ordered to harass Jews in any way possible. The violent socialization of German policemen throughout the 1930s is a factor that is often overlooked, which may help to explain the ease with which many officers were able to participate in mass murder in the occupied east during the war.[109]

Yet, the Berlin documents also demonstrate that a full segregation of Jews and non-Jews was never accomplished, not even during the war, and many ties between non-Jews and Jews persisted. The mass deportations proved to be a litmus test for personal relationships. Friends, acquaintances, neighbors could all offer help or denounce fleeing or hiding Jews. The new sources also challenge the widespread notion of the passivity of the victims. The sheer number of complaints filed by Jews with the police against their attackers suggests a different reality. Even individual protests by Jews in public are documented.[110]

This microstudy of individual participation in violence and plunder, or in opposition and resistance, shows both the possibilities and the limits of the Nazi regime's attempt to control and mobilize the inhabitants of an urban metropolis, as well as the possibilities and the limits of trying to integrate Berliners into the Nazi peoples (and persecution) community.

Wolf Gruner holds the Shapell-Guerin Chair in Jewish Studies and is professor of history at the University of Southern California, Los Angeles, where he is also director of the Center for Advanced Genocide Research at the USC Shoah Foundation. He is the author of eight books on the Holocaust, among them *Jewish Forced Labor under the Nazis: Economic Needs and Nazi Racial Aims* (Cambridge, 2008) and *The Persecution of the Jews in Berlin 1933–1945: A Chronology of Measures by the Authorities in the German Capital* (Berlin, 2014). He has recently coedited the volume *The Greater German Reich and the Jews: Nazi Persecution Policies in the Annexed Territories 1935–1945* (New York, 2015), and his study *Parias de la Patria. El mito de la liberación de los indígenas en la República de Bolivia 1825–1890* has been published with Plural Editores (La Paz, Bolivia) in 2015.

Notes

1. Hans Fallada, *Alone in Berlin*, 1st English edn (New York, 2009).
2. Historians assumed either a widespread radical anti-Semitism in the German population, passive complicity, or the dominance of indifference regarding the fate of the Jews, while some saw limited opposition in parts of the society. Peter Longerich, *"Davon haben wir nichts gewusst!" Die Deutschen und die Judenverfolgung 1933–1945* (Munich, 2006).
3. *Gesetz gegen heimtückische Angriffe auf Staat und Partei und zum Schutz der Parteiuniformen*, 20 December 1934; *Reichsgesetzblatt*, 1934 I, 1269.
4. Bernward Dörner, *"Heimtücke": Das Gesetz als Waffe. Kontrolle, Abschreckung und Verfolgung in Deutschland 1933–1945* (Paderborn, 1998); Robert Gellately, *The Gestapo and German Society: Enforcing Racial Policy, 1933–1945* (Oxford, 1991).
5. Konrad Kwiet, "Problems of Jewish Resistance Historiography," *Leo Baeck Institute Yearbook* 24 (1979): 43–45.
6. For Berlin 1933–45, see Rüdiger Hachtmann, Thomas Schaarschmidt, and Winfried Süss, eds, *Berlin im Nationalsozialismus. Politik und Gesellschaft 1933–1945,* Beiträge zur Geschichte des Nationalsozialimus 27 (Göttingen, 2011); Michael Wildt and Christoph Kreutzmüller, eds, *Berlin 1933–1945* (Munich, 2013).
7. Wolf Gruner, *Judenverfolgung in Berlin 1933–1945. Eine Chronologie der Behördenmaßnahmen in der Reichshauptstadt,* 2nd edn (Berlin, 2009), 171; see also the English edn: *The Persecution of the Jews in Berlin 1933–1945: A Chronology of Measures by the Authorities in the German Capital* (Berlin, 2014).
8. For details, see Gruner, *The Persecution of the Jews in Berlin.*
9. *The Times,* 3 April 1933, 14. Cf. Antoni Graf Sobański, *Nachrichten aus Berlin* (Berlin, 2007), 70–71, 80; Hannah Ahlheim, *"Deutsche, kauft nicht bei Juden!" Antisemitismus und politischer Boykott in Deutschland 1924 bis 1935* (Göttingen, 2011), 154–62; Christoph Kreutzmüller, *"Ausverkauf": Die Vernichtung der jüdischen Gewerbetätigkeit in Berlin 1930–1945* (Berlin, 2012), 92–105.
10. Saul Friedländer, *Nazi Germany and the Jews*, vol. 1, *The Years of Persecution, 1933–1939* (New York, 1997); Wolf Gruner, "Local Initiatives, Central Coordination: German Municipal Administration and the Holocaust," in *Networks of Nazi Persecution: Bureaucracy, Business, and the Organization of the Holocaust*, eds Gerald D. Feldman and Wolfgang Seibel (New York, 2005), 269–94.
11. Armin Nolzen, "The Nazi Party and Its *Violence* against the Jews 1933–1939: *Violence* as a Historiographical Concept," *Yad Vashem Studies 31* (2003): 245–85; Michael Wildt, *Volksgemeinschaft als Selbstermächtigung. Gewalt gegen Juden in der deutschen Provinz 1919 bis 1939* (Hamburg, 2007), 211–13.
12. Peter Longerich, *Politik der Vernichtung: eine Gesamtdarstellung der nationalsozialistischen Judenverfolgung* (Munich, 1998), 70–101 (English edn: *Holocaust: The Nazi Persecution and Murder of the Jews* [Oxford, 2010]); Ahlheim, *"Deutsche, kauft nicht bei Juden,"* 379–90; Kreutzmüller, *"Ausverkauf,"* 133–41; Gruner, *The Persecution of the Jews in Berlin,* 81–84; idem, "Die Berliner und die NS-Judenverfolgung. Eine mikrohistorische Studie individueller Handlungen und sozialer Beziehungen," in Hachtmann, Schaarschmidt and Süss, *Berlin im Nationalsozialismus,* 57–87, here 60–68.

13. Landesarchiv Berlin (hereafter LA Berlin), A Rep. 408, no. 3, folio 118: Police logbook, entry no. 407, 14 July 1935. The flyer was cited on 25 September 1935 by the *Basler Nationalzeitung* and later published as a facsimile in *Der gelbe Fleck. Die Ausrottung von 500.000 deutschen Juden*, preface by Lion Feuchtwanger (Paris 1936), 165.

14. LA Berlin, A Pr.Br.Rep. 030, no. 21638, folio 367: Logbook 133rd police precinct, entry, 16 July 1935. Cf. *Neue Zürcher Zeitung* (evening edn), 16 July 1935, printed in *Die Verfolgung und Ermordung der europäischen Juden durch das nationalsozialistische Deutschland*, vol. 1, *Deutsches Reich: 1933–1937*, ed. Wolf Gruner (Munich, 2008), doc. no. 176, 452.

15. Helldorf "Gegen Einzelaktionen," in *Völkischer Beobachter* (North German edn), no. 209, 28 July 1935, 2; see also Gruner, *The Persecution of the Jews in Berlin*, 84.

16. LA Berlin, B Rep. 020, Acc. 1124, no. 6943, folio 647: 177th police precinct, Friedenau, no. 205, entry, 21 July 1935; see also ibid., folio 645: 177th police precinct, Friedenau, no. 201, entry, 16 July 1935; ibid., folio 648: 177th police precinct, Friedenau, no. 206, entry, 21 July 1935.

17. LA Berlin, A Pr.Br.Rep. 030, no. 21640, fols 601–602RS: report on a political incident to Stapo, 21 July 1935. An example from Kreuzberg: ibid., no. 21637, folio 91: Note, 29 July 1935, to Stapo. See for another case on Invalidenstrasse in Mitte: ibid., A Rep. 408, no. 3, folio 130: Police logbook, entry no. 430, 26 July 1935.

18. According to the Berlin police reports, Hitler Youth activists were usually between sixteen and eighteen years old, i.e., longtime members, and obviously similar to the SA in their eagerness to launch anti-Jewish violence. Nolzen has emphasized their systematic integration into party actions: Armin Nolzen, "Der Streifendienst der Hitlerjugend und die 'Überwachung der Jugend,' 1934–1945," in *Beiträge zur Geschichte des Nationalsozialismus* 16 (2000): 13–51, here 36–37; idem, *Violence*, 269, cf. Wildt, *Volksgemeinschaft*, 211–13.

19. Courts increasingly stopped prosecution of anti-Jewish violence by party members "on duty." See Nolzen, *Violence*, 271; see also Wildt, *Volksgemeinschaft*, 363.

20. 22 August 1933, doc. no. 69, in Gruner, *Verfolgung*, 228–29.

21. The source does not reveal the outcome of this matter. LA Berlin, B Rep. 020, Acc 5179, no. 8496, no fols: Logbook 205th police precinct, Tempelhof, Paradeplatz, entry no. 213, 4 May 1934.

22. Ibid., A Pr.Br.Rep. 030, no. 21638, folio 274: 133rd police precinct, report, 12 February 1934, to Marine-SA.

23. See, for example, ibid., no. 21637, folio 109: Note, 23 December 1935, to Stapo.

24. Ibid., A Rep. 408, no. 3, no folio: Insert note, 30 July 1935; and ibid, folio 135: Logbook 5th police recinct Mi., entry no. 439, 30 July 1935.

25. On self-empowerment, see Wildt, *Volksgemeinschaft*, 370–74.

26. LA Berlin, A Rep. 408, no. 3, folio 637–638: entry no. 509, 18 August 1936. For other cases, see ibid., B Rep. 020, Acc 5179, no. 8496, no fols: Logbook 205th police precinct, Tempelhof, Paradeplatz, entry 16 September 1933 and 21 April 1934.

27. LA Berlin, A Pr.Br.Rep. 030, no. 21638, folio 387: Note, 133rd police precinct, no. 811, 5 September 1935, to Stapo.
28. *Das Schwarze Korps,* 7 August 1935, printed in Gruner, *Verfolgung,* vol. 1, doc. 185, 466–67. On the criminalization of the German Jews, see Michael Berkowitz, *The Crime of My Very Existence: Nazism and the Myth of Jewish Criminality* (Berkeley, 2007), 24–44.
29. LA Berlin, A Pr.Br.Rep. 030, no. 21638, folio 395: Note, 133rd police precinct, no. 921, 2 October 1935, to Stapo.
30. No record of the outcome is available; ibid., folio 411: report, 133rd police precinct, no. 1108, 2 December 1935 to Stapo. Another similar case: ibid., folio 421: report, 133rd police precinct, Kripo, no. 1653, 24 December 1935, to Stapo.
31. Ibid., A Rep. 408, no. 13, no fols: Logbook Kripo precinct 71, entry no. 338, 14 August 1934.
32. Ibid., no fols: Logbook Kripo precinct 71, entry no. 395, 25 September 1934.
33. Ibid., no fols: Logbook Kripo precinct 71, entry no. 391, 12 December 1935.
34. Ibid., no. 8, folio 208RS: Logbook Kripo 63rd police precinct, 1935–38. People filed complaints even for being called a jumping jack or a silly ass; see examples in ibid., no. 38, no. fols: Logbook Kripo precinct 285, Weißensee, 1941–42.
35. LA Berlin, A Rep. 355, no. 4181, no fols: Judgement, 9 June 1936, 1–36.
36. See, for example, LA Berlin, A Pr.Br.Rep. 030, no. 21619, folio 135.
37. For more details, see Longerich, *Politik,* 175–80; Gruner, *The Persecution of the Jews in Berlin,* 30–31, 106–11; Christian Dirks, "Die 'Juni-Aktion' 1938 in Berlin," in *Juden in Berlin 1938–1945. Begleitband zur gleichnamigen Ausstellung in der Stiftung Neue Synagoge Berlin–Centrum Judaicum Mai bis August 2000,* eds Beate Meyer and Hermann Simon, (Berlin 2000), 33–43; Christoph Kreutzmüller, Hermann Simon and Elisabeth Weber, eds, *Ein Pogrom im Juni. Fotos antisemitischer Schmierereien in Berlin 1938* (Berlin, 2013).
38. LA Berlin, A Pr.Br.Rep. 030, no. 21619, folio 176–177RS: 64th police precinct, report on a political incident, 20 June 1938, to Stapo.
39. Ibid., folio 173–174RS: 141st police precinct, report on a political incident, 20 June 1938.
40. Wolf Gruner, *Der Geschlossene Arbeitseinsatz deutscher Juden. Zur Zwangsarbeit als Element der Verfolgung 1938 bis 1943* (Berlin, 1996), 43. For eyewitness testimonies on the June arrests and internments, see Ben Barkow, Raphael Gross, and Michael Lenarz, eds, *Novemberpogrom 1938. Die Augenzeugenberichte der Wiener Library, London* (Frankfurt, 2008), 45–91. See also the recent work *Die „Juni-Aktion" 1938. Eine Dokumentation zur Radikalisierung der Judenverfolgung,* ed. Christian Faludi (Frankfurt, 2013).
41. Gruner, *The Persecution of the Jews in Berlin,* 109.
42. Guidelines printed in *Verfolgung und Ermordung der europäischen Juden,* vol. 2, *1938–1939,* ed. Susanne Heim (Munich, 2009), 234–43; cf. Gruner, *The Persecution of the Jews in Berlin,* 111–12.
43. See eyewitness testimonies in Barkow, Gross, and Lenarz, *Novemberpogrom 1938,* 105–6, 115.

44. LA Berlin, A Rep. 355, no. 4774 Wilk, Chaskil (9 February 1911), no fols: General prosecutor at the dictrict court Berlin to Special Court, indictment, 21 July 1933. See Judgement Special Court Berlin, 5 January 1934, in Dörner, *Heimtücke*, 325–27.
45. LA Berlin, Rep. 020, Acc. 1124, no. 6943, fols 222–225: 177th police precinct, Friedenau, Entry no. 545, 6 November 1933.
46. LA Berlin , A Pr.Br.Rep. 030, no. 21638, folio 296: 133rd police precinct, report, 17 March 1934 to SA-Standarte.
47. Ibid, folio 383: Note, 133rd police precinct, 22 August 1935, to Stapo.
48. Ibid., folio 386: Note, 133rd police precinct, no. 800, 4 September 1935, to Stapo.
49. By contrast, see the critical voices mentioned in administrative reports and the Sopade reports; Longerich, *"Davon haben wir nichts gewusst!,"* 85–92.
50. LA Berlin, A Pr.Br.Rep. 030, no. 21619, vol. 4, folio 149RS: report, 106th police precinct, 17 June 1938. For another case in Lichtenberg, see ibid., folio 158.
51. Ibid., folio 167–168RS: 121st police precinct, report on political incident, 20 June 1938 to Stapo. For a similar case at the same day and same street, see ibid., folio 165–166RS. For a case in Neukölln, see ibid., folio 171–172RS: 216th police precinct, report on political incident, 20 June 1938 to Stapo.
52. Ibid., folio 180: report 107. R.HT, 21 June 1938.
53. *Die Judenpolitik des SD 1935–1938. Eine Dokumentation,* ed. Michael Wildt (Munich, 1995), 57, 66–67; Yad Vashem Archives Jerusalem, 051/OSOBI, no. 88 (Moscow 500/1/261), folio 40–41RS: Hagen (SD II 112) to SD-OA Süd, 29 June 1938.
54. LA Berlin, A Rep. 408, no. 1, folios 521–522: Logbook 5th police precinct, entry no. 239, 28 June 1938.
55. Eyewitness reports in Barkow, Gross, and Lenarz, *Novemberpogrom 1938,* 215–50; *Sopade—Deutschland-Berichte der Sozialdemokratischen Partei Deutschlands 1934–1940,* ed. Klaus Behnken, vol. 5, 1938, 7th printing (Salzhausen, 1989), 1194–95; LA Berlin, A Pr.Br.Rep. 030, Tit. 95, no. 21620 vol. 5, folio 65RS. For a recent authoritative account, see Alan E. Steinweis, *Kristallnacht 1938* (Cambridge, MA, 2009).
56. Cited in Irene Alenfeld, *Warum seid Ihr nicht ausgewandert? Überleben in Berlin 1933–1945* (Berlin, 2008), 118.
57. For critique on the research controversy, see Wolf-Arno Kropat, *"Reichskristallnacht." Der Judenpogrom vom 7.–10. November 1938—Urheber, Täter, Hintergründe* (Wiesbaden, 1997), 156–69; Alexander Korb, *Reaktionen der deutschen Bevölkerung auf die Novemberpogrome im Spiegel amtlicher Berichte* (Saarbrücken, 2007), 6–16.
58. For an analysis of these reports, see Korb, *Reaktionen,* 59–65. For the use of the argument see Longerich, *"Davon haben wir nichts gewusst!,"* 130–33; Frank Bajohr, "Über die Entwicklung eines schlechten Gewissens. Die deutsche Bevölkerung und die Deportationen," in *Die Deportation der Juden aus Deutschland. Pläne-Praxis-Reaktionen 1938–1945,* eds Birthe Kundrus and Beate Meyer, Beiträge zur Geschichte des Nationalsozialismus 20 (Göttingen, 2004), 180–195, here 182.

59. Cf. the mentioning of critical voices, yet also of the fear to make comments in public: Barkow, Gross, and Lenarz, *Novemberpogrom 1938*, 120, 228, 232, 242, 260. For reactions to the pogrom and critique, see also *Sopade*, vol. 5, November 1938, 1194–95, 1207. For the national level, see Korb, *Reaktionen*.
60. LA Berlin, A Pr.Br.Rep. 030, Tit. 95, no. 21620 vol. 5, fols 74–105. See also *Sopade*, no. 11, November 1938, 1207–8; and report Brazilian embassy, 21 November 1938, in Hermann Simon, "Bilder, die sich Dante nicht vorstellte, denn die Höllenpeinigungen haben das Raffinement ihres jeweiligen Jahrhunderts," in *Vom Pogrom zum Völkermord. November 1938*, Dokumentation einer Veranstaltung des Vereins Porta Pacis am 7. November 1998 im Gedenken an die Reichspogromnacht vor 60 Jahren (Berlin 1999), 33.
61. LA Berlin, A Pr.Br.Rep. 030, no. 21620, fols 72–73RS: 180th police precinct Schöneberg, report on a political incident, 10 November 1938, to Stapo. See similar incident ibid., folio 80: 180th police precinct, report on a political incident, 10 November 1938, to Stapo.
62. Ibid., fols 78–79RS: 113th police precinct, report on a political incident, 10 November 1938 to Stapo. Cf. ibid., fols 83–84RS: entry, 81st police precinct, 10 November 1938.
63. LA Berlin, A Pr.Br.Rep. 030, no. 21620, fols 74–75RS: 180th police precinct Schöneberg, report on a political incident, 10 November 1938 to Stapo. Cf. a similar case: ibid., folio 76: 180th police precinct Schöneberg, report on a political incident, 10 November 1938 to Stapo. Cf. also ibid., B Rep 020, Acc 1201, no. 6949, fols 440–441; Simon, "Bilder, die sich Dante nicht vorstellte," 20. By contrast, Klaus Hesse claimed that pictures were taken only by perpetrators or by voyeurs. Klaus Hesse, "'Vorläufig keine Bilder bringen.' Zur bildlichen Überlieferung des Novemberpogroms," in *Es brennt! Antijüdischer Terror im November 1938*, eds Andreas Nachama, Uwe Neumärker and Hermann Simon (Berlin 2008), 136–44.
64. LA Berlin, A Rep. 408, no. 9, folio 61: Logbook Kripo precinct 63, entry no. 267, 10 November 1938.
65. LA Berlin, A Pr.Br.Rep. 030, no. 21620, folio 103: 108th police precinct, report, 12 November 1938, to Stapo. Cf. the similar behavior of a resistant custodian in *Juden in Berlin-Mitte. Biografien, Orte, Begegnungen*, ed. Verein zur Vorbereitung einer Stiftung Scheunenviertel Berlin e.V. (Berlin, 2000), 71.
66. LA Berlin, A Pr.Br.Rep. 030, no. 21620, fols 92–93RS: 142nd police precinct Spandau, report on a political incident, 11 November 1938, to Stapo. Cf. ibid., folio 100: 103rd police precinct, report, 12 November 1938; ibid., fols 106–107RS: 216th police precinct, Neukölln, report on a political incident, 14 November 1938, to Stapo.
67. On 25 November 1938, the student Walter Rutkowski took pictures of the destroyed synagoge in Spandau; ibid., folio 121: 141st police precinct, Spandau, report, 25 November 1938, to Stapoleitstelle D.
68. Ibid., folio 128: 49th police precinct, report, 27 November 1938, to Stapo inspection III.
69. Cabel Chief Order Police, 10 November 1938, in *Verfolgung, Vertreibung, Vernichtung. Dokumente des faschistischen Antisemitismus 1933–1942*, ed. Kurt Pätzold (Leipzig, 1983), 170, doc. 127. For examples, see LA Berlin, A Rep.

Wolf Gruner

358-02, no. 2542, fols 3–5: General prosecutor at the dictrict court to local court Berlin, indictment, 2 January 1940; ibid., folio 10: Judgement, local court Berlin, 10 May 1940. Cf. several eyewitness reports about looting in Berlin: Barkow, Gross, and Lenarz, *Novemberpogrom 1938,* 153, 224, 227.

70. LA Berlin, A Pr.Br.Rep. 030, no. 21620, fols 65–71: 251st police precinct, Lichtenberg, report on a political incident, 10 November 1938, to Stapo; ibid., A Rep. 358-02, no. 2874, no fols: General prosecutor at the dictrict court to *Schnellschöffengericht* Berlin, Indictment, 26 January 1939; ibid., folio 29: handwritten note, 5 July 1939.

71. Some of the teenagers got away with just warnings; ibid., no. 118439, fols 3–5RS: ordinance to Reich Minister of Justice via General prosecutor Berlin, 25 May 1939; ibid., folio 2: NSDAP Gau court Kurmark to Gestapo Potsdam, 31 January 1939; ibid., fols 11–13: Indictment, 24 August 1939; ibid., folio 21RS: court proceedings, 11 September 1939; ibid., fols 22–23RS: report to RJM, 9 November 1939; ibid., folio 26: General prosecutor to RJM, 29 November 1939.

72. LA Berlin, A Rep. 408, no. 1, fols 674–675: Logbook 5th police precinct, entry no. 462, 24 November 1938. For more cases of looting schoolkids in Berlin, see Barkow, Gross, and Lenarz, *Novemberpogrom 1938,* 153, 224.

73. Stenographic protocol of parts of the meeting on 12 November 1938, in Heim, *Verfolgung und Ermordung,* vol. 2, doc. 146, 408–37, here 419.

74. Cf. Dörner, *Heimtücke,* 133–35.

75. LA Berlin, A Rep. 355, no. 5744, no fols: Judgement Special Court II Berlin,15 August 1939.

76. The Vienna police also established such patrols; see Heim, *Verfolgung und Ermordung,* doc. 133, p. 386.

77. LA Berlin, A Pr.Br.Rep. 030, no. 21620, fols 85–86RS: 108th police precinct SO 36, report on a political incident, 11 November 1938, to Stapo; ibid., no. 21620, fols 94–95RS: 108th police precinct, report on a political incident, 11 November 1938, to Stapo.

78. Ibid., A Pr.Br.Rep. 030, no. 21620, folio 105: 121st police precinct, Charlottenburg, report, 14 November 1938.

79. *Verordnung zur Ausschaltung der Juden aus dem deutschen Wirtschaftsleben,* 12 November 1938; *Reichsgesetzblatt* 1938 I, 1580.

80. Gruner, *The Persecution of the Jews in Berlin,* 35. On the Aryanization of businesses in Berlin, see Kreutzmüller, *"Ausverkauf."*

81. *Gesetz über Mietverhältnisse mit Juden,* 30 April 1939; *Reichsgesetzblatt* 1939I, 864.

82. LA Berlin, A Rep. 358-02, no. 7657, folio 2: anonymous denunciation, 1 June 1939; ibid., folio 3: Note, 6 July 1939.

83. Ibid, no. 7674, fols 2–3: letter Ludwig Lenz to the Gestapo, 6 June 1939; ibid., fols 4+RS: filed complaint of 7 June 1939; ibid., fols 11–14RS: statement Friedrich Soller, pensioner, 3 August 1939; ibid., fols 22RS–23: final report, 27 August 39; ibid., folio 27: Note, no date.

84. LA Berlin, B Rep. 020, Acc. 1201, no. 6948, folio 134: 211th police precinct, Neukölln, logbook entry no. 359, 25 August 1941; ibid., folio 135: 211th police precinct, Neukölln, entry no. 362, 28 August 1941. For the orders to

– 80 –

limit shopping times in Berlin, see Gruner, *The Persecution of the Jews in Berlin*, 136–38.

85. LA Berlin, A Rep. 408, no. 28, folio 719: Logbook 254th police precinct, Lichtenberg, entry no. 77, 11–13 April 1941. On Jewish forced labor, see Wolf Gruner, *Arbeitseinsatz;* idem, *Jewish Forced Labor under the Nazis: Economic Needs and Racial Aims (1938–1944)* (New York, 2006; rev. paperback edn 2008).

86. LA Berlin, A Rep. 355, no. 5465, no fols: General prosecutor to Special Court, 1 October 1940, indictment, 1; ibid.: Judgement, 21 October 1940, 1–6. Cf. a similar case of relationships between Jewish and non-Jewish tenants: ibid., A Rep. 358-02, no. 3952, folio 3: Note, Stapo, 20 October 1941.

87. Bankier had already emphasized the fact that according to contemporary statements in many Berlin apartment buildings, non-Jews and Jews still had good relationships in 1941–42. David Bankier, *The Germans and the Final Solution: Public Opinion under Nazism* (Oxford, 1992), 119, 125.

88. For the ambivalent situation, see the entries in Erna Becker's diary of 1940–41, in *"Ich fürchte die Menschen mehr als die Bomben." Aus den Tagebüchern von drei Berliner Frauen 1938–1946,* eds Angela Martin and Claudia Schoppmann (Berlin, 1996), 23, 30–31.

89. Longerich, *"Davon haben wir nichts gewusst!,"* 181, 399.

90. Kundrus and Meyer, *Die Deportation der Juden aus Deutschland.* For more details on Berlin, see Wolf Gruner, *Widerstand in der Rosenstraße. Die Fabrik-Aktion und die Verfolgung der "Mischehen" 1943* (Frankfurt, 2005).

91. Ian Kershaw promoted the "indifference argument", Otto Dov Kulka talked about a "silent agreement," and Bankier already underlined the interests of the Germans in the deportations. Bankier, *The Germans and the Final Solution,* 130–38. For examples of critique, see Dörner, *Heimtücke,* 146–48; idem, *Die Deutschen und der Holocaust. Was niemand wissen wollte, aber jeder wissen konnte* (Berlin, 2007), 316–18, 428–29.

92. Gertrud Roensch received two years in prison for "Jew-friendly" comments under article 2 of the *Heimtücke* law. LA Berlin, A Rep. 355, no. 5728, fols 1–8. Excerpt printed in Dörner, *Die Deutschen,* 291.

93. Beate Kosmala, "Zwischen Ahnen und Wissen. Flucht vor der Deportation (1941–1945)," in Kundrus and Meyer, *Die Deportation der Juden aus Deutschland,* 135–59, here 142–50; Anna Fischer, *Erzwungener Freitod. Spuren und Zeugnisse in den Freitod getriebener Juden der Jahre 1938–1945 in Berlin* (Berlin, 2007).

94. Fischer, *Erzwungener Freitod,* 15–16, 35.

95. See, for example, LA Berlin, B Rep. 020, Acc. 1201, no. 6948, folio 266: 211th police precinct, Neukölln, no. 214, 24 August 1942.

96. LA Berlin, A Rep. 408, no. 10, no fols: Logbook Kripo 63rd precinct, entry no. 61, 22 March 1943.

97. More details in Gruner, "Berliner," 81–82.

98. Susanne Willems, *"Der entsiedelte Jude." Albert Speers Wohnungsmarktpolitik für den Berliner Hauptstadtbau* (Berlin, 2002).

99. LA Berlin, B Rep. 020, Acc. 1124, no. 6941, no fols: Logbook 173rd police precinct, Schöneberg, entry no. 174, 1 March 1943.

100. Ibid., fols 45, 54, 75–76, 80: 173rd police precinct, Schöneberg, entries of 24 February, 7 March 1943, 9 March 1943, 12 March 1943.
101. Ibid., folio 90: 173rd police precinct, Schöneberg, entry no. 224, 16 March 1943.
102. LA Berlin, A Rep. 408, no. 4, no fols: Logbook Kripo 17th precinct, entry no. 258, 8 March 1943. See also ibid.: Logbook Kripo 17th precinct, entry no. 21, 7 January 1943 and entry no. 246, 5 March 1943.
103. Gruner, *Widerstand,* 77–84; Claudia Schoppmann, "Die 'Fabrikaktion' in Berlin. Hilfe für untergetauchte Juden als Form humanitären Widerstandes," *Zeitschrift für Geschichtswissenschaft* 53, no. 2 (2005): 138–48.
104. Kosmala, "Zwischen Ahnen und Wissen," 138–39; Marnix Croes and Beate Kosmala, "Facing Deportations in Germany and the Netherlands: Survival in Hiding," in *Facing the Catastrophe: Jews and Non-Jews in Europe during World War II,* eds Beate Kosmala and Georgi Verbeeck (Oxford, 2011), 97–158, here 115–39. For Berlin examples, see Beate Kosmala, "The Rescue of Jews: Resistance by Quite Ordinary Germans, 1941–1945," in *Nazi Europe and the Final Solution,* eds David Bankier and Israel Gutman (Jerusalem, 2003), 93–107; Claudia Schoppmann, "Rettung von Juden. Ein kaum beachteter Widerstand von Frauen," in *Überleben im Untergrund: Hilfe für Juden in Deutschland 1941–1945,* eds Beate Kosmala and Claudia Schoppmann (Berlin, 2002), 109–26; Leonard Gross, *Versteckt. Wie Juden in Berlin die Nazi-Zeit überlebten* (Reinbeck, 1988).
105. LA Berlin, A Rep. 408, no. 4, no fols: Logbook, Kripo 17th precinct, entry no. 785, 30 August 1943.
106. Ibid.: Logbook Kripo 17th precinct, entry no. 971, 4 November 1943.
107. LA Berlin, A Rep. 355, no. 4571, fols 1–18: Judgement, 26 August 1943. See also Dörner, *Heimtücke,* 237. For other cases: ibid., no. 4461, fols 1–24, and ibid., A Rep. 358-02, no. 1992, no fols. See also Longerich, *"Davon haben wir nichts gewusst!,"* 201–304; and in more detail: Dörner, *Die Deutschen.*
108. The Special Court materials used here reveal that German newspapers and broadcasts were often perceived as not trustworthy. Communication research confirms that people seldom react directly to media information, as here to Nazi press and radio, unless they receive such news via personal channels. Mark S. Granovetter, "The Strength of Weak Ties," *American Journal of Sociology* 78, no. 6 (1973): 1360–80, here 1374.
109. This side is left out in the discussion between "eliminationist anti-Semitism" and group dynamic as the main positions to explain the active participation of policemen in mass murder. Christopher R. Browning, *Ordinary Men: Reserve Police Battalion 101 and the Final Solution in Poland* (New York, 1992); Daniel Jonah Goldhagen, *Hitler's Willing Executioners: Ordinary Germans and the Holocaust* (New York, 1996).
110. Wolf Gruner, "'The Germans Should Expel the Foreigner Hitler': Open Protest and Other Forms of Jewish Defiance in Nazi Germany," *Yad Vashem Studies* 39, no. 2 (2011): 13–53. For more cities, see Wolf Gruner, "Defiance and Protest: A Micro Historical Re-evaluation of Individual Jewish Responses towards Nazi Persecution," in *Microhistory of the Holocaust,* ed. Tal Bruttmann and Claire Zalc (forthcoming).

Selected Bibliography

Ahlheim, Hannah. *"Deutsche, kauft nicht bei Juden!" Antisemitismus und politischer Boykott in Deutschland 1924 bis 1935*. Göttingen, 2011.

Bankier, David. *The Germans and the Final Solution: Public Opinion under Nazism*. Oxford, 1992.

Barkow, Ben, Raphael Gross, and Michael Lenarz, eds. *Novemberpogrom 1938. Die Augenzeugenberichte der Wiener Library, London*. Frankfurt, 2008.

Berkowitz, Michael. *The Crime of My Very Existence: Nazism and the Myth of Jewish Criminality*. Berkeley, 2007.

Dörner, Bernward. *"Heimtücke": Das Gesetz als Waffe. Kontrolle, Abschreckung und Verfolgung in Deutschland 1933–1945*. Paderborn, 1998.

Gellately, Robert. *The Gestapo and German Society: Enforcing Racial Policy 1933–1945*. Oxford, 1990.

Gruner, Wolf. *Der Geschlossene Arbeitseinsatz deutscher Juden. Zur Zwangsarbeit als Element der Verfolgung 1938 bis 1943*. Berlin, 1996.

Gruner, Wolf. *The Persecution of the Jews in Berlin 1933–1945: A Chronology of Measures by the Authorities in the German Capital*. Berlin, 2014.

Gruner, Wolf. *Widerstand in der Rosenstraße. Die Fabrik-Aktion und die Verfolgung der "Mischehen" 1943*. Frankfurt, 2005.

Hachtmann, Rüdiger, Thomas Schaarschmidt, and Winfried Süss, eds. *Berlin im Nationalsozialismus. Politik und Gesellschaft 1933–1945*. Beiträge zur Geschichte des Nationalsozialimus 27. Göttingen, 2011.

Kreutzmüller, Christoph. *"Ausverkauf": Die Vernichtung der jüdischen Gewerbetätigkeit in Berlin 1930–1945*. Berlin, 2012.

Kropat, Wolf-Arno. *"Reichskristallnacht." Der Judenpogrom vom 7.–10. November 1938—Urheber, Täter, Hintergründe*. Wiesbaden, 1997.

Kundrus, Birthe, and Beate Meyer, eds. *Die Deportation der Juden aus Deutschland. Pläne-Praxis-Reaktionen 1938–1945*. Beiträge zur Geschichte des Nationalsozialismus 20. Göttingen, 2004.

Longerich, Peter. *"Davon haben wir nichts gewusst!" Die Deutschen und die Judenverfolgung 1933–45*. Munich, 2006.

Steinweis, Alan E. *Kristallnacht 1938*. Cambridge, MA, 2009.

Wildt, Michael. *Hitler's Volksgemeinschaft and the Dynamics of Racial Exclusion: Violence against Jews in Provincial Germany, 1919/1939*. New York, 2012.

Wildt, Michael, and Christoph Kreutzmüller, eds. *Berlin 1933–1945*. Munich, 2013.

Figure 5. "He is to blame for the war!" A propaganda poster holding the Jews collectively responsible for the Second World War, 1943.

Chapter 4

BABI YAR, BUT NOT AUSCHWITZ

What Did Germans Know about the Final Solution?

———— ❧ ————

Peter Fritzsche

PETER LONGERICH BEGINS HIS FINE study of the "Germans and the Persecution of the Jews" with the familiar postwar claim "That"—the Holocaust—"we didn't know anything about." He comments, "It is noteworthy that what is being denied is not that one didn't hear something or suspect something, but *knowledge* at the time. The categorical statement, that we did not *know* or after further questioning that we didn't *really* know, does not exclude rumors, clues, and partial information about the murder of the Jews."[1] Longerich's opening is a fine example of how to think about the way Germans as bystanders and as perpetrators spoke, denied, concealed, and revealed—sometimes, as in this composite case example, all at once. A careful analysis of language reveals a great deal about the state of knowledge in the 1940s; it was composed of stark details, vague suspicions, dire warnings, and sometimes repressed or forgotten eyewitness confirmations. Scholars agree that Germans knew far more about the murderous persecution of German and European Jews than the lapidary "That we didn't know anything about" would suggest.[2]

At the same time, the object of knowledge, the "that," is not a self-evident reference. Seventy years later, "that" is taken to be the Holocaust, the implementation of the Final Solution over the course of the years 1941–45. But the comprehensive and systematic nature of the murder of European Jews was not self-evident until the end of the war. Only with their liberation did Jewish survivors in Theresienstadt understand the full extent of the disaster; likewise, American and British troops were not prepared for the scenes they witnessed when they liberated the concentration camps in Buchenwald and Bergen-Belsen.[3] The exculpatory commentary of German contemporaries is not without elements of shock and surprise once it was clear that all the wartime news about deportations, massacres, and atrocities added up to systematic state-sponsored program of extermination. The twin assumptions that atrocities (horrible but not necessarily related events) occurred in war and that German atrocities had been exaggerated in World War I further impeded understanding of what was happening to the Jews in World War II.[4] The partial and deformed nature of knowledge, which Jews, Germans, and Allied soldiers all shared in different ways, needs to stay in view. Even Victor Klemperer, who did know about Auschwitz and had heard about gassing, continued to associate the murder of Jews with the retreat of German soldiers. He thus interpreted Nazi actions as reactive rather than proactive and planned.[5] If Jewish observers pieced together the comprehensive nature of the Nazis' murderous intentions when able-bodied men and women were deported from the ghettos in 1942,[6] Germans did so when they contemplated their own collective demise when Germany's defeat became increasingly possible to imagine. Even so, facts did not always add up to systematic understanding, because such understanding defied the rational premises by which contemporary observers generally evaluated the evidence of Nazi crimes. Until well after 1945, historians themselves reproduced the partial nature of knowledge about the Holocaust by assigning it a relatively marginal role in their narratives and explanations of the war.[7]

While the linguistic and epistemological tropes in which the Final Solution was discussed changed between 1941 and 1945, and while many proved resistant to a more complete understanding of events, there are identifiable, socially verifiable complexes of knowledge that can be outlined. I identify four: (1) the basically shocking news of the murder of Jewish civilians behind the advancing line of German invaders in the Soviet Union in the summer and fall of 1941; (2) the sight of the deportation of German Jews into this eastern killing field in the fall of 1941 and again in the summer of 1942; (3) the fact of the general disappearance of the Jews combined with the experience of intense aerial bombardment, which eroded knowledge of the Final Solution but also embellished "urban legends" about Jewish revenge; (4) the increasingly public "Strength through Fear" campaign after 1943, in which the regime both concealed and admitted the fact that a great crime had taken place for which Germans would not be forgiven, a situation that not only precluded the option of surrender but required struggle to the bitter end. These four complexes in turn structured the way Germans thought about the Jews after the war, in part exculpating themselves from the crimes, but also denying knowledge of the Holocaust. Longerich's excavation of "rumors, clues, and partial information" behind the denial of knowledge is smart but also limited, because Germans not only found out about the Final Solution, but were often told about it, although never in great detail. To my mind, the 1943–44 campaign to get Germans to understand that "the bridges have burned behind us" is an explicit admission that a great crime—at least from the Allied point of view—had been committed. This crime can refer only to the murder of Jews and other innocent civilians in German-occupied Europe. It is important to remember that most of the six million Jews who were murdered were murdered before the Battle of Stalingrad, which for contemporaries marked the turning point of the war.

First News of Mass Murder

The Germans invaded the Soviet Union on 22 June 1941. In just a few weeks, news about the murder of Jewish men and ferocious pogroms—often instigated by Germans, but carried out by locals—in Ukraine, Poland, and Lithuania began to circulate. By the beginning of August, six weeks into the military campaign, rumors, reports, and eyewitness accounts confirmed that the SS death squads had commenced with the extermination of entire Jewish communities—men, women, and children. Rumors spread through Germany like wildfire in late summer and fall 1941 even though the vast majority of the millions of troops mustered in the Soviet Union did not go back home on leave and would not do so until the following spring. Even so, there was traffic back and forth to the front: wounded soldiers went west, while supplies and reserve forces as well as rehabilitated soldiers returned to the east. Information was traded in train compartments and railway stations. Letters to loved ones back home also reported on pogroms, shootings, and the murder of Jewish civilians. Usually the news was second- or third-hand or at least it was passed on in that form. Just to take one example of the open talk along the home front: the city employee who came to read Anna Haag's water meter in a Stuttgart suburb at the end of November 1941 "told about a relative, an SS man, who reported that he had had to shoot down five hundred Jews, including women and children, in

Poland, that many were not dead, but others were just thrown on top, and that he could not take it anymore."[8] Communities of special interest sometimes knew more because they were expertly placed. Working with the General Staff, which necessitated travel to Poland, Helmuth von Moltke wrote to his wife, Freya, in mid-November 1941, "I have a hard time remembering these last two days. Russian prisoners, evacuated Jews, evacuated Jews, Russian prisoners, executed hostages, the gradual spread into the Reich of measures 'tried and tested' in the occupied territories, evacuated Jews, Russian prisoners, a mental sanatorium where those SS soldiers who broke down after executing women and children are treated. This was the world of my two days."[9] German Jews also had special interests and means of communication. Although Victor Klemperer did not make mention of the massacres in Kiev—the murder of more than thirty thousand Jews at Babi Yar at the end of September 1941—until several months after the event, Willy Cohn, a Jewish high-school teacher in Breslau, heard about a "big bloodbath" in Kiev already on 11 October 1941.[10]

The rumors in fall 1941 generally had three parts: (1) the inclusion of women and children among the victims; (2) the fact that victims undressed and went to their deaths naked or partly naked; (3) the indication that SS shooters sometimes went mad. These parts suggest that the news were passed on and received as news of something very, very terrible. It is hard to imagine that most Germans were not shocked and even frightened by the news of the mass murder of civilians. That the rumors foregrounded "women and children" meant that the information was generally not wrapped up in a justification of the general horrors of war or the specific threat posed by partisans. At the same time, "women and children" was central to the SS endeavor not to leave behind any potential future "avengers." The SS was proud that it had the strength and determination to murder "women and children." For this reason, the SS camera lingered on the figures of women and children, as we see in Lili Jacob's *Auschwitz Album* or in the iconic picture of the boy with raised arms in the Stroop Report on the liquidation of the Warsaw Ghetto.[11] Of course, rumors did not come in uniform shapes and sizes, but it is noteworthy that the identity of the shooters was often clarified: the SS. Already in the fall of 1941, a division of labor was in place to distribute blame, with the SS acting in a way that set it apart from what would become regarded as the "clean" Wehrmacht.

However, letters and photographs also indicated that the German Wehrmacht participated in massacres of civilians, aided in an organizational capacity, and certainly witnessed actions. The German high command had to explicitly prohibit soldiers from taking photographs, because so many snapshots of the killing sites were circulating in fall 1941.[12] At home, German parents and wives and children had an inkling of what their soldiers had seen or had undertaken at the front, but until spring 1942, the home front and the battlefront did not have to confront each other. In the summer of 1942, and this is the German version of the "Summer of '42,"[13] the two fronts encountered each other when the first (and last) large wave of home leaves was granted. The moment was tricky. How would civilians question soldiers, and how would soldiers answer back? A few conversations can be reconstructed.

When Walter Kassler came home to Celle on leave from the Soviet Union in June 1942, he had a mishmash of contradictory views about the genocidal actions he had witnessed there. "Walter emphasized repeatedly, 'We can be happy that we are not Jews.'" This was the swaggering, victorious warrior speaking, one who knew something about the extent of the killing, since Jews in general were admitted to be targets, but Kassler was now at home with his sister and brother-in-law and probably needed to provide a little more in the way of moral justification. "At first I didn't understand," he explained, "but now I know, it is a matter of existence or nonexistence." Still, his brother-in-law Karl Dürkefäldens, an old Social Democrat, pressed the point: "But that is murder." Certainly the rest of the world would consider the shooting of civilians murder, a realization that made Kassler briefly evaluate the actions of the Germans from the perspective of the enemy. He replied to Karl, "Certainly it has gone so far that they will do to us as it was done to them, if we should lose the war." Interestingly, when Walter passed along the report of a scene of murder, he did so as a witness ("I was standing twenty meters away"), not as a perpetrator, yet he used the first person plural when contemplating the revenge that might be sought on "us," the Germans. Walter understood that he would be regarded as guilty of murder in the eyes of the Allies, although he tried to justify the anti-Jewish actions. Even so he was not completely sure how to talk about the murder, especially when pressed by his inquisitive brother-in-law, Karl Dürkefäldens, who transcribed the exchange in his diary.[14]

Joseph Goebbels himself anticipated troubled encounters such as the one between Walter and Karl. He published a piece in *Das Reich* in summer 1942 titled "Conversations with Front Soldiers," in which he addressed relatives back home. Goebbels admitted that soldiers who returned home on leave appeared in many ways to have become strangers to their families. This was so because combatants were participating "in a gigantic struggle of worldviews." "It is understandable" that "uncompromising thinking about the war, and its causes, consequences, and aims" would produce "points of friction" with "life at home." Therefore it was necessary for families to "live up" to the brutal "face of the war."[15] What "points of friction" was Goebbels referring to? It is hard to imagine any other answer than the fact that soldiers had witnessed and even participated in the killing of civilians. Goebbels's admonition was part of the forth-and-back conversation the regime conducted with the German population with regard to the Final Solution. As it was, most encounters went well enough, since the leaves in the summer of 1942 were followed by a mini baby boom in late winter 1943. This is a noteworthy generation, which disproportionately grew up without fathers (many of whom were killed after returning from leave) or even grandfathers (who had fallen in World War I) and retired from the German workforce only in 2008.[16]

It should be noted that in summer and fall of 1941, though much less so as the war ground on in 1942, there was an urgent desire among combatants to document the war and their place in it. Soldiers pleaded with relatives to take extra care in developing and enlarging photographs—"A 6 x 9 format. Preferably, silk smooth matte finish"—which were also traded with other comrades in the unit.[17] Jewish subjects were part and parcel of this vernacular national photo album.[18] Indeed, a documentary zeal animated the high command. On 1 August 1941, SS death squads were directed to send "particularly interesting visual material" to Berlin "as quickly as possible," such as "photographs, placards, leaflets, and other documents."[19] Himmler went so far as to recruit novelists Hanns Johst and Edwin Erich Dwinger and filmmakers and photographers to accompany SS missions. In all likelihood, a film was made to document the murder of Jews in Minsk that Himmler witnessed on 15 August 1941.[20] Stationed in Paris in spring 1942, Ernst Jünger registered the accumulation of reports about SS massacres, which he described as "ghost festivals, with the murder of men, children, women. The gruesome booty is quickly interred, then other ghosts arrive to dig it out again; they film the dismembered, half-decomposed carcasses with a nightmarish glee. And then they screen these films for others."[21]

In the end, attentive Germans knew in 1941 and 1942 about the systematic murder of civilians, many knew about extraordinarily deadly operations such as Babi Yar, and most were probably shocked, given the repeated references to murdered women and children, naked bodies, and madness. The knowledge of Babi Yar absorbed enough of the shock so that it may have barred future knowledge about Auschwitz. It was a shock and a shock absorber. Babi Yar may also have been categorized as an atrocity that by definition was exceptional.

Knowledge of the Deportations

The second complex of knowledge was laid down in October, November, and December 1941 when the deportation of German Jews made eyewitnesses and informants out of thousands of their non-Jewish German neighbors. It is important to realize that the deportations to the "east" took place after the rumors of the activity of the death squads in precisely that same "east" had begun to sweep across the country. What is striking about the information circulated about the deportations was the attention to detail. Detail is usually allied with empathy, and it is jarring in the conversations in the Third Reich.[22] But empathetic detail was also often followed by the effort to snuff out the detail by other narrative means. Two examples are revealing.

On 25 September 1941, Paulheinz Wantzen, Münster's newspaper editor and a Nazi Party member, encountered a Jew marked with the star for the first time: "The man, who wears it on the left side of his coat, hugs the side of the houses with great timidity." The description indicated a flicker of pity, but soon enough Jews were, in Wantzen's renditions, accomplices to their own fate. Later in Berlin, he observed, Jews were "still remarkably well-dressed," a muddle of words around the derivative root "mark," which unconsciously transformed the star into a suit ("*noch ausgezeichnet angezogenen Jüdinnen*"). Jews did not give the impression "that they are walking around in a funk." Once Wantzen knew the Jews to be wearing the star in a "very blithe, almost ostentatious" fashion, he had succeeded in purging himself of any sympathy for Jews. "Gentlemen" might criticize vulgar Nazi policies, but the "voice of the people" played along. "You hear," Wantzen continued, passing on gossip from the street, that "the Jews now have a penchant for holding their attaché cases or purses under the left arm so that the star is as hidden from view as possible."[23] Wantzen's diary also recorded the deportation of the last of Münster's Jews, which occurred on 30 July 1942. It turned out that "a university professor … struggled with his hands and feet against being transported, while the others went willingly and gave generous tips to several men from the Security Service [Sicherheitsdienst—SD] who helped them with their heavy suitcases, since some of these Jews were already just too flabby. One SD man is said to have made ninety marks."[24] Like his diary entry of what "you hear" about marking Jews with the Star of David, Wantzen's writing passed along gossip circulating at the time. It was precisely the kind to hold in check empathy, which is tellingly compared to a sickness from which Wantzen found himself to be "cured." Gossip introduced the misbehaved professor and flabby, suckered Jews.

A second example: Isa Kuchenbuch wrote to her soldier husband Fritz at the end of November 1941. Before that, in July, as the initially victorious Germans began their offensive against the Soviet Union, she had asked for "a silk 'Jewish dress'"—"but it's got to be plenty big!" since she wanted to give it to her supersized aunt. Yet Isa struggled with the news of the deportation of her Jewish neighbors a few months later:

> They are being sent to Poland, to Lodz. In Bremen, in our neighborhood, they had to assemble in two big schools, right near Heinz and Alma. There they reside with kit and caboodle and they look just terrible. They are allowed 100 M travel money. The railway journey costs 90 M, so 10 M has to cover necessities for an eight-day period. They leave the Reich as the poorest of the poor. ... Many find this bitter hard and some were okay. But now they all have to take responsibility for their kind. Now I have given enough "honor" to the Jews, having sacrificed half a page of writing paper on their account. So let's change the subject.[25]

The alleged sins of the collective repeatedly justified the acknowledged sufferings of individual Jews. The assignment of collective guilt also allowed wives to participate in the rigors of war.

It is almost possible to hear the doubts and justifications that animated the discussions among neighbors as they confronted the news of the deportations of German Jews. A secret police report recounted the following scene when elderly Jews were deported from Detmold in July 1942:

> It could be observed that a large number of older people's comrades generally criticized the measure to transport the Jews out of Germany. All sorts of arguments were made more or less openly to argue against the transport. It was argued that the Jews in Germany were condemned to die out as it was. ... Even comrades who had proved their National Socialist convictions ... stood up for the Jews. From among

those loyal to the church came the warning: "that the German people do not one day await God's judgment." National Socialist loyalists tried to make it clear to those who thought differently that the action was completely justified and urgently necessary. They were contradicted with the argument that the old Jews can't do us any harm anymore because they wouldn't "hurt a fly."[26]

In this case, the discussions seemed to veer off in a more critical direction. Local Nazis themselves may well have felt besieged because the party probably received what must have been thousands of appeals on behalf of individual Jews in fall 1941; the concrete result of this wave of exceptionalism to Nazi policies against the Jews was Theresienstadt, which allowed the "friends" of the Jews to imagine their former neighbors incarcerated in an *Endlager* or "old-age ghetto," not a death camp. Himmler was still smarting from the overall lack of resolve among Germans when he bitterly denounced in his October 1943 Posen speech all the "A-1 Jews" that even Nazi Party members seemed to have.[27]

To discuss the Jews and to pass on details about their fate did indicate critical responses, but the interactions among neighbors also ended in justifications that allowed the home front to stand firm alongside the battlefront, as Goebbels had wished in his July 1942 article, "Conversations with Front Soldiers." That the deportations took place in the middle of a ferocious anti-Jewish campaign in which new ration cards came with notices blaming the Jews for the deaths of German soldiers in Russia and a whole new layer of anti-Jewish signs blocking access to countless shops made it easier for citizens to accept deportations and certainly made it difficult to overlook them.[28] Many Germans probably shared the empathy of Isa Kuchenbach, who retailed heartrending details, as well as her desire, formulated in the admonitory scene-changing word "now," which was repeated twice, to justify the operation as a whole so that the idea of the Third Reich would remain untarnished.

The feeling that the German cause was righteous found further confirmation in the zeal to document the deportations. In Berlin, Goebbels hoped to film deportations, and in Stuttgart and Nuremberg, authorities in fact filmed the assembly and entraining of Jews in November 1941. In Bad Neustadt, local Nazis photographed elderly, malnourished Jews on 22 April 1942 as they stood before the fountain on the marketplace and even choreographed group shots before marching them to the train station for deportation. They later enlarged the photographs and hung them in picture windows in the center of town to document the successful action.[29] In Münster, Wantzen mobilized himself "to gather material and get details. Later, that will be very interesting."[30] All this added up to the first draft of the history of the Final Solution.

Allied Bombing and the Disappearance of the Jews

The third complex of knowledge regarding the murder of the Jews was laid down during the first intense bombing campaign that the Allies conducted beginning in the Ruhr in spring 1942 and later across Germany to Hamburg, Kassel, Berlin, and elsewhere over the course of 1943. This was also the time when German Jews were no longer disappearing in regular deportations but had in fact already disappeared. With the Jews gone, the anti-Jewish signs on stores, park benches, and swimming pools were superfluous and were taken down. The sights and sounds of anti-Jewish propaganda dimmed in 1942 and 1943 as well—at least compared to fall 1941. The coincidence of the presence of the bombing campaign and the absence of the Jews might well have ended up eroding the shocking knowledge in 1941 about murder pits and deportations. In any case, Germans certainly felt they had troubles of their own, and however disproportionate these were to the fate of the Jews, the bombs were nearer at hand. What is more, the faltering fortunes of the war in autumn 1942, with defeats in North Africa and the Sixth Army stalled and then surrounded at Stalingrad—a drama the German public anxiously followed—also diminished the zeal to document Germany's military record, actions that were a major byway of information about anti-Jewish actions.[31] Once the war soured, the Final Solution no longer seemed so interesting. In this context, news about the Jews was also more "toxic" because it threatened to contaminate the projected postwar self.

Yet the Jews were talked about, and the bombings in fact replenished discussions about murder, revenge, and responsibility. The relatively light destruction of the first British bomber runs in 1941 had, in some western German cities, served as a premise for demands to deport Jews.[32] By the middle of 1942, when more than half of Germany's Jews had already been deported and the first major air raids against Hamburg and Cologne had taken place, the argument shifted in reverse and Jews were blamed for the bombing, which then served as an argument or justification for their dispossession and deportation. What is interesting, however, is that while regime propaganda simply put the blame on international Jewry, talk on the street went further and blamed the Jews who, from their powerful positions abroad, were taking revenge on Germany for the cruel treatment Jewish neighbors had suffered. (See Appendix F.) Or else, the Allies were punishing Germany or Germany was being punished in some sort of divine reckoning for persecuting the Jews. The vernacular path of cause and effect was circumstantial and moral, while the regime explained Allied motivations via the essence of the Jews. With these ideas of retaliation, public opinion established a link between what had happened to Jews (in 1941 and 1942) and what was happening to Germans (in 1942 and 1943). Rumors even circulated that cities such as Würzburg had not been bombed because the synagogue there had been spared in November 1938 (which was not true—all seven were destroyed or damaged in the Kristallnacht pogrom) or that the city had suddenly become vulnerable once it had deported its last Jew, who was said to have told the townspeople as much upon his departure.[33]

The connection between the air war and the persecution of the Jews rested on the knowledge that the deportations (which were chronologically prior) were as extensive as the bombing raids, a cycle (however tendentiously imagined) of injury and revenge that involved every city and, by extension, almost every person in Germany. Thus the comprehensiveness of the air campaign against Germany implied the prior comprehensiveness of the Nazi war against the Jews in which the deportations ended where the killing fields of the SS death squads began. The "Jewishness" of the air war admitted the idea that the Jews had been systematically murdered in a way that established the complicity of the German people. Moreover, in whatever moral register, the rumors constituted a German "us" and a Jewish "them," which functioned either to bind together the beleaguered *Volksgemeinschaft* (national community) or to democratize and spread out guilt among Germans, or, of course, both.

Urban legends such as those circulating in Würzburg could and did imply fundamental criticism of the deportations. Interestingly, as the air raids grew worse, the German crime with which they were implicitly linked remained large enough to sustain the equivalency all the way to the end of the war. In these wild scenarios, no one ever said that Jews went overboard in the destruction they meted out. Therefore, these urban legends contained knowledge of the comprehensiveness of the crime against the Jews. But if popular reactions to the air raids revealed guilty knowledge, the association between persecution and bombing also enabled Germans to relieve themselves of guilt because they had become victims too—the equivalency worked both ways. This was particularly the case after the war, so that the critical edge of the rumors before 1945 turned exculpatory after 1945. What is more, since the rumors fantasized about the sheer power of super-Jews to take revenge from across the sea, they relied on the most blatant anti-Semitic stereotypes.[34]

"Strength through Fear"

The connection between Jews and the air war began in 1941, with German Jews taking the blame for Allied actions, but it gained legs in 1942 and 1943, with Jews taking revenge for what Germans had done. The switch in the direction of blame could not have pleased Nazi loyalists, and the rumors implied that Germans were indeed complicit in a great crime. But as the inability of Germany to win the war became more and more evident over the course of 1943, the Nazis used the toxic knowledge that Germans had about the murder of the Jews to bolster morale and discipline. The complicity of Germans in the Holocaust was made explicit to demand the continued loyalty of Germans in a campaign British intelligence dubbed "Strength through Fear," a play on the "Strength through Joy" leisure program. This is the fourth and most mediated complex of knowledge about the Holocaust.

The Nazis encouraged and justified murder by asking soldiers to imagine themselves as the potential victims of their actual victims. In summer 1942, when he was visiting home on leave, Walter Kassler explained to his relatives that he had come to understand that the murder of the Jews was "a matter of existence or nonexistence." This stark choice, "us or them," had justified the Nazis' preemptory actions against innocent civilians since the beginning of the war and continued to echo in its last days when the "either/or" was expressed as *"Friss, oder du wirst gefressen!"* ("Devour them, or you will be devoured!").[35] By 1943, however, references to the Final Solution had become quite concrete and were aimed quite explicitly at German civilians—a nod to the state of ethnic emergency by which the Nazis imagined and conducted the war. In his infamous "total war" speech that he gave at the Sportpalast on 18 February 1943, Goebbels outlined what would happen to the German people in the event they lost the war: "the liquidation of our educated and political elite," "forced labor battalions in the Siberian tundra," and "Jewish liquidation commandos," which closely approximated what the Nazis had already done to Jews.[36] Six months later, Hermann Goering applied Germany's racial judgment on the Jews onto German civilians, who would be totally exposed to the wrath of the Jews if the Allies won the war. "Whoever you were, whether a democrat or a plutocrat or a Nazi or a Social Democratic or a Communist, that won't matter at all. The Jew sees only the German," he explained. "He intends to destroy what is racially pure, what is Germanic."[37] Delivered in Berlin's Sportpalast on 4 October 1943, Goering's speech indicated that biology or Germanness was destiny, just as Goebbels had insisted that there is "no difference between a Jew and a Jew" in his scurrilous November 1941 article "The Jews Are Guilty!" in *Das Reich*. Germans were asked to imagine themselves as the "Jews" the Nazis themselves had created and implicitly to imagine the fate of the Jews for themselves.

In these threatening tirades, the Holocaust that had occurred was only hinted at but provided the detail for the Holocaust that would befall the Germans in the future in the event of defeat. However, in the most compelling image of the "Strength through Fear" campaign, the bridges that Germany had burned behind itself, the actual murder of the Jews and other civilians, was made explicit to compel Germans to continue to fight to the bitter end. "A movement and a people who have burned the bridges behind them fight with much greater determination than those who are still able to retreat," noted Joseph Goebbels in his diary in early March 1943.[38] To master the crisis of confidence in spring and summer 1943, in the aftermath of Stalingrad, the Allied invasion of Italy, and the end of the "brutal alliance" with Mussolini, prominent Nazis workshopped the news of the Final Solution in dozens of meetings with local political elites to stiffen the will to resist the approaching enemy. On the road in western Germany in April and May 1943, Alfred Rosenberg explained to a *Gauschulungstagung* (district indoctrination meeting) on 8 May in Trier, "Today our task is to make Germany and Europe clean again. After two thousand years of parasitical activity, Europe must be liberated from Jewish leprosy. That is not brutality, but clean, biological humanitarianism. Better that eight million Jews disappear than eighty million Germans. The bridges have been broken behind us, and there is no way back anymore."[39] These revelations did not reach all Germans, of course, but Goebbels published the frightening watchwords that the Germans had "broken the bridges behind us" in *Das Reich*, which had a circulation of 1.4 million on 14 November 1943. "We will either go down in history as the greatest statesmen of all time, or as the greatest criminals," he concluded.[40] The Nazis came close to conceding that Germans might be fitting objects of revenge.

Ordinary Germans could not have misunderstood that the burned bridges were anything but an explicit reference to the murder of the Jews and other innocent civilians across Europe. What is remarkable about this propaganda is that it required Germans to see themselves as the Allies did, as criminals, who to save themselves would push themselves further into the moral wilderness of the Third Reich. For the "Strength through Fear" campaign to work, Germans needed as much knowledge about the Final Solution as the Allies had; Germans needed to simulate Allied moral outrage in order to properly arm themselves. "Goebbels has allowed so much information on German crimes to filter through," commented a Swedish correspondent in August 1943, "that everyone is conscious of shared responsibility and guilt, and afraid of personal retaliation."[41] However, the generation of fear could also recoil against the Nazis if frightened listeners distanced themselves from the belligerent broadcasters, which would have had the effect of unfastening rather than fastening, as the regime had intended, the identification of Germans with Nazis. As a result, many Germans might well have started imagining themselves as the naive dupes of a small clique of monstrous Nazis—Goebbels, Goering, Himmler. Knowledge of the Final Solution had become inextricably tied to fear and guilt, which deformed the comprehension of the Holocaust for many decades after 1945.

When Germans in the Third Reich had a final opportunity to contemplate the Jews who had been persecuted and murdered, they conjured up not the super-Jews who had allegedly taken revenge against the Germans in the air war, but the emaciated, starved survivors of the concentration camps who recalled the great crime the Nazis had committed. It was not always clear what sort of prisoners constituted the death marches, Jews or Allied prisoners of war or political prisoners from around Europe, but the sight of the columns marched across the German landscape in winter 1945 provoked feelings of unease; German civilians had every interest in making sure the death marches left the vicinity or resulted in death, and both the SS and civilians participated in the murder of prisoners in the last weeks of the war. Having burned bridges, the perpetrators continued to burn barns and sheds if for no other reason than to destroy the evidence.[42] If this is so, then Germans not only *did* see the death marches, but quite possibly saw the frightening prospect that they might find themselves in the ranks of similar marches a few weeks hence.[43] Evidence was certainly tampered with across German-occupied Europe. It is striking how limited the documentary archive of the Final Solution is, although the Germans were at first quite energetic in preparing such an archive. Of course there are extraordinary batches of evidence, including the protocol of the Wannsee Conference, all manner of deportation lists maintained at local and Reich levels, the Stroop Report, even blueprints for the gas chambers in Auschwitz. But the vast majority of evidence was destroyed in the last weeks and months of the war. Martin Bormann in the Reich Chancellery was in charge of party affairs, and he gave repeated and detailed orders about the security and, if necessary, disposal of party documents. Most local officials followed Bormann's guidelines and destroyed the evidence. In Mecklenburg, for example, a total of thirteen district and 629 local party organizations burned or otherwise got rid of party records.[44] Countless Germans purged the evidence of their past as well. "When you have two military brothers and a like-minded brother-in-law, you can image what sort of stuff has collected around the house," wrote one woman in besieged Gleiwitz in late January 1945 as she tore up incriminating photographs before the arrival of the Russians.[45] The writer Günter Kunert remembers the same thing as a child in Prenzlauer Berg, his Berlin neighborhood. He recounted what happened when word spread that the Russians were about to arrive: "Turmoil ensued—papers are taken out, documents, passports, photographs, any indication of one's own complicity … straight into the fires of purgatory with all that incriminating material."[46] As a result, self-protection blocked the way to self-incrimination, but the destruction of evidence also was the effect of what ended up being a self-immolating and thus silent form of self-incrimination. Tampering with the evidence made it possible to say "That we didn't know anything about" with a measure of plausibility.

In the end, the knowledge of the Final Solution was extensive, but deformed. First, much of the knowledge was contained in documentary efforts designed to celebrate the Final Solution. These endeavors lost their pertinence halfway through the war. Second, many Germans had quite precise knowledge of Babi Yar, which, I think, they found shocking, but which was also shock absorbing. Three, outside of the Wartheland and the highest levels in Berlin, there is little evidence of semi-public or public knowledge about Auschwitz or gas chambers. Obviously Auschwitz was discussed in the town of Auschwitz itself and in the "German casinos" that dotted Poland. And rumors about gas, gas vans, gas in trains, and gas in tunnels did circulate, but never as extensively as the news about the death squads in fall 1941 or the rumors about super-Jews in the Allied bombing campaigns in 1942 and 1943. Hitler in *Mein Kampf* and others mentioned Jews and gas, but the context was World War I, not World War II. In his 1943 Posen speeches, Himmler did not mention either Auschwitz or gas chambers. Four, knowledge about the great crime that the Germans had committed could be regime critical ("All guilt avenges itself on earth," to quote Goethe), but also self-exculpatory (the moral balance sheet is even, given Allied air raids) and even useful for regime purposes, as in the "Strength through Fear" campaign (know yourself as they do, so you will stay with us). The implication of this knowledge was that discussions about the Jews was always accompanied by deliberation about the justifiability of the murderous actions. Five, although almost every aspect of the Holocaust was known in the United States by the end of summer 1942, the facts were not put together to produce systematic knowledge about the Final Solution. Even the well-informed Jewish diarist Victor Klemperer thought in terms of event-based atrocities. And where a sense of comprehensiveness was acknowledged—for example, in the connection between Allied bombing of city after city and Germany's deportation of basically all Jews (as in the reference to the "last Jew" to leave)—it often worked to settle accounts, not to achieve deeper insight into Nazi racism. Six, the news of anti-Jewish actions was generally associated with the SS so that the specifically Nazi crime in the war did not have a clear German provenience.

Finally, as a matter of speculation, I wonder if Germans didn't know more about the Final Solution in 1941 than in 1945. Is it possible that this knowledge, produced in part by shock, but also by the desire to celebrate, eroded over the course of the war? Did Germany's eminent defeat make moral outrage at Nazi actions or a sense of moral triumphalism at the moment of victory—which had now been denied—irrelevant? Is it possible that once the imminent loss of the war destroyed the ideal of the Third Reich, the murder of the Jews could no longer function either to endanger or to guarantee its durability, and the murder simply became one more dramatic register of the overall catastrophe of war and destruction? In the end, knowledge about the Final Solution was heavily mediated by the desire to continue to live in the Third Reich. In the years 1941–45, Germans told the story of their own complicity themselves, whether out of consent or out of fear.

Peter Fritzsche has been a professor at the University of Illinois at Urbana-Champaign since 1987. He is the author of numerous books including *Stranded in the Present: Modern Time and the Melancholy of History* (Cambridge, MA, 2004), *Life and Death in the Third Reich*

(Cambridge, MA, 2008), and *The Turbulent World of Franz Göll: An Ordinary Berliner Writes the Twentieth Century* (Cambridge, MA, 2011). He is currently at work on a cultural history of World War II.

Notes

1. Peter Longerich, *"Davon haben wir nichts gewusst!" Die Deutschen und die Judenverfolgung 1933–1945* (Berlin, 2006), 7.
2. In addition to Longerich, Bernward Dörner, *Die Deutschen und der Holocaust. Was niemand wissen wollte, aber jeder wissen konnte* (Berlin, 2007); and David Bankier, *The Germans and the Final Solution: Public Opinion under Nazism* (Oxford, 1992).
3. Peter Fritzsche, *Life and Death in the Third Reich* (Cambridge, 2008), 294–95; Robert H. Abzug, *Inside the Vicious Heart: Americans and the Liberation of the Nazi Concentration Camps* (New York, 1987).
4. Paul Fussell, *The Great War and Modern Memory* (New York, 1975), 316.
5. See, for example, entries for 27 February 1943 and 24 October 1944, Victor Klemperer, *I Will Bear Witness 1942–1945: A Diary of the Nazi Years* (New York, 1998), 204, 371.
6. Alexandra Garbarini, *Numbered Days: Diaries and the Holocaust* (New Haven, 2006), 89.
7. Dan Diner, "The Destruction of Narrativity: The Holocaust in Historical Discourse," in *Catastrophe and Meaning: The Holocaust and the Twentieth Century,* eds Moishe Postone and Eric Santner (Chicago, 2003), 69, 72. The key example is Gordon Craig, *Europe since 1815* (New York, 1961), which does not mention the Holocaust.
8. Entry for 26 November 1941, in "Kriegstagebuch," in Anna Haag, *Leben und gelebt werden* (Tübingen, 2003), 252–53.
9. Letter dated 13 November 1941 in Helmuth James von Moltke, *Briefe an Freya 1939–1945,* ed. Beate Ruhm von Oppen (Munich, 1988), 318.
10. Entry for 11 October 1941 in Willy Cohn, *Als Jude in Breslau 1941,* ed. Joseph Walk (Gerlingen, 1984), 106. On Klemperer, see entry for 19 April 1942, Victor Klemperer, *I Will Bear Witness 1942–1945: A Diary of the Nazi Years* (New York, 1998), 41.
11. *The Auschwitz Album: Lili Jacob's Album,* ed. Serge Klarsfeld (New York, 1980); Jürgen Stroop, *The Stroop Report: The Jewish Quarter of Warsaw Is No More!* (New York, 1979).
12. Bernd Boll and Hans Safrian, "On the Way to Stalingrad: The 6th Army in 1941–42," in *War of Extermination: The German Military in World War II, 1941–44,* eds Hannes Heer and Klaus Naumann (New York, 2000), 249.
13. A reference to Robert Mulligan's "coming of age" film, *Summer of '42* (Warner Bros., 1971).
14. Karl Dürkefälden, *"Schreiben, wie es wirklich war ..." Aufzeichnungen Karl Dürkefäldens aus den Jahren 1933–1945,* eds Herbert and Sibylle Obenaus

(Hannover, 1985), 110. See also Christopher Browning, *Ordinary Men: Reserve Police Battalion 101 and the Final Solution in Poland* (New York, 1992), 58.

15. Goebbels, „Gespräche mit Frontsoldaten," *Das Reich,* 26 July 1942.

16. Jürgen Reulecke, "'Vaterlose Söhne' in einer 'Vaterlosen Gesellschaft': Die Bundesrepublik nach 1945," in *Vaterlosigkeit: Geschichte und Gegenwart einer fixen Idee,* ed. Dieter Thomä (Suhrkamp, 2009), 142–59.

17. Albert to Agnes Neuhaus, 30 November 1941, in *Zwischen Front und Heimat: Der Briefwechsel des Münsterischen Ehepaares Agnes und Albert Neuhaus 1940–1944,* ed. Karl Reddemann (Münster, 1996), 362–63.

18. Kathrin Hoffmann-Curtius, "Trophäen in Brieftaschen–Fotografien von Wehrmachts-, SS- und Polizei-Verbrechen," *kunsttexte.de* 3 (2002), accessed 9 October 2012 at http://edoc.hu-berlin.de/kunsttexte/download/poli/hoffmann-curtius.PDF.

19. Christian Gerlach, *Kalkulierte Morde: Die deutsche Wirtschafts- und Vernichtungspolitik in Weißrußland 1941 bis 1944* (Hamburg, 2000), 574.

20. Ibid., 573–74; Klaus Hesse, "'… Gefangenenlager, Exekution, … Irrenanstalt … ' Walter Frentz' Reise nach Minsk im Gefolge Heinrich Himmlers im August 1941," in *Das Auge des Dritten Reiches: Hitlers Kameramann und Fotograph Walter Frentz,* ed. Hans Georg Hiller von Gaertringen (Munich, 2007), 180–86; Rolf Düsterberg, *Hanns Johst: "Der Barde der SS." Karrieren eines deutschen Dichters* (Paderborn, 2004), 302–14.

21. Entry for 12 March 1942, Ernst Jünger, *Strahlungen* (Tübingen, 1955), 90.

22. See Thomas W. Laqueur, "Bodies, Details, and the Humanitarian Narrative," in *The New Cultural History,* ed. Lynn Hunt (Berkeley, 1989).

23. Entries for 25 and 28 September and 19 October 1941, in Paulheinz Wantzen, *Das Leben im Krieg 1939-1946. Ein Tagebuch* (Bad Homburg, 2000), 551, 567, 594. This "local knowledge" would become propaganda soon enough. See Maurer, "Wie sich die Juden tarnen," *Der Stürmer,* 20 November 1941.

24. Entry for 8 August 1942, Wantzen, *Das Leben im Krieg,* 916.

25. Isa to Fritz Kuchenbuch, 8 July and 23 November 1941, Kempowski Archive, 5483, Akademie der Künste, Berlin.

26. Cited in Longerich, *"Davon haben wir nichts gewusst!,"* 219–20. See also Hans G. Adler, *Der verwaltete Mensch. Studien zur Deportation der Juden aus Deutschland* (Tübingen, 1974), 332.

27. Heinrich Himmler, "Rede in Posen," 4 October 1943, NS19/4010, Bundesarchiv Berlin.

28. Howard K. Smith, *Last Train from Berlin* (New York, 1942), 197.

29. Entry for 27 April 1942 in Joseph Goebbels, *Die Tagebücher von Joseph Goebbels. Sämtliche Fragmente,* ed. Elke Fröhlich (Munich, 1994), part 2, vol. 4, 184; on Nuremberg, Beate Meyer, "Handlungsspielräume regionaler jüdischer Repräsentanten (1941–1945): Die Reichsvereinigung der Juden in Deutschland und die Deportationen," in *Die Deportation der Juden aus Deutschland: Pläne, Praxis, Reaktionen 1938–1945,* Beiträge zur Geschichte des Nationalsozialismus 20, eds Birthe Kundrus and Beate Meyer (Göttingen, 2004), 77; on Stuttgart, Roland Müller, *Stuttgart zur Zeit des Nationalsozialismus* (Stuttgart,

1988), 405; and on Bad Neustadt, Herbert Schultheis, *Juden in Mainfranken 1933–1945* (Bad Neustadt, 1980), 467–68.

30. Entry for 15 December 1941, in Wantzen, *Das Leben im Krieg*, 651–52.

31. On Stalingrad and Tobruk, see the entries for 14 and 29 November 1942 in Lore Walb, *Ich, die Alte – ich, die Junge: Konfrontation mit meinen Tagebüchern 1933–1945* (Berlin, 1997), 249, 253. The avid amateur photographer on the eastern front, Albert Neuhaus, lost interest in taking snapshots of his experiences, at least as registered by a growing lack of interest in the diary entries. See *Zwischen Front und Heimat*.

32. The Gauleiter of Hamburg, Karl Kaufmann, was especially vociferous on this issue. See Christopher Browning, *The Origins of the Final Solution: The Evolution of Nazi Jewish Policy, September 1939–March 1942* (Lincoln, NE 2004), 324–25.

33. Longerich, *"Davon haben wir nichts gewusst!,"* 284–85; Nicholas Stargardt, "Opfer der Bomben und der Vergeltung," in *Ein Volk von Opfern? Die neue Debatte um den Bombenkrieg 1940–45*, ed. Lothar Kettenacker (Berlin, 2003), 56–71; Frank Bajohr, "Über die Entwicklung eines schlechten Gewissens: Die deutsche Bevölkerung und die Deportationen 1941–1945," in Kundrus and Meyer, *Deportation der Juden aus Deutschland*, 190–92.

34. See also my analysis of the United States Strategic Bombing Survey interviews after the war in Fritzsche, *Life and Death in the Third Reich*, 260–61.

35. *Das Schwarze Korps*, 22 February 1945.

36. Günter Moltmann, "Goebbels' Rede zum totalen Krieg am 18. Februar 1943," *Vierteljahrshefte für Zeitgeschichte* 12, no. 1 (1964): 22.

37. Goering on 17 November 1943, quoted in Dörner, *Die Deutschen und der Holocaust*, 143.

38. Goebbels's diary entry for 2 March 1943 cited in Bajohr, "Über die Entwicklung eines schlechten Gewissens," 194.

39. Entry for 9 May 1943 in Wantzen (who attended the meeting), *Das Leben im Krieg*, 1093.

40. Quoted in Hans-Ulrich Thamer, *Verfolgung und Gewalt. Deutschland 1933–1945* (Berlin, 1986), 679.

41. Christian T. Barth, *Goebbels und die Juden* (Paderborn, 2003), 238.

42. Gordon J. Horwitz, *In the Shadow of Death: Living Outside the Gates of Mauthausen* (New York, 1990); Daniel Blatman, *The Death Marches: The Final Phase of Nazi Genocide* (Cambridge, 2011), especially 405.

43. Ruth Kluger leaves behind a compelling account in which Germans did not see the death marches that passed through their community. See *Still Alive: A Holocaust Girlhood Remembered* (New York, 2001), 146.

44. Michael Buddrus, "Einleitung," in *Mecklenburg im Zweiten Weltkrieg: Die Tagungen des Gauleiters Friedrich Hildebrandt mit den NS-Führungsgremien des Gaues Mecklenburg 1939–1945. Eine Edition der Sitzungsprotokolle*, ed. Michael Buddrus (Bremen, 2009), 9–10, 16.

45. Quoted in Walter Kempowski, *Das Echolot: Fuga furiosa* (Munich, 1999), 2:650.

46. Günter Kunert, *Erwachsenenspiele* (Munich, 1997), 85.

Selected Bibliography

Abzug, Robert H. *Inside the Vicious Heart: Americans and the Liberation of the Nazi Concentration Camps.* New York, 1987.

Bajohr, Frank, and Dieter Pohl. *Der Holocaust als offenes Geheimnis. Die Deutschen, die NS-Führung und die Alliierten.* Munich, 2006.

Bankier, David. *The Germans and the Final Solution: Public Opinion under Nazism.* Oxford, 1992.

Dörner, Bernward. *Die Deutschen und der Holocaust. Was niemand wissen wollte, aber jeder wissen konnte.* Berlin, 2007.

Dürkefälden, Karl. "Schreiben, wie es wirklich war ..." Aufzeichnungen Karl Dürkefäldens aus den Jahren 1933–1945. Edited by Herbert and Sibylle Obenaus. Hannover, 1985.

Fritzsche, Peter. *Life and Death in the Third Reich.* Cambridge, MA, 2008.

Garbarini, Alexandra. *Numbered Days: Diaries and the Holocaust.* New Haven, 2006.

Gerlach, Christian. *Kalkulierte Morde: Die deutsche Wirtschafts- und Vernichtungspolitik in Weißrußland 1941 bis 1944.* Hamburg, 2000.

Klemperer, Victor. *I Will Bear Witness 1942–1945: A Diary of the Nazi Years.* New York, 1998.

Kluger, Ruth. *Still Alive: A Holocaust Girlhood Remembered.* New York, 2001.

Kundrus, Birthe, and Beate Meyer, eds. *Die Deportation der Juden aus Deutschland. Pläne-Praxis-Reaktionen 1938–1945.* Beiträge zur Geschichte des Nationalsozialismus 20. Göttingen, 2004.

Longerich, Peter. *"Davon haben wir nichts gewusst!" Die Deutschen und die Judenverfolgung 1933–1945.* Munich, 2006.

Moltke, Helmuth James von. *Briefe an Freya 1939–1945.* Edited by Beate Ruhm von Oppen. Munich, 1988.

Reddemann, Karl, ed. *Zwischen Front und Heimat: Der Briefwechsel des Münsterischen Ehepaares Agnes und Albert Neuhaus 1940–1944.* Münster, 1996.

Walb, Lore. *Ich, die Alte – ich, die Junge: Konfrontation mit meinen Tagebüchern 1933–1945.* Berlin, 1997.

Wantzen, Paulheinz. *Das Leben im Krieg 1939-1946. Ein Tagebuch.* Bad Homburg, 2000.

Figure 6. Bernhard K., who survived the Holocaust in hiding, with his protector, his neighbor Kathi S., Munich 1942.

Chapter 5

SUBMERGENCE INTO ILLEGALITY

Hidden Jews in Munich, 1941–45

————— ∞ —————

Susanna Schrafstetter

IN THE EARLY HOURS OF 20 November 1941, 999 Jewish men, women, and children boarded a train at the Milbertshofen station, a remote cargo terminal in the north of Munich. Their destination was the Lithuanian town of Kovno, where, five days later, every single one of them would be shot by an SS *Einsatzkommando.* In Munich, 20 November 1941 marked the beginning of the deportations of the city's remaining Jewish population. On forty-three transports that left the city between November 1941 and February 1945, approximately 3,500 Jews were sent to Kovno, Piaski, Auschwitz, and Theresienstadt. Few of the deportees survived. Only 160 Jews from Munich were liberated in Theresienstadt in 1945.[1] Even fewer had managed to escape the deportations, flee, and survive in hiding. When the Americans liberated the former capital city of the Nazi movement, "there were only a few Jews here and there" in the city.[2] Valerie Wolffenstein was one of them. "When at last, the scourge of Nazism was wrestled to the ground and the Americans made their victorious entry into Munich, I could finally breathe again and resurface together with my sister and start a new life," she wrote later. [3]

In all of Germany, Jews reemerged from hiding in May 1945 after years on the run, but their numbers were tiny. An estimated ten to fifteen thousand had gone underground beginning in 1941. There are no precise numbers of how many survived. Figures vary between three thousand and five thousand.[4] In their efforts to submerge, these Jewish *U-Boote,* or "submarines," as they called themselves, depended on the help of non-Jewish relatives, friends, neighbors, colleagues, and in many cases, even complete strangers. Dozens of people were often involved in the rescue of a single person.[5] Both the Jews who avoided deportation and their non-Jewish helpers fought against a central goal of the regime: the deportation and annihilation of the Jewish population. Hence, helping Jews to survive is seen as part of the history of resistance in Nazi Germany; in German it is known as *Rettungswiderstand*, "rescue as a form of resistance."[6] However, the term *Rettungswiderstand* is also problematic. Typically, when Jews attempted to go into hiding, a lot more people were involved in the process than just the Jews and their rescuers. There were some genuinely heroic rescuers, but the pathos of the term *Rettungswiderstand* obfuscates the complexity of the process. Some people made small gestures of help (e.g., donating ration cards, acting as messengers), some witnessed the hiding of a person and remained silent, others used this opportunity to blackmail or to denounce. Some people helped for reasons that had nothing to do with resistance. Hence, flight attempts need to be seen as part of the complex social history of the deportation of the German Jews.

Many of those who helped Jews had kept their distance from Nazism, and some were outright political opponents of the regime. But recent research has unearthed a complex web of motivations of the non-Jewish helpers. Among the helpers were members of the Nazi Party, the SA, and even the SS. In many cases non-Jews supported Jewish family members or close friends. But even complete strangers received aid from people who did so out of humanitarian sentiment or out of a spontaneous impulse to help save a life. In a considerable number of cases, less than altruistic motives were paramount. Some Germans were willing to help for financial reward or in return for free labor. The expectation of sexual favors sometimes played a role, and Jews were sometimes confronted with pressure to convert.[7] "I had to work from seven in the morning until eleven at night without much of a break, in the house, in the kitchen, in the garden. In the morning I also had to attend a prayer service because my host had been instructed to convert me,"[8] wrote Lilly Neumark about her time with a pastor's family in the Weserbergland. Ilse Stillmann, on the run in Berlin beginning in 1943, later remarked dryly "women were interested in a cheap maid, men in a mistress."[9] Even if the motives of the rescuers included an element of personal gain, the helpers still acted in defiance of the regime. However, some Germans tried to exploit the distress of Jews and demanded enormous amounts of money in return for aid—which then did not materialize. Apparently, using false promises of aid to rob desperate people of their last possessions was so widespread in Berlin that Berliners coined a sarcastic term for it: *Judenfledderei,* "the looting of Jews."[10] The word *Fleddern* is usually associated with bodies—*Leichenfledderei,* "the looting of the dead."

Jews in Hiding in Germany: Key Questions and Sources

Most of the hidden Jews who survived did so in Berlin, which had been by far the largest Jewish community in Germany. By 1941, 73,000 of Germany's remaining 170,000 Jews lived in the capital. Around 7,000 of these went into hiding in Berlin, of whom up to 2,000 survived.[11] Numerous non-Jewish inhabitants were in one way or another involved in the rescue of the city's Jews. Still, the rescuers were a tiny minority within a city of approximately four million people, but nowhere else in Germany was their number nearly as big as in Berlin. Given that Berlin was the center of Jewish rescue, it is no surprise that historical research has concentrated on the German capital.[12] Berlin, however, was unique. Other major cities such as Hamburg, Frankfurt, Breslau (Wroclaw), Cologne, Leipzig, or Munich also had sizable Jewish communities, albeit much smaller than that of Berlin. We still know comparatively little about Jews who went into hiding and their helpers in those places. How many Jews escaped the deportations in these cities? How did they manage to survive? Studies of the city of Frankfurt—in 1933 home to the second largest Jewish community in Germany—suggest that the number of those who survived in hiding there was comparatively small.[13]

With regard to Munich, only a couple of rescue cases have received attention,[14] and only a few Munichites have been honored as "Righteous among the Nations" by Yad Vashem. Most likely, no more than 100 Jews survived in hiding in and around Munich.[15] But if we keep in mind that in the fall of 1941 only 3,200 Jews had remained in Munich, and roughly 100 of these hid successfully once the deportations had begun, then the percentage of Munich Jews who survived in hiding is approximately the same as the percentage of successfully hidden Jews in Berlin, where out of 73,000 Jews who had lived in the capital in late 1941, probably no more than 2,000 survived in hiding.[16]

This chapter will look at individual flights as well as more general patterns of flight in the context of the deportations from Munich. How did the citizens of Munich react to the deportations? Under what circumstances did the Jews go into hiding? Who were some of the Munich Jews who resisted deportation, and who were the non-Jewish Munichites who were willing to help and why? What kinds of strategies of concealment did they pursue together? How did the circumstances in Munich differ from those in Berlin? How high was the risk of being betrayed or denounced?

In analyzing some of the rescue cases in the Bavarian capital, we can gain insights into the relationship between Jews and non-Jews in Germany during the years 1941–45. The differences between Berlin and Munich reveal some of the regional particularities in the social history of the deportations from Germany. While in Munich, like in Berlin, people from all social backgrounds both helped and betrayed hidden Jews, it will become clear that the conditions under which Jews went underground in Berlin were different from those in Munich. Jews in Berlin were deported somewhat later than those from Munich. More so than in Munich, Berliners developed structures designed to help and to offer services to those who attempted to go underground.

Often it was the survivors who wrote to Yad Vashem to ask for an official recognition of their rescuers.[17] In other cases, we know the stories from memoirs or diaries of survivors. Sometimes there is nothing more than anecdotal reference to the survival of family members. For example, Walter Bloch, a Jewish boy from Munich who was on the Kindertransport to England, casually mentions in his memoir how his aunt, Gretel, survived in hiding in her Munich apartment supported by all of the other residents of the building.[18] Margarethe (Gretel) B. survived the war, but she never talked about this experience, nor did her neighbors. In many cases, survivors simply did not want to talk about their harrowing experiences, preferring instead to get on with their lives. The rescuers also did not want publicity. It would have marked them as outsiders in postwar Germany, where living examples of Germans who had demonstrated that one had been able to do something against the marginalization, persecution, and deportation of people from within their communities were not particularly welcome. Consequently, many of the rescue stories were forgotten. In some cases, the rescuers even had to fear repercussions for what they had done. When it emerged that the girl who had come to live with a Franconian peasant family was Jewish, and not the illegitimate child of a family member (as everyone in the village had assumed), the family received hate mail and even death threats.[19]

Aside from memoirs and survivor testimony, there are two sets of sources in particular that can provide information about rescue efforts: postwar claims for compensation by survivors, in which they had to explain how and where they survived; and de-Nazification files, in which

Jews who were helped testified on behalf of their rescuers. The latter, however, have to be treated with particular caution, as many testimonies about help for Jews were made up after the war.[20] Germans had to undergo the process of de-Nazification after the war and account for their activities in the years 1933–45. Many Germans sought testimonies about their supposed anti-Nazi activity to help clear their names.[21] In addition, court and police records can provide some clues; however, here the main problem is that the Gestapo files for Munich, and for most parts of Germany, were largely destroyed before the end of the war.[22]

From the November 1938 Pogrom to the Deportations

In 1933, 9,005 Jews had lived in Munich. In a city of approximately 800,000 people, they constituted just slightly more than 1 percent of the overall population. In the same year, a total of 9,522 Jews were registered for all of Upper Bavaria, which meant that in the rural areas surrounding the Bavarian capital a mere 500 Jews could be found.[23] From 1933 to 1938, thousands of Jews left Munich to escape discrimination, expropriation, and violence. Yet the size of the Jewish community in Munich shrank only slightly, as a significant number of Jews from small towns, particularly from Franconia, moved into the city. They hoped that life under the Nazis would be more bearable in a bigger Jewish community. Emigration peaked after the November 1938 pogrom ("Kristallnacht"). Munich's main synagogue had been demolished in June 1938 on Hitler's personal order.[24] The remaining two synagogues were vandalized and burnt during the night of 9 November 1938. In Munich, over a thousand male Jews were arrested in the aftermath of the pogrom, twenty-six of whom died from mistreatment at the Dachau concentration camp.[25] Officially, eighteen suicides were recorded in the wake of November 9, but the real figure is probably higher.[26]

Reactions to the pogrom in Munich were very mixed. Some people looked at the destruction with glee, making derisive comments about Jews, while others looked on in silence.[27] As Jews were not allowed to shop for several days after the pogrom, some people provided spontaneous help. Many Munich Jews recalled instances where neighbors and even shop owners brought them food.[28] At least one woman was denounced by a neighbor for doing this.[29] Some hid their Jewish friends and neighbors until the wave of arrests were over; among them was a Gestapo official who warned his Jewish doctor. Else Behrend-Rosenfeld's husband found shelter with her seamstress.[30] The pogrom of November 1938 was not the first chapter of the Holocaust, but it was the first time that large numbers of Jews sought to escape arrest and go in search of places to hide.

By November 1941, just before the start of the deportations, the number of Jews in Munich had dwindled to 3,200 individuals. Many of them had been confined to a number of "Jew houses" (*Judenhäuser*) and two makeshift camps at the edge of the city. One camp was located within the compound of the convent of the Sisters of Mercy in Berg-am-Laim, a suburb to the east of Munich. Around 300 people were confined there in squalid conditions, although the nuns did what they could to make life bearable for the Jews. The second camp, a set of barracks in the north of Munich, the *Barrackenlager* Milbertshofen, housed around 1,100 people.[31] The cargo terminal Milbertshofen, from which the first deportation trains departed, was close to the barracks, and the deportees had to walk to the station in the early morning. In other words, these deportations in 1941–42 took place largely out of sight of Munich's population, in contrast to later deportations, on a smaller scale, which took place from within the city.[32]

This did not mean that the residents of Munich remained ignorant of the first, larger wave of deportations. Jews were collected by trucks disguised as moving vans from *Judenhäuser* and from the camp in Berg-am-Laim. Neighbors watched as individuals and families with a few belongings had to board the trucks. With the liquidation of the Jewish hospital in June 1942, patients, including the severely sick and dying, were dragged onto a moving van in broad daylight.[33] "Nobody stopped it, nobody looked at this, nobody asked any questions," commented Judith Hirsch, whose father worked as janitor in the hospital.[34] When Gerty Spies received her deportation notification, it was late in the evening, and she had just come home from work. She was alone at home, and she wanted to talk to friends about what lay ahead of her. She decided to ask the friendly neighbors whether they would let her use their phone:

> I rang the doorbell. Rang again. … The man opened. "Excuse me," I said, "I have a big favor to ask—might I use your phone?" He stared at me, didn't say a word. Perhaps he found me impertinent? I had to explain, win his heart. I brought myself to say, "I—I will be sent away—with a transport—I—" At that point, the man shook his head, looked at me sadly and closed the door. I ran outside. … I asked

a complete stranger to light a match in a phone booth for me so that I could see. He wanted to know why. I told him, he got terrified, lit a match for me, and then ran away.[35]

These stories reveal both a profound sense of not wanting to know as well as a fear of any form of contact with those who were being excluded from the *Volksgemeinschaft* (national community). The aversion to learning more about a fate that was clearly perceived as horrifying was compounded by fears of denunciation.

The majority of Jews from Munich and the surrounding areas had been deported by the summer of 1942. Following two mass transports in November 1941 (to Kovno) and April 1942 (to Piaski) and a series of smaller transports to Theresienstadt between June and August 1942, only around 650 Jews remained in Munich by the end of the year.[36] One last transport of 220 individuals left Munich for Auschwitz in March 1943. At that point, the camp in Berg-am-Laim was closed, while the Milbertshofen camp had been closed earlier.

In Berlin the situation was very different. Early in 1943, over fifteen thousand Jewish forced laborers were still living in the city. This means that a significant number of Jews were still present at a time when rumors about mass murder in the east were abundant.[37] When they were scheduled for deportation in the infamous *Fabrikaktion* (factory raid) in late February 1943, thousands fled and attempted to go into hiding. During the *Fabrikaktion,* which lasted for about a week, more than 7,000 Jews were rounded up and deported, many of whom were forced laborers who were arrested at their factories.[38] Whereas in Berlin 3 percent and 34 percent of all flights of Jews occurred in 1941 and 1942, respectively, well over 50 percent took place in 1943.[39] Munich did not see a mass flight in 1943. An estimated two dozen Jews went underground in 1941–42. From among the last remaining Jews scheduled for deportation in March 1943, only a handful attempted to flee.

Smaller deportations from Munich to Theresienstadt continued until February 1945.[40] These later deportations comprised mainly groups of Jews who until 1943 had been exempt from deportation, such as Jews whose "mixed marriages" had been ended through divorce or the death of the non-Jewish spouse. Jewish spouses of mixed marriages were scheduled for deportation in February 1945.[41] Only at this point did mass flights of Jews, ignoring their deportation orders, occur in Munich. In this respect Munich was by no means unique. Deportation orders in the final stages of the war were disregarded in other cities as well.[42] In some cities, deportations could no longer be carried out properly because of extensive war damage.[43]

Several hundred of Munich's Jews decided to avoid deportation by committing suicide. Dr Else Behrend-Rosenfeld, who was in charge of household matters at the Berg am Laim camp, mentioned in her diary that suicides had become a regular occurrence. [44] In some cases, however, the suicide was only feigned. Faking suicide was a common tactic of those who were planning to flee. It bought precious time as the police had to search for a body, which could be difficult, especially if people had announced that they would drown themselves in a river.

In Hiding: Cases from Munich

Such was the case with Meta L., a middle-aged Jewish woman who lived alone in Munich. Her neighbor, Stanislaus H., spread her clothes and documents on the banks of the river Isar in Munich after he had found a hiding place for her. She was brought to a former business partner of her brother,[45] where she stayed in a toolshed in the garden that Stanislaus H., a carpenter, had made barely habitable. Herr H. already had experience in hiding people. A Communist activist, he had provided shelter for a fellow comrade in 1933. This had earned him a fourteen-month stay at the Dachau concentration camp.[46] This punishment did not, however, stop him from offering help to his Jewish neighbor. He organized a series of hiding places for her, and at times she stayed in the tiny apartment where he lived with his family. Some people were willing to take Meta L. for a modest financial reward, but it is not clear why others agreed to give her shelter. Apart from Stanislaus H. and the business partner of Meta L.'s brother, the following individuals were among her helpers: her former cleaning lady, a housewife, a distant relative, a woman who had in the past been married to a Jew and was willing to help old acquaintances from those days, and a retired teacher who lived with his ailing niece.[47] While we do not know what motivated all of them, they made for a rather heterogeneous group of helpers.

In 1948 Stanislaus H. had to face de-Nazification procedures. He had joined the National Socialist Motor Corps (NSKK) so that he would be able to check out a series of potential hiding places in the countryside without attracting attention. Asked by the de-Nazification court why he had decided to help his neighbor, Herr H. said, "I was not interested in Frau L. personally; we had just happened to know each other. I only did this to help a human being who was doomed to extinction because of her race."[48]

Stanislaus H. ran an extremely high risk in helping Meta L. As a repeat offender and Communist, he would have been sent back to the Dachau concentration camp had he been found out. For others the risk was more difficult to assess. Punishment for what the Nazis called *Judenbegünstigung,* "preferential treatment of Jews," ranged from having no consequences at all to imprisonment in a concentration camp.[49] In the Nazi-occupied areas of Europe, people who hid Jews could expect a death sentence. However, within the Reich, the situation was different. A decree from October 1941 specified that so-called Aryans who exhibited friendly relations with Jews in public should be taken into "protective custody" (*Schutzhaft*) for up to three months. The Nazi Special Courts (*Sondergerichte*) dealt with some cases of *Judenbegünstigung,* but more often no court became involved, as an order to take someone into "protective custody" could be issued without a court warrant.[50] Sometimes people were charged for other offenses, such as "malicious gossip." Elisabeth Bocks got away with a hefty fine for sheltering a Jewish woman for several weeks. In her case, the formal charge was that she had failed to register her tenant with the police.[51] Karl Schörghofer, the (non-Jewish) keeper of the Jewish cemetery in Munich, also had to pay a big fine. He was told that if he caused any more trouble, he would be sent to Dachau concentration camp.[52] Schörghofer had hidden a number of Jews on the grounds of the cemetery during the final stages of the war. However, others who helped Jews went to prison or were sent to concentration camps.[53] Thus, while hiding Jews did not carry an automatic death sentence in Germany, there was the possibility of having to suffer imprisonment in a concentration camp, where death rates were very high during the war. The actual risk may be difficult to calculate in retrospect, but the perceived risk at the time was certainly very high.[54]

Like Meta L., Paula, Sophie, and Elisabeth Mayer left suicide notes before disappearing in July 1942, with the hope that the Gestapo would believe them to be dead. The three women escaped from the Berg am Laim camp after Paula had learned that she was on the list for the next transport. Paula and her younger daughter Elisabeth were on their way to a location near Deggendorf in Lower Bavaria. Sophie, Paula's older daughter, went to Lenggries, a small town in the Alps. An acquaintance, Maria Lethnar, had secured them hiding places with relatives.[55] Paula and Elisabeth Mayer did, however, eventually commit suicide, drowning themselves in the nearby Danube river. Sophie Mayer, who stayed with Maria Lethnar's sister Rosa and her husband, Paul Mayer (no relation), in Lenggries, survived the war. According to Sophie, when she, her mother, and her sister turned to Maria Lethnar for help, the latter resolutely declared that "it was out of the question that we would be sacrificed to those beasts."[56]

Maria's sister Rosa and her husband, Paul, readily agreed to hide a complete stranger. Paul Mayer, a member of the Nazi Party and local police chief in Lenggries, was involved in a multitude of resistance activities. He warned local opponents of Nazism who were about to be arrested, organized hiding places for a number of people, and regularly ignored orders. Paul Mayer helped foreign forced laborers who had fled their workplaces, and at the end of the war he sent messengers to the Americans to inform them about SS hideouts. Sophie Mayer was not the only Jewish person he helped. In another case, he simply refused to arrest a local Jew and send him to Munich. Later, Sophie Mayer wrote, reflecting on her time in Lenggries, "The Mayers took exceptionally good care of me, there was never a sign of impatience, never did they let me know in what danger I put them."[57] (See Appendix H.) The entire family showed an enormous amount of courage and audacity. For almost three years, Sophie Mayer hid in the same house where the police station was located while SS men came and went. The Mayers had a ten-year-old son to whom they tried to explain the presence of a stranger and the necessity of not mentioning her to anyone. And he did not. The Mayers, like other rescuers, had to feed a person who had no ration cards. Rosa Mayer and Maria Lethnar used their connections to local farmers to boost the family rations.

In 1946 Sophie Mayer testified on behalf of Paul Mayer's de-Nazification. Mayer had been a member of the Nazi Party since 1937. Sophie Mayer was able to explain not only that the family had hid her beginning in 1943, but that she also knew about Mayer's other resistance activities, which were confirmed by several inhabitants of Lenggries. His application to join the Nazi Party might be explained by fears over losing his job. Mayer had already run into trouble with the party in 1935 and 1936. In fact, his position in Lenggries was the result of a transfer from the town of Eggenfelden for disciplinary reasons.[58] Sophie Mayer was adamant: "If today I reflect on the fact that this man was a member of the party and will be thrown into the same pot with those who wore the same party badge, I have to say, that in this case, it was not a party comrade who did something good, but that it was a good brave man who was forced to wear a party badge."[59]

Sophie Mayer's case reflects the image that people have of Jews in hiding, living in crammed attics or tiny rooms for prolonged periods of time—an image reinforced by the famous story of Anne Frank.[60] However, this form of hiding was rather unusual. Typically people had to move around, changing hideouts frequently, in some cases every few days. This can be seen in the case of Max Krakauer, who had sixty different hiding places.[61] Some embarked on odysseys over great distances. Many of those in hiding were constantly on the move and therefore not entirely invisible.[62] Dr Behrend-Rosenfeld, the manager of the Berg-am-Laim camp, fled from Munich to Berlin, from there to Freiburg, and then across the Swiss border. She claimed later that when she prepared for flight in August 1942, she understood that deportation meant death.[63] She could rely on a network of close friends whom she knew from her time at university, highly educated women, all with PhDs, independent, resourceful, and contemptuous of the regime.[64] They used their contacts across the country, scouting out different escape routes and hiding places.[65] Behrend-Rosenfeld went to Berlin, where she stayed with a series of hosts and was able to obtain fake papers and plan her next steps supported by friends across the country. Eventually, she traveled to Freiburg, a town close to the border with Switzerland, where she was able to stay with the family of a journalist. In April 1944 she successfully escaped across the border to Switzerland.[66] Friends of hers had organized a paid guide who brought her to the border.[67]

Else Behrend-Rosenfeld was not the only Munich "submarine" who went to Berlin to seek anonymity and access to false papers. Others followed a different strategy, leaving the Bavarian capital to seek shelter in the surrounding areas of Upper Bavaria or in remote villages in Lower Bavaria. These regions were not affected by Allied bombing raids, so obtaining food without ration cards was easier. During the later stages of the war, strangers could pass as bombed-out city dwellers, and children from the cities were a common sight. Some farmers who hosted Jews hoped that God would reward a good deed.[68] At the same time, many Jews who went into hiding in Berlin left the city after they had obtained some kind of fake identity. Some tried to make it to Switzerland, while others came to Upper Bavaria to seek shelter in some secluded village at the foothills of the Alps. Many hidden Jews crisscrossed the country to cover their traces.

Valerie and Andrea Wolffenstein went into hiding in Berlin in January 1943. The daughters of Jewish parents who had converted, they were raised as Lutherans and considered themselves as such. Belonging to the group of people the Nazis dubbed "non-Aryan Christians," they were persecuted as Jews. As members of the Confessing Church, they could rely on an extensive network of friends from religious circles who provided them with false documents and organized a series of hiding places. After a short period in hiding in and around Berlin, during which they obtained false documents, Andrea went to Pomerania, and Valerie to Bavaria. Valerie's friend, Esther Seidel, who had moved to Munich some time earlier, worked with another old friend, a nun, to find people willing to accept Valerie into their homes. After a couple of weeks with a peasant family, Valerie came to the family of Rudolf Ammann, an employee at the BMW factory in Munich.[69] Like Paul and Rosa Mayer, Rudolf Ammann and his wife agreed to house a complete stranger. From mid-1943 onward, Valerie Wolffenstein hid with the Ammanns and their six children, as well as at a series of other locations in and around Munich. Valerie Wolffenstein later remarked that about one hundred people all across Germany were involved in the rescue operation to save her.[70] Some of these people also helped her sister and other Jews. In the last months of the war, the Ammann family in Munich hosted both sisters. Most of the helpers acted out of religious motives, and many of them may well have seen the sisters as persecuted fellow Christians rather than as Jews. For some people it made a difference whether the rescue operation was in support of a Jewish or a Christian soul, and some hidden Jews later spoke of pressure to convert and of the open anti-Semitism of their helpers.[71] However, for many Christians, the background of the hidden person did not matter. Rudolf Ammann and his wife, devout Catholics and former Center Party activists, had hidden a wanted Socialist in 1933, before they sheltered Valerie and Andrea Wolffenstein.[72]

People who helped Jews go underground in Munich came from every possible social background. There were Communist workers, like Stanislaus H.; employees, like Rudolf Ammann; writers and artists, businessmen, cleaning ladies, doctors, priests, publishers, secretaries, and housewives. Typically they were of middle age, and many had Jewish friends or family connections. Some displayed a remarkable presence of mind. In Munich, a woman, on seeing the arrival of the Gestapo van from her window, rang the doorbell of her neighbor, a single Jewish woman, grabbed the Jewish woman who opened the door, pushed her into her apartment, and slammed the door shut behind them.[73] In Berlin, somewhat more women than men seem to have been involved in rescue operations, although in Munich a similar gender imbalance is not discernible.[74] A number of cases involved non-Jewish Germans who hid their Jewish boyfriends and girlfriends. The owner of a factory that employed Jewish forced laborers hid one of them, Benno Schülein, the former lawyer of the company, whom he had known for some time.[75] The lawyer, in turn, defended the factory owner at the latter's postwar de-Nazification trial. (See Appendix G.)

Benno Schülein was one of the very small number of individuals who escaped before the last mass transport left Munich for Auschwitz in March 1943.[76] The transport contained 220 people, while only 4 seem to have fled upon receiving their deportation notice. Why did more of them not try to go underground at a time when rumors about the fate of Jews in the east were abundant? In Berlin, the large number of Jews in the city and the late deportation schedule allowed networks of helpers and some degree of organized support to emerge. Berlin was unique in its level of opposition against the regime, serving as the base for a high number of dissenters, as well as for organized resistance circles who also started to help Jews.[77] Given the relatively high number of Jews in Berlin, many more people were confronted with cases of Jews needing help. In Berlin, Jews were not ghettoized in Jewish camps and *Judenhäuser*. The degree of separation from the population was therefore lower than in Munich. Berlin developed an infrastructure to address the plight of thousands of people. Helpers formed networks, and a shadow economy for hiding Jews emerged. Graphic designers produced fake documents and ration cards, hideouts were scouted out, contacts in the city and across the country were activated.[78] This included the development of commercial structures. People offered accommodations, ration cards, and fake papers of varying quality, while smugglers offered to bring people across borders. Some Berliners sold their passports to Jews, who took them to graphic designers to be counterfeited.[79] Even Nazi Party and Gestapo officials took part in these activities. Elisabeth Zimmermann could buy ration cards from her Nazi *Blockwart* (block warden) for extortionate amounts of money.[80] A high-ranking SS officer demanded money in exchange for his silence—which he received in monthly installments.[81] Needless to say, not all of these helpers were honest dealers. *Judenfledderei*, the looting of Jews, became a widespread practice. People promised aid and shelter for payment, only to take the money and deliver the Jews to the Gestapo.[82] Overall, conditions developed that allowed Jews who went into hiding in Berlin to rely on a mix of altruistic non-Jewish helpers and various forms of paid aid. They could also rely on a thriving black market, especially if they had managed to hide away some money, although there was a high risk of falling victim to fraud, blackmail, and betrayal. In Berlin, Jews found themselves in a terrible situation, but they felt less alone and isolated than Jews elsewhere in Germany. They were still living among the population, with access to friends and potential helpers. Almost all of them knew someone who had dared to flee but who had not (yet) been found. Valerie Wolffenstein felt encouraged as people around her went into hiding, and the example helped her muster the courage to do the same.[83] By comparison, among the small number of Munich Jews left in 1943, few knew someone who had already fled, and few could think of anyone to whom to turn.

Jews in Hiding: The Dangers

At the same time, cases of *Judenfledderei* seem to have been less widespread in Munich than in Berlin. As thousands of Berlin Jews looked for help, the opportunity to make fast money at their expense must have been widely recognized throughout the city. In Munich, with a much smaller number of Jews remaining, this "business idea" occurred only to a few individuals. But even in Munich, where few Jews were on the run, Jews were promised help and were asked for their last possessions, only in the end to be betrayed to the Gestapo.[84]

Given that so many more Jews were on the run in Berlin than anywhere else, the effort that went into the pursuit of runaway Jews was higher than in other places. Raids and searches were frequent. In addition, there was the omnipresent danger posed by *Greifer*, Jewish collaborators who hunted down hidden Jews in the hope of saving their own lives.[85] *Greifer* or *jüdische Fahnder* (Jewish searchers) were employed only in Berlin and Vienna. As Konrad Kwiet and Helmut Eschwege have noted, nearly all the testimonies of Jews who had survived in hiding in Berlin talked about this particular danger or mentioned narrow escapes. Most notorious among the *Greifer* was a young woman, Stella Kübler-Isaaksohn, who probably betrayed over a hundred 'submarines'.[86] In addition, in Berlin many "submarines" perished in the frequent Allied air raids. Often they did not dare to use shelters, as they feared being recognized and there could be controls at the entrances. Bert Lewyn, who was in hiding in Berlin, usually took refuge in public shelters, but sometimes he was questioned about his identity by the warden. Whenever this happened, he had to run outside as soon as the bombing had stopped, in order to avoid arrest. Once, he had to flee into the street while bombs were still falling.[87] These factors help explain why out of seven thousand individuals who went into hiding in Berlin, only fifteen hundred to two thousand survived. We do not know how many perished in Munich, but the chances of survival were better, particularly as most of those who did go into hiding did so in the final stages of the war. In early 1945, flight and hiding occurred under very different conditions than two or even three years earlier. In fact, the late flights of 1945 comprised the majority of successful rescue efforts in Munich and other cities, such as Hamburg.[88]

All of this did not mean that the danger of betrayal or denunciation was smaller in Munich than in Berlin. It was considerable. Strangers, neighbors, colleagues, and even family members made use of that option. Sometimes the reasons were personal. Jealousy, revenge, personal dislike, and the desire to destroy a business competitor all served as motives. In some cases the grounds for denunciation were ideological. In many cases no real incentive or motive is apparent.[89] In the years up to 1941, denunciations of Jews often had to do with accusations of "race defilement," derogatory remarks about Nazi leaders, or an effort to achieve economic gain. Although only a small number of Jews went underground in Munich, many of them were denounced at one point or another. In the case of Benno Schülein, multiple denunciations occurred. One helper was denounced by a neighbor, another was denounced by two of his employees, and a third was blackmailed by her cook.[90] Else Behrend-Rosenfeld was denounced by a neighbor. Luckily, the policeman who filed the denunciation report warned the family that sheltered her in Freiburg.[91] The danger of denunciation by neighbors seems to have been very high, but in many instances the people who went to the police preferred to remain anonymous. In one case, a married woman had provided shelter for a Jewish woman against her husband's will. The Jewish woman stayed with them for several months, despite threats by the husband to denounce her.[92]

Hence it is not surprising that fear of denunciation was extraordinarily high. Hugo Holzmann, who worked as forced laborer in a nursery in Munich, mentioned that he regularly tried to get lunch at a certain inn. The owner tried to pass him extra food or ration cards when the waitress was not around. The waitress did the same when the owner and his wife were not around.[93] Both the landlord and the waitress shared a mutual fear of betrayal. Holzmann and his mother fled Munich just before young *Geltungsjuden*[94] like himself were deported to Theresienstadt.

He survived the last months of the war on an isolated farm in Lower Bavaria that belonged to relatives of his neighbors in Munich.[95]

Leonie von Seuffert, a Jewish forced laborer in Munich, recalled that a high-level employee of the company for which she had to work had offered to hide her. Von Seuffert, who barely knew the woman, reflected, "Even if I did not take her up on the offer … it contributed to my ability to believe in people, their decency and their goodness."[96] Stories of rescue against the odds can be inspiring. In Munich, like all across Germany, we see extraordinary individuals who welcomed complete strangers into their families, who had the presence of mind and the courage to snatch their neighbors from the Gestapo. Yet we also see those who went straight to the Gestapo upon hearing unfamiliar voices coming out of the apartment next door. While in November 1938 some families spontaneously hid Jewish men to save them from arrest, others watched blazing synagogues with glee.

Much more common than these two groups were Munichites who were preoccupied with the daily concerns of a society at war, such as air raids, husbands and sons killed in the war, and meager food rations. From their windows, they looked on as their Jewish neighbors were hauled onto vans with a few belongings. Some bought the household goods of their deported neighbors, which were regularly auctioned off to the population.[97] They preferred not to ask whose goods they had bought and what had become of the former owners. They did not want to be confronted with the victims. Judith Hirsch described her walk through Munich to the train station from where she would be deported: "Nobody from the population looked at us; it was as if we didn't exist."[98] Later they would say, *"Davon haben wir nichts gewusst!"*: "We didn't know anything about that!"[99]

Susanna Schrafstetter is associate professor of history at the University of Vermont. Her publications include *Die dritte Atommacht. Britische Nichtverbreitungspolitik im Dienst von Statussicherung und Deutschlandpolitik, 1952–1968* (Munich, 1999) and (with Stephen Twigge) *Avoiding Armageddon: The United States, Western Europe and the Struggle for Nuclear Non-Proliferation, 1945–1970* (New York, 2004). She has published a number of articles on German compensation to the victims of Nazism and on the post-1945 careers of Nazi-era officials. She has recently completed a book-length study about Jews who avoided deportation and went underground in Munich and the surrounding region during the early 1940s.

Notes

1. Andreas Heusler, "Verfolgung und Vernichtung (1933–1945)," in *Jüdisches München. Vom Mittelalter bis zur Gegenwart*, eds Richard Bauer and Michael Brenner (Munich, 2006), 183. On the deportations from Munich see Maximilian Strnad, "Die Deportationen aus München," in *Münchner Beiträge zur Jüdischen Geschichte und Kultur* 8, no. 2 (2014) ed. Alan E. Steinweis, 76–96.

2. Anthony Kauders and Tamar Lewinsky, "Neuanfang mit Zweifeln (1945–1970)," in Bauer and Brenner, *Jüdisches München*, 185.

3. Valerie Wolffenstein and Andrea Wolffenstein, *Erinnerungen von Valerie Wolffenstein bis 1945, Andrea Wolffenstein 1938 bis 1945*, (no place of publication, 1979), 168.

4. Claudia Schoppmann, "Rettung von Juden: ein kaum beachteter Widerstand von Frauen," in *Überleben im Untergrund. Hilfe für Juden in Deutschland 1941–1945. Solidarität und Hilfe für Juden während der NS-Zeit*, vol. 5, eds Beate Kosmala and Claudia Schoppmann (Berlin, 2002), 114.

5. Ibid., 115.

6. Arno Lustiger coined the term *Rettungswiderstand*. See Wolfram Wette, "Vorwort," in Arno Lustiger, *Rettungswiderstand. Über die Judenretter in Europa während der NS-Zeit* (Göttingen, 2011), 13.

7. For a survey of different motives, see Wolfgang Benz, "Juden im Untergrund und ihre Helfer," in *Überleben im Dritten Reich. Juden im Untergrund und ihre Helfer*, ed. Wolfgang Benz (Munich, 2003), 41–48.

8. Lilly Neumark, quoted in Wolfgang Benz, "Gegenleistungen. Stationen eines Kirchenasyls zwischen Weserbergland und Lausitz," in Benz, *Überleben im Dritten Reich*, 221.

9. Ilse Stillmann, quoted in Schoppmann, "Rettung von Juden," 125.

10. See also Benz, "Juden im Untergrund," 24.

11. The most recent estimates range from fifteen hundred to two thousand survivors in Berlin. Marnix Croes and Beate Kosmala, "Facing Deportation in Germany and the Netherlands: Survival in Hiding," in *Facing the Catastrophe: Jews and Non-Jews in Europe during World War II*, eds Beate Kosmala and Georgi Verbeek (Oxford, 2011), 142.

12. Kosmala and Schoppmann, *Überleben in Untergrund*; Benz, *Überleben im Dritten Reich*; Croes and Kosmala, "Facing Deportation in Germany and the Netherlands."

13. Monica Kingreen, "Verfolgung und Rettung in Frankfurt am Main und der Rhein-Main-Region," in Kosmala and Schoppmann, *Überleben im Untergrund*, 167–90. Petra Bonavita, *Mit falschem Pass und Zyankali. Retter und Gerettete aus Frankfurt am Main in der NS-Zeit* (Stuttgart, 2009). In 1933, 160,564 Jews lived in Berlin, 26,158 in Frankfurt, and 20,202 in Breslau. Andreas Heusler and Tobias Weger, *"Kristallnacht." Gewalt gegen die Münchner Juden im November 1938* (Munich, 1998), 16.

14. These are the cases of Karl Schörghofer, Franz Herda, and Paul Mayer. See, for example, Peter Widmann, "Die Kunst der Frechheit. Ein Maler und das Überleben in München," in Benz, *Überleben im Dritten Reich*, 278–88. Benedikt

Weyerer, "Retter unter Einsatz des eigenen Lebens—Die Familie Schörghofer," in *Ausgegrenzt—Entrechtet—Deportiert. Schwabing und Schwabinger Schicksale 1933 bis 1945,* ed. Ilse Macek (Munich, 2008), 393–95.

15. It is impossible to provide concise numbers. The author is currently aware of seventy-five individuals who at some point between October 1941 and May 1945 were in hiding in and around Munich and who survived the war. Some of them came to Munich or Upper Bavaria from other regions of Germany; many of those who fled the deportations in Munich left the city. Fourteen unsuccessful flight attempts have been identified resulting in deportation or suicide. The actual numbers are almost certainly higher.

16. However, it is important to note that in Berlin, many Jews who had gone into hiding during the final stages of the war were not subsequently registered "as having survived in hiding," Croes and Kosmala, "Facing Deportation," 124.

17. See, for example, the cases of Rosl Vetter and Sophie Mayer. Yad Vashem, Record Group M.031, files 694 and 394b.

18. Walter Bloch, "Ich war schon froh als es hieß: Auswandern in ein Land, in dem man nicht verfolgt wird," in *Der olle Hitler soll sterben. Erinnerungen an den jüdischen Kindertransport nach England,* ed. Anja Salewsky (Munich, 2001), 110.

19. Lustiger, *Rettungswiderstand,* 68. On the silence of the helpers see Dennis Riffel, *Unbesungene Helden Die Ehrungsinitiative des Berliner Senats 1958 bis 1966* (Berlin, 2007), 29–30.

20. On this point, see also Atina Grossmann, *Juden, Deutsche, Alliierte. Begegnungen im besetzten Deutschland* (Göttingen, 2012), 184–85.

21. These testimonies were known as *Persilscheine,* literally "Persil slips," named after a popular laundry detergent.

22. Robert Gellately, *The Gestapo and German Society: Enforcing Racial Policy 1933–1945* (Oxford, 1990), 14–15.

23. Baruch Ophir and Falk Wiesemann, *Die jüdischen Gemeinden in Bayern, 1918–1945* (Munich, 1979), 33. These figures should be treated as estimates. The actual numbers were probably higher, as Jews who were not members of their religious communities were not included in these figures. Compare these figures to the numbers given in Maximilian Strnad, *Zwischenstation "Judensiedlung." Verfolgung und Deportation der jüdischen Münchner 1941–1945* (Munich, 2011), 178. He lists the number of Jews in Munich as 10,737 in 1933.

24. Heusler and Weger, *"Kristallnacht,"* 37. On the November 1938 pogrom in Munich, see Heusler and Weger, *"Kristallnacht."* On emigration see Heusler, "Verfolgung und Vernichtung," 177–79.

25. Heusler and Weger, *"Kristallnacht,"* 131–33.

26. Heusler, "Verfolgung und Vernichtung," 176.

27. Heusler and Weger, *"Kristallnacht,"* 149.

28. Ophir and Wiesemann, *Gemeinden,* 53, and Peter Hanke, *Zur Geschichte der Juden in München zwischen 1933 und 1945* (Munich, 1967), 218.

29. Marion Detjen, *"Zum Staatsfeind ernannt ..." Widerstand, Resistenz und Verweigerung gegen das NS-Regime in München* (Munich, 1998), 321.

30. On these cases: Hanke, *Geschichte der Juden in München,* 218; Else Behrend-Rosenfeld, *Ich stand nicht allein. Erlebnisse einer Jüdin in Deutschland 1933–1944* (Munich, 1988), 65. See also Heusler and Weger, *"Kristallnacht,"* 124, 150.

31. On both camps, see Strnad, *Zwischenstation "Judensiedlung."*
32. Ibid., 125–26.
33. Ilse Macek, "Judith Hirsch, heute Judy Rosenberg," in Macek, *Ausgegrenzt,* 119.
34. Ibid.
35. Gerty Spies, *Drei Jahre Theresienstadt* (Munich, 1984), 33–34.
36. Strnad, *Zwischenstation "Judensiedlung,"* 178. For a list of the individual transports, see ibid., 182.
37. See chapter 4 in this volume.
38. For the *Fabrikaktion,* see Wolf Gruner, *Widerstand in der Rosenstraße: Die Fabrik-Aktion und die Verfolgung der „Mischehen" 1943* (Frankfurt, 2005), and Claudia Schoppmann, "Die "Fabrikaktion" in Berlin. Hilfe für untergetauchte Juden als Form humanitären Widerstandes," *Zeitschrift für Geschichtswissenschaft* 53, no. 2 (2005): 138–48.
39. Beate Kosmala, "Gedenkstätte Stille Helden, ein Erinnerungsort in Berlin," in *Helfer im Verborgenen. Retter jüdischer Menschen in Südwestdeutschland,* ed. Irene Pill (Heidelberg, 2012), 172–73.
40. Strnad, *Zwischenstation "Judensiedlung,"* 182.
41. According to a Reich Security Main Office decree dated 15 January 1945, Jews in existing mixed marriages were to be sent to Theresienstadt by 15 February 1945. Wolf Gruner, *Der Geschlossene Arbeitseinsatz deutscher Juden. Zur Zwangsarbeit als Element der Verfolgung, 1938–1943* (Berlin, 1997), 328.
42. Beate Meyer, *Tödliche Gratwanderung. Die Reichsvereinigung der Juden in Deutschland zwischen Hoffnung, Zwang, Selbstbehauptung und Verstrickung, 1939–1945* (Göttingen, 2011), 389.
43. Gruner, *Der geschlossene Arbeitseinsatz,* 328.
44. Else Behrend-Rosenfeld and Siegfried Rosenfeld, *Leben in zwei Welten. Tagebücher eines jüdischen Paares in Deutschland und im Exil,* eds Erich Kasberger and Marita Krauss (Munich, 2011), 188.
45. Bayerisches Landesentschädigungsamt (BLEA), EG 1220, Protokoll der öffentlichen Sitzung, 11 November 1955.
46. BLEA, BEG 67 271 and Staatsarchiv München (StaM), SpkA, K 621, Stanislaus H., Spruch, 3 January 1950.
47. BLEA, EG 1220, Protokoll der öffentlichen Sitzung, 11 November 1955.
48. StaM, SpkA, K 621, Stanislaus H., Aussage von Stanislaus H., 3 January 1949.
49. Benz, "Juden im Untergrund," 40–41.
50. Ibid., 39–40.
51. StaM, AG 47166, Strafbefehl, 3 August 1943.
52. Weyerer, "Retter unter Einsatz des eigenen Lebens," 394.
53. StaM, WB I A 4279, Protokoll der öffentlichen Sitzung, 4 February 1953, Zeugenaussage von Frau K. Archiv der Gedenkstätte Dachau, DA Deutsche Häftlinge, A 1493, List, Heinrich.
54. On this point, see also Beate Kosmala, "Mißglückte Hilfe und ihre Folgen: die Ahndung der 'Judenbegünstigung' durch NS-Verfolgungsbehörden," in Kosmala and Schoppmann, *Überleben im Untergrund,* 205–21.
55. Yad Vashem, M.31, file 394b, Letter from Sophie Mayer, 27 March 1966.
56. StaM, SpkA, K 3643, Mayer, Paul, Eidesstattliche Erklärung, Dr Sophie Mayer, 15 May 1946.

57. Ibid.

58. StaM, SpkA, K 3643, Mayer, Paul, Eidesstattliche Erklärung, Paul Mayer, 10 April 1946.

59. StaM, SpkA, K 3643, Mayer, Paul, Eidesstattliche Erklärung, Dr Sophie Mayer, 15 May 1946.

60. See Richard Lutjens, "Vom Untertauchen: 'U-Boote' und Berliner Alltag 1941–1945," in *Alltag im Holocaust. Jüdisches Leben im Großdeutschen Reich 1941–1945,* eds Andrea Löw, Doris Bergen, and Anna Hajkova (Munich, 2013), 49–63.

61. Konrad Kwiet and Helmut Eschwege, *Selbstbehauptung und Widerstand. Deutsche Juden im Kampf um Existenz und Menschenwürde, 1933–1945* (Hamburg, 1984), 154

62. Lutjens, "Vom Untertauchen," 52–53.

63. Marita Krauss, "Zur Einführung," in Behrend-Rosenfeld and Rosenfeld, *Leben in zwei Welten,* 17.

64. Ibid.

65. Behrend-Rosenfeld, *Ich stand nicht allein,* 173–74, 179–81.

66. Ibid., 257–58.

67. Behrend-Rosenfeld, *Ich stand nicht allein,* 255–57.

68. Stefanie Hajak and Jürgen Zarusky, "Verfolgung, Zerstörung, Neuanfang. Ein Gespräch mit Charlotte Knobloch," in *München und der Nationalsozialismus. Menschen Orte Strukturen,* eds Stefanie Hajak and Jürgen Zarusky (Berlin, 2008), 388.

69. Wolffenstein and Wolffenstein, *Erinnerungen,* 139–45.

70. Ibid., 44.

71. Benz, "Gegenleistungen," 221–23.

72. StaM, SpkA, K 22, Ammann, Rolf, Ammann an die Spruchkammer X, 2 June 1948.

73. BLEA, EG 65146, Eidesstattliche Versicherung von Marion V., undated.

74. Schoppmann, "Rettung von Juden," 122.

75. StaM, SpkA, K 633, Kammerer, Rudolf, Benno Schülein: Meine Tätigkeit und meine Erfahrungen bei der Firma Kammerer, 5 October 1946.

76. So far only four individuals could be identified.

77. See, for example, the resistance circle that called itself "Onkel Emil": Ruth Andreas-Friedrich, *Der Schattenmann. Tagebuchaufzeichnungen, 1938–1945* (Berlin, 1947); and Karin Friedrich, "'Er ist gemein zu unseren Freunden …' Das Retternetz der Gruppe 'Onkel Emil,'" in Benz, *Überleben im Dritten Reich,* 97–112.

78. See, for example, Cioma Schönhaus, *Der Passfälscher. Die unglaubliche Geschichte eines jungen Grafikers, der im Untergrund gegen die Nazis kämpfte* (Frankfurt, 2004) and Andreas-Friedrich, *Schattenmann.* On the lower degree of segregation in Berlin see also chapter 3 in this volume.

79. Christine Zahn, "'Nicht mitgehen, sondern weggehen!' Chug Chaluzi—eine jüdische Jugendgruppe im Untergrund," in *Juden im Widerstand. Drei Gruppen zwischen Überlebenskampf und politischer Aktion, Berlin 1939–1945,* ed. Wilfried Löhken and Werner Vathke (Berlin, 1993), 169.

80. Benz, "Gegenleistungen," 224–25.

81. Marion Neiss, "'Herr Obersturmbannführer lässt daran erinnern, dass die Rate noch nicht da ist.' Eine Rettung auf Abzahlung," in Benz, *Überleben im Dritten Reich*, 202–4.
82. Benz, "Juden im Untergrund," 24.
83. Wolffenstein and Wolffenstein, *Erinnerungen*, 102.
84. For such cases, see Detjen, *Staatsfeind*, 323.
85. On the "Fahnder" who were both persecutees as well as persecutors, see Doris Tausendfreund, "'Jüdische "Fahnder.' Verfolgte, Verfolger und Retter in einer Person," in Benz, *Überleben im Dritten Reich*, 239–58; and Doris Tausendfreund, *Erzwungener Verrat. Jüdische "Greifer" im Dienst der Gestapo 1943–1945* (Berlin, 2006).
86. Kwiet and Eschwege, *Selbstbehauptung und Widerstand*, 158. On Stella Kübler-Isaaksohn, see Tausendfreund, *Erzwungener Verrat*, 142–52.
87. Bert Lewyn and Bev Saltzman Lewyn, *Versteckt in Berlin. Eine Geschichte von Flucht und Verfolgung 1942–1945* (Berlin, 2009), 208.
88. Meyer, *Tödliche Gratwanderung*, 389.
89. On denunciations, see Inge Marszolek, "Denunziation im Dritten Reich. Kommunikationsformen und Verhaltensweisen," in Kosmala and Schoppmann, *Überleben im Untergrund*, 89–108; Eric Johnson, *Nazi Terror: The Gestapo, Jews, and Ordinary Germans* (New York, 1999); Gellately, *Gestapo*; Robert Gellately, *Backing Hitler: Consent and Coercion in Nazi Germany* (Oxford, 2001).
90. StaM, SpkA, K 816, Jordan, Otto, Schülein an die Spruchkammer VIII, Eidesstattliche Versicherung von Otto und Anny Jordan, 14 April 1947.
91. Behrend-Rosenfeld, *Ich stand nicht allein*, 248–49.
92. Bayerisches Hauptstaatsarchiv, LEA 13 085 (EG 39193), Feststellungsverfahren, Zeugenvernehmung, Emmy R., 11 May 1954.
93. Hugo Holzmann, *Woman Courageous*, unpublished memoir, courtesy of the author, 238. An earlier version is available in Stadtarchiv München, Judaica, Memoiren 22.
94. *Geltungsjuden* were half-Jews who practiced the Jewish religion, were married to a Jew, or who had been born out of wedlock to a Jewish and a non-Jewish German. Many young *Geltungsjuden* were deported with their Jewish parent in February 1945. See Beate Meyer, *"Jüdische Mischlinge." Rassenpolitik und Verfolgungserfahrung 1933–1945* (Hamburg, 1999); Maria van der Heydt, "'Wer fährt denn gerne mit dem Judenstern in der Straßenbahn?' Die Ambivalenz des 'geltungsjüdischen' Alltags zwischen 1941 und 1945," in Löw, Bergen, and Hajkova, *Alltag im Holocaust*, 65–80; and Michaela Raggam-Blesch, "'Mischlinge' und 'Geltungsjuden.' Alltag und Verfolgungserfahrungen von Frauen und Männern halbjüdischer Herkunft in Wien 1938–1945," in Löw, Bergen, and Hajkova, *Alltag im Holocaust*, 81–98.
95. Holzmann, *Woman Courageous*, 357.
96. Stadtarchiv München, Judaica, Memoiren 9, Leonnie von Seuffert.
97. Christiane Kuller, *Finanzverwaltung und Judenverfolgung. Die Entziehung jüdischen Vermögens in Bayern während der NS-Zeit* (Munich, 2008), 111–36.
98. Macek, "Judith Hirsch," 123.

99. "We didn't know anything about that!" (*Davon haben wir nichts gewusst!*) was the standard German response to questions about what they had known about the fate of the Jews. Peter Longerich, *"Davon haben wir nichts gewusst!" Die Deutschen und die Judenverfolgung, 1933–1945* (Munich, 2006); Frank Bajohr and Dieter Pohl, *Der Holocaust als offenes Geheimnis. Die Deutschen, die NS-Führung und die Alliierten* (Munich, 2006).

Selected Bibliography

Andreas-Friedrich, Ruth. *Der Schattenmann. Tagebuchaufzeichnungen, 1938–1945.* Berlin, 1947.

Bauer, Richard, and Michael Brenner, eds. *Jüdisches München. Vom Mittelalter bis zur Gegenwart.* Munich, 2006.

Behrend-Rosenfeld, Else, and Siegfried Rosenfeld. *Leben in zwei Welten. Tagebücher eines jüdischen Paares in Deutschland und im Exil.* Edited by Erich Kasberger and Marita Krauss. Munich, 2011.

Benz, Wolfgang, ed. *Überleben im Dritten Reich. Juden im Untergrund und ihre Helfer.* Munich, 2003.

Benz, Wolfgang, and Beate Kosmala, eds. *Solidarität und Hilfe für Juden in der NS-Zeit.* 7 vols. Berlin, 1996–2004.

Gruner, Wolf. *Der Geschlossene Arbeitseinsatz deutscher Juden. Zur Zwangsarbeit als Element der Verfolgung 1938 bis 1943.* Berlin, 1996.

Heusler, Andreas, and Tobias Weger. *"Kristallnacht." Gewalt gegen die Münchner Juden im November 1938.* Munich, 1998.

Kosmala, Beate, and Claudia Schoppmann, eds. *Überleben im Untergrund. Hilfe für Juden in Deutschland 1941–1945.* Solidarität und Hilfe für Juden während der NS-Zeit, vol. 5. Berlin, 2002.

Kosmala, Beate, and Georgi Verbeeck, eds. *Facing the Catastrophe: Jews and Non-Jews in Europe during World War II.* Oxford, 2011.

Löw, Andrea, Doris Bergen, and Anna Hajkova, eds. *Alltag im Holocaust. Jüdisches Leben im Großdeutschen Reich 1941–1945.* Munich, 2013.

Lustiger, Arno, ed. *Rettungswiderstand. Über die Judenretter in Europa während der NS-Zeit.* Göttingen, 2011.

Macek, Ilse, ed. *Ausgegrenzt—Entrechtet—Deportiert. Schwabing und Schwabinger Schicksale 1933 bis 1945.* Munich, 2008.

Meyer, Beate. *Tödliche Gratwanderung. Die Reichsvereinigung der Juden in Deutschland zwischen Hoffnung, Zwang, Selbstbehauptung und Verstrickung, 1939–1945.* Göttingen, 2011.

Ophir, Baruch, and Falk Wiesemann. *Die jüdischen Gemeinden in Bayern, 1918–1945.* Munich, 1979.

Spies, Gerty. *Drei Jahre Theresienstadt.* Munich, 1984.

Strnad, Maximilian. *Zwischenstation "Judensiedlung." Verfolgung und Deportation der jüdischen Münchner 1941–1945.* Munich, 2011.

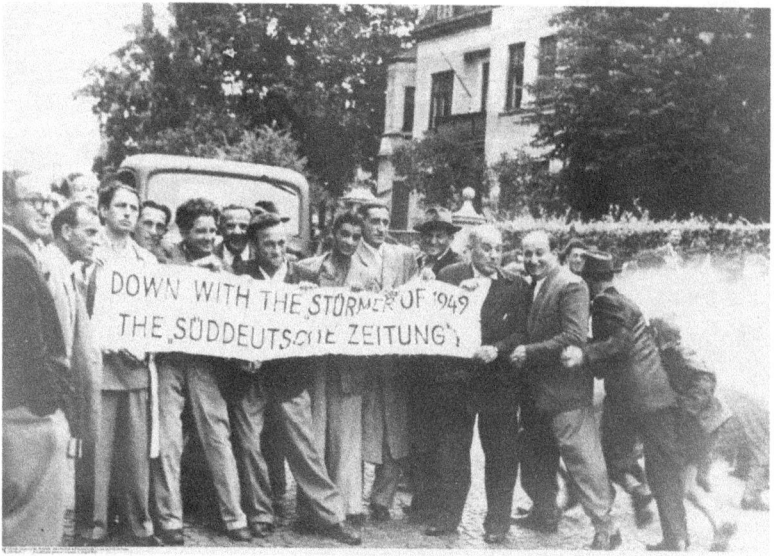

Figure 7. Jewish displaced persons protesting the publication of an anti-Semitic letter in the *Süddeutsche Zeitung* newspaper, Munich, August 1949.

Chapter 6

WHERE DID ALL "OUR" JEWS GO?

Germans and Jews in Post-Nazi Germany

———— ∞∞∞ ————

Atina Grossmann

IN 1933, AT THE BEGINNING of the National Socialist regime, Germany counted approximately half a million Jews. In 1946–47, three years after Germany had been declared *judenrein* (cleansed of Jews), some quarter of a million Jews resided in Germany, albeit on occupied and defeated territory, mostly in the American zone.[1] Only about fifteen thousand of them were German Jews, almost half of them in Berlin, former citizens of a nation that had been, for most of them, an unquestioned home, even as anti-Semites referred to the post–World War I Weimar Republic as a *Judenrepublik*.[2] Some had survived in hiding or disguised as so-called Aryans, a few returned from forced labor, death, and concentration camps. Most had managed a precarious aboveground existence in "privileged" mixed marriages or as *Mischlinge* (partial Jews); they often owed their survival to close "Aryan" connections and a distanced relationship to the Jewish community. Still others were returned émigrés, many of them now in occupier uniform and serving as translators, interrogators, and civil affairs and cultural officers in all four Allied, especially the American, armed forces.

The majority, however, were eastern European Jews, traumatized survivors on "blood-soaked soil" classified by the victors as "displaced persons" (DPs). As the months passed, this remnant was augmented by tens of thousands of Jewish "infiltrees" who poured into the American zone from Eastern Europe, reluctantly accepted by the occupiers and viewed with resentment and suspicion by the defeated Germans. These predominantly Polish Jews included camp and death-march survivors, who had been liberated in Germany but initially returned to their home-towns hoping, generally in vain, to find lost family members or reclaim property, as well as Jews who had survived among the partisans, in hiding, or "passing" as non-Jews. The largest—and the least studied—cohort of European survivors of the Final Solution comprised perhaps two hundred thousand Jews who had been repatriated to Poland from their harsh but lifesaving exile in the Soviet Union and then fled again when postwar anti-Semitism convinced them, especially after a notorious pogrom in Kielce on 4 July 1946, that there was no future for Jews in the "vast graveyard" that was Communist-occupied Eastern Europe. Jewish life in postwar Germany reflected therefore, in ways that are only beginning to be adequately examined by historians, highly diverse wartime trajectories, from European towns and cities to Nazi ghettos and camps but also—for the majority—to labor camps in the Soviet interior and a difficult exotic and utterly alien refuge in Soviet Central Asia.[3]

Unexpected Postwar Encounters

Between 1945 and 1949, contrary to all expectation and instinct, Jewish DPs in occupied Germany, gathered in and around large refugee camps near Munich and Frankfurt and in Berlin, as well as smaller centers throughout the American zone, generated a unique transitory society.[4] In this liminal period from war's end to 1949, and the establishment of the Federal Republic, Germans and Jews lived, as they often claimed, in different worlds on the same terrain, divided by memory, experience, and mutual antagonism. But, regulated and observed by their (mostly) American occupiers and international relief organizations, they also continually interacted, in uneasy, sometimes cordial, and always pragmatic ways, in black-market enterprises and the general stuff—the nitty-gritty—of everyday life: feeding people, taking care of children and the sick, establishing local businesses and administering the camps, engaging in sports and education, and even entertainment and sexual relations. Policed and protected by the American occupiers, Jews lived side by side and among defeated Germans, who were now themselves confronting a mass influx of ethnic German refugees from the east and the collapse of the Nazi system that most had defended to the bitter end. Germans were almost universally preoccupied with their own miseries and self-perception as victims: of Hitler and the Nazis, who had misled them; of the Allies, who imposed an arbitrary victors' justice; and indeed of the Jewish survivors, who now insistently claimed space, rations, and the assistance of the occupiers. In constant tension with these odd, even perverse, surroundings, whether the almost painfully peaceful and picturesque Bavarian lakes and Alps or the rubble landscapes of the cities, there emerged over several years a new and self-conscious Jewish collectivity, which named itself the *She'erit Hapletah*, invoking biblical references to the surviving remnant that has escaped destruction and "carries the promise of a future."[5]

For the vast majority of Jewish DPs and a significant number of German Jews, however, that possible future meant—and this is key also for understanding the under-studied question of German responses to their discomfiting unexpected presence—emigration, as soon as possible, from "bloodstained, cursed" German soil. In the meantime, however, the years of postwar limbo as displaced persons, supported by the U.S. Military Government, the UNRRA (United Nations Relief and Rehabilitation Administration), and international Jewish aid organizations, notably the American Joint (Jewish) Distribution Committee (JDC, the Joint), provided a frustrating—but also in many ways necessary—interregnum, a space between the trauma of war, genocide, and displacement and the burdens of starting new lives in new homelands, generally outside of Europe, in the United States, Israel, Australia, and Canada.[6] DP life in the American zone of occupied Germany, whether within the protected gates of refugee camps or outside, in German villages and cities, gave the overwhelmingly young Jewish survivors time to recover physically, reestablish contact with or (more likely) mourn lost family members, and establish a lively and contentious autonomous political and cultural life. They became agents in the broader landscape of postwar retribution, revenge, and justice, ranging from internal Jewish "honor courts" to extralegal acts of revenge and Nazi-hunting, as well as intensive, mostly "behind the scenes," involvement as prosecutors, interrogators, interpreters, journalists, psychologists, and witnesses in Allied war crimes trials. From the beginning, campaigns for material restitution and cultural reconstruction, efforts to rescue and reclaim the material remnant of European Jewry, in the form of property, books, and ritual objects, as well as calls for monetary compensation were on the agenda. At the same time, the frustrations of stateless refugee existence also promoted a Zionist consciousness that served to give Jews a sense of agency and hope for the future regardless of their eventual destination.

Shadowed by a traumatic recent past and under the most "abnormal" of circumstances survivors began to construct a kind of quotidian

"normality," with rapid marriage and childbirth leading to the formation of new families but, paradoxically perhaps, also through the fraught
yet frequent negotiation of encounters, both confrontational and harmonious, with defeated Germans. Jewish-German encounters in the
years immediately following the war and Holocaust—always, it must
be stressed, mediated by the formal power of Allied occupiers—were
marked by dizzying paradoxes and contradictions, one reason certainly
why they have been so marginalized and difficult to narrate in both
German and Jewish memory and historiography.

Jews and Germans had little choice but to cooperate in a wide variety
of ordinary activities: in medical and child care; in the black-market
and gray-market trade on which everyone—German, Jews, and DPs of
all nationalities—relied; as employers and employees in the DP camp;
and in German vocational training programs and universities. Jews
who lived in German towns and cities routinely hired German house-
keepers and nannies. Although officially off-limits to Germans, local
residents with permits also entered the DP camps daily to perform a
wide variety of menial, skilled, and professional tasks, working as baby
nurses, cleaning personnel, drivers, mechanics, plumbers, locksmiths,
photographers, secretaries, teachers, and doctors. They met in the many
cafés and bars run by DPs, whose neon-lit names—Hawaii, Alabama,
or California—evoked fantasies, for both Jews and Germans trapped in
war-torn Europe, of the America from which GIs hailed. Perceived by
Germans as centers for illicit trade and petty crime, traditionally associated with eastern European Jews, and part of a *Rotlicht Milieu* ("red-
light" districts) often servicing especially African American GIs, these
Jewish-owned or, more likely, leased establishments in fact catered to
Germans as well as occupiers.[7] The thriving Yiddish-language press relied on the equipment, facilities, and skills of German printers. German
farmers sold their cows and equipment to young Jewish DPs preparing
for aliyah to Palestine on Zionist collective farms in the German countryside (*kibbutzim* and *hachscharot*). Some 20 percent of these settle-
ments had German managers, farmhands, and agricultural instructors.
Germans and Jews attended DP boxing matches in Munich's Krone
Arena; Jewish soccer teams sometimes included German players, train-
ers, and referees. Bavarian Radio carried Yiddish-language programs,
and Berlin Radio broadcast the stirring Sabbath liturgies of Estrango
Nachama, an Auschwitz survivor from Salonika who became Germany's leading postwar cantor. Between five hundred and eight hundred
young DPs attended German universities, especially in technical fields

like medicine, dentistry, or engineering, their tuition paid for by German state restitution funds and their food rations provided by the DP camps. Despite resistance from local residents and strict German trade laws, determined Jewish DPs managed to pass craft exams and set up businesses.[8] And there were of course sexual and romantic encounters between Jewish men and German women, stigmatized and difficult to document, except for the approximately one thousand marriages registered up until 1950. Over time, almost 25 percent of DP Jews left the safe but confining space of the camps and became "free-livers," living with German neighbors in German towns and cities.

Jews and Germans in postwar occupied Germany navigated, therefore, a tenuous balance between relatively harmonious everyday encounters and the persistence, indeed reawakening and reworking, of anti-Semitic sentiment and expression, tendencies that became more pronounced with the additional influx of eastern European Jewish refugees starting in late 1945. There were violent and sometimes even murderous confrontations between Germans and Jews, although most were contained by American authorities. Tensions festered and occasionally erupted around precisely the basic everyday necessities that brought Jews and Germans into close contact, such as housing and food as well as appropriation of public space, reparations, sexual entanglements, and the contest for political and economic support from the occupiers. Jews and antifascists diagnosed an "enigma of German irresponsibility," or in Hannah Arendt's astute observation in 1950, "a deep-rooted, stubborn, and at times vicious refusal to face and come to terms with what really happened"; they saw "sullen" (a remarkably common characterization) Germans, undeservedly well-fed and housed, remarkably unscathed but unrepentant.[9] (See Appendix I.) Germans for their part quickly positioned their former Jewish victims as "privileged." They resented Jews' guaranteed access to rations from the UNRRA, which was charged by the Military Government with the "care and control" of refugees displaced by the Nazis (excluding thereby all German "expellees" from Central and Eastern Europe), the generosity of individual American Jewish soldiers and their chaplains, and the much-envied supplements from the American Jewish relief organization JDC, which provided the chocolates, coffee, and above all, the American cigarettes that were key to successful informal (black) market trading. Local German officials were particularly frustrated by the semi-autonomous status, relatively free of German administrative and police authority, granted by the Americans in the aftermath of a scathing report in August 1945 by President Truman's special envoy, Earl Harrison, which demanded dramatically improved conditions for Jews in the American zone.

Jewish activity on the "black" market, in reality only a small percentage of this dominant postwar economy, reinforced timeworn stereotypes about Jewish speculators and illicit business practices, even as the "exotic" bazaars of the Möhlstrasse in Munich or the Hermannplatz in Berlin were gratefully frequented by Germans and Allied soldiers, seeking coffee, tea, and cigarettes or luxury items such as liquor and well-tailored dresses made by Jewish artisans. German shoppers congregated in the many Jewish-run cafés, restaurants, and bars, provoking agitated resentment from local storekeepers incensed at "unfair competition" from Jews who, ostensibly privileged and protected by the Americans, were able to disregard with relative impunity regulations about building permits, sales taxes, import duties, or opening hours.

Rehearsing a toxic mixture of lingering Nazi stereotypes and renovated traditional prejudices against eastern European Jews (*Ostjuden*), emboldened right-wing politicians and local officials fulminated against Jewish "crooks" and "black market hyenas," presenting DP camps and markets as cauldrons of contagion for corruption and immorality, including, in a familiar trope, sexual threats to German women. Male DPs were arrested with some frequency and charged with black-market trading or possession of stolen property. In most cases, they were quickly released, often with the helpful intervention of JDC or Jewish military legal officers, but not before having spent time in jail, losing possessions, and earning a criminal record that could compromise chances for emigration.

Allied requisition of German homes and apartment blocks to house survivors and then the increasing population of Jewish "infiltrees" from Eastern Europe further inflamed German rancor. While Jews complained bitterly, with more or less success, to occupation and relief agency authorities about anti-Semitic discrimination by landlords or storekeepers in German towns and cities, Germans often imagined DP camps as a "magic kingdom" (*Schlaraffenland*) of "sugar and spam, margarine and jam, plus cigarettes and vitamized chocolate bars" unavailable to decent, honest Germans.[10] They were outraged by American orders to vacate, often on very short notice, their homes for occupancy by scruffy homeless Jews. In the lakeside town of Feldafing near Munich, site of a large DP camp, residents had to watch the dismantling and plunging down the stairs of a still elegant villa of a "glorious Bechstein" grand piano to make room for considerably less luxurious basic necessities like beds and lockers.[11] By 1947, the keen sense of unfair and arbitrary treatment by the victors led the Council of German Towns and Cities (Deutsche Städtetag) to avail itself of the new occupier-provided rhetoric of democratization and explicitly protest such evictions as human rights violations.

To be sure, Germans also complained about the disruptive influx of their uprooted compatriots from the east and labeled them "dirty and untidy" as well as "ungrateful." Bavaria alone, which was the center of DP life, with three major and numerous smaller Jewish DP camps and communities, took in some two million ethnic Germans who had fled or been expelled from Soviet-occupied territory. But the arrival of these German refugees did not seem to arouse as much resentment and fear as the numerically much smaller incursion of ragged Jewish survivors and infiltrees. Indeed, the presence of two "outsider" refugee groups, foreign displaced persons and ethnic Germans refugees, may have helped to reconstitute German identity and a sense of *Volksgemeinschaft* (national community) in opposition to non-German others.[12]

Germans were aggrieved by the startling arrival of tens of thousands of eastern European Jewish infiltrees who crossed the border into American-occupied Germany via semi-clandestine routes and after the cutoff date for entry of official "DPs." If Germans were accused of "irresponsibility" or willful ignorance of Nazi crimes, they felt even less guilt—or, as some historians have recently reformulated, shame—about these postwar refugees, who were neither direct camp survivors nor former Germans Jews, and could therefore be labeled as victims of Communism rather than Nazism.[13] Or conversely, the very fact of their survival in the Soviet Union associated the infiltrees with the Communist Cold War enemy. Jews' very obvious presence, their astonishingly rapid (at least superficial) recovery and high birthrate, their takeover of requisitioned housing, and their entrepreneurship in black-market commerce in an economy of scarcity produced resentment, bewilderment, and sometimes contentious confrontation.

Conflict and Coexistence in Bavaria

In a not atypical case, a riot broke out in spring 1946 in the small Bavarian town of Oberrammingen, where 120 Jewish DPs, many more Jews than had ever lived there before the war, were quartered in a schoolhouse and scattered apartments in a village of only 500. Coping with their own war losses and the arrival of bedraggled ethnic German refugees and expellees, Oberrammingen's inhabitants were blindsided and disturbed by the presence of these alien, Yiddish-speaking *Ostjuden*. It may well be that the placement of Jewish DPs in small groups or in a small designated "camp" area in the midst of German towns or cities generated more mutual insecurity and mistrust than the large, well-patrolled and well-organized DP camps on the outskirts of cities. UNRRA and Military Government files, which admittedly are more likely to record criminal or unruly behavior than the countless experiences of nondramatic daily interchange, document numerous occasions for conflict, such as demonstrative actions by Jews in otherwise quiet German towns, including exhumations and reburials of Jewish victims of nearby labor and concentration camps, or militant marches, often led by mothers brandishing baby carriages, demanding open emigration to Palestine. They report the circulation of anti-Semitic pamphlets, protests by youths outside a Jewish orphanage, or threats against individual families, demanding that they decamp immediately for their true "homeland" in Palestine—ironically a goal that was shared by many Jews as well as Germans and occupiers.[14]

In Oberrammingen, the precise reasons for the confrontation were obscure and the details murky, but the uneasy peace quickly unraveled. According to one account provided by the Jewish affairs liaison officer to the U.S. Military Government, the unfamiliar sight of two Jews ostentatiously racing through town on macho motorcycles was sufficient to provoke a brawl with four or five Germans. Apparently seeking revenge, one of the motorcyclists and some of his buddies entered German homes searching for their attackers and "beat up" two Germans. As this news traveled through a town already on edge, the mayor supposedly sounded an alarm, summoning a volatile crowd of some one hundred residents. Armed with sticks and stones, they "surrounded" the schoolhouse shelter, after having attacked several Jews on their way, "shouted threats, broke some of the windows and the door, and assaulted another DP" inside the building until German police from a nearby village dispersed the crowd.[15] In the somewhat more neutral version recorded by the American military investigating the case, local German police apparently looked on as a crowd gathered and fights broke out but did not intervene, preferring to await the arrival of American MPs, who prudently arrested the "ringleaders" on both sides, the town's mayor and the leader of the Jewish DP community, a survivor of Auschwitz and Mauthausen, who had lost his two children and now lived with his wife in this Bavarian community. They were brought into an American military courtroom, where each side was free to articulate its grievances, producing a transcript that offers insight into the nature of both confrontation and coexistence between Germans and Jews right after the war, and the ways in which the Americans tried to mediate and control that bizarre situation.

The responses of Germans and Jews to their interrogation revealed the profound difference in wartime experiences and postwar attitudes among these reluctant neighbors. To the key question "What is your nationality?" the DP defendants answered, "Jewish." When asked, "Of what country are you a citizen?" they unabashedly responded, "I want to go to Palestine." Paradoxically, Jews embraced their stateless status to highlight their demands for a new kind of proto-citizenship in a nation that did not yet exist. For the German witnesses and defendants, who actually lived in an occupied non-sovereign nation, the nationality question was nonetheless quite clear: they were German. A standard query about "family" status also exposed drastically different circumstances. The Jews' testimony was curt and dramatic: Are you married? "Yes." Do you have children? "No, they were killed." The local Germans on the stand, all men, lived with their wives and children, although the lost war did cast its shadow. One farmer said he had three children, one of whom was still missing. Unlike the technically unemployed DPs dependent on UNRRA rations and JDC supplements, the Germans all reported solid rural occupations; as farmers or dairy workers, they were likely to see the Jews' dependence on UNRRA and JDC assistance as the "parasitic privilege" of those who refused to work for their living. The Jews in turn, who vividly recalled the forced labor to which the Nazis had subjected their victims (as well as the grueling conditions in the Soviet Union), had no interest in supporting the revival of an autonomous German economy with their labor.

Ultimately, the U.S. military court rejected all claims of innocence and victimization and sentenced the mayor and the informal head of the DP community to one year in prison; it is not clear whether or for how long the terms were served. The court then pronounced, "Both elements are advised that they must get along together until better conditions prevail for both." All involved hoped and expected that this was a temporary situation and the Jews would soon leave Germany. But in the meantime Germans and Jews were admonished to be "practical" and encounter one another in a civil manner. They had to, whether they wanted to or not, live with or at least alongside each other, and for the most part they did, sometimes reluctantly and sullenly, mostly with a matter-of-fact pragmatism, sometimes with genuine warmth. Indeed, it is important to note that while this was an angry confrontation in which people beat each other up, no shots were fired, order was restored, and expediency, no matter, how grudging, prevailed.[16]

Perhaps the surprise is not that there were violent encounters and intense mutual suspicion or that, as the Berlin Jewish community's journal *Der Weg* noted with mixed sorrow and anger—as if any readers in 1946 needed reminding—that "despite all efforts the anti-Semitic poison that Hitler infused into the German *Volk,* and not only since his *coup d'état,* has not yet been everywhere totally eliminated,"[17] but that there were so relatively few such incidents. Seeking no doubt to downplay the tensions he was assigned to prevent or moderate, Jewish affairs officer Philipp Bernstein was also largely accurate when he insisted in a speech in New York that "it is the sensational isolated incident which is featured by the press whereas the daily, quiet living together never makes the headlines. However, they do live together for the most part in an unbroken though uneasy peace."[18] Another careful observer noted that Jews had "as little to do with Germans as possible, carrying on whatever relations may be necessary in a purely formal and business-like manner" but simultaneously acknowledged that "individually they carry on business relations, sex relations and there are even some cases of intermarriage." "Jews' 'bitterness,'" he added, "has rarely led to active conflict with Germans."[19] As these convoluted assessments suggest, the rather forced insistence on distanced and instrumental relations did not capture the everyday reality, and it was precisely in the "individual" basic and intimate arenas of food, reproduction, and sexuality that relations were both most fraught and most close. Indeed, within this broader context, it is entirely likely that the day after the riot in Oberrammingen, Jewish women handed their babies over to German nannies, who also washed the DPs' laundry. Animosities notwithstanding, they traded American Quaker Oats and white bread for the farmers' fresh milk and vegetables or haggled over the price of a cow they wanted to clandestinely slaughter according to kosher rituals banned as "unhygienic" and disorderly. Such were the paradoxes of German/Jewish life in occupied Germany.

Indeed, the counterintuitive revival of Jewish life in the land of the murderers—albeit under the protection of reluctant but determined occupiers—was conceived from the outset as temporary, a transit station "on the way" (as some DP journals were called) to new homes. It was an emergency relief and rehabilitation measure that depended for its success on the firm belief among all parties involved—Jews, Germans, and Americans—that it would be short-lived and that substantial numbers of Jews would never again become part of a reconstructed German polity. It depended also on the curious circumstance that for many DPs their most recent experiences of either persecution or aid had been with Russians and Poles, not Germans. Moreover, as Jews focused more on a putative future in an imagined Jewish state than on their transitional present on German soil, the British, who tried to keep the doors to Palestine tightly closed, became the "hangmen," the new enemy. Within a year of the DPs' arrival in occupied Germany, Haman, the villain of the Purim carnival, determined to wipe out the Jews until foiled by Queen Esther, had changed his costume from that of Hitler to British foreign secretary Bevin. In another curious twist, many Bavarians, whose capital had after all been the incubator of the Nazi movement, nevertheless deemed Nazism to have been a Prussian intruder, therefore exempting themselves still further from direct association with, or responsibility for, the genocidal regime. This position was reinforced by the Bavarian minister-president Wilhelm Hoegner, a Social Democrat who had himself been in Swiss exile and therefore had no compunctions about announcing to the first major conference of "Liberated Jews in Bavaria" in the Munich City Hall in January 1946 that while "the extermination of a great part of the Jewish people by the National Socialists was one of the most terrible events in the history of a humanity already rich in horrors," he was now pleased to greet "the liberated Jews in a Bavaria liberated from the coercive dominance of the National Socialists." In a by no means unusual move, albeit by someone with genuine antifascist credentials, he reminded the gathering of survivors that the Germans too had suffered in the war and insisted that for the Nazi "criminals" the persecution of the Jews had been only a "means to incite and control their own *Volk*," managing therefore to present the murder of the Jews as just a facet of the great betrayal perpetrated on the German *Volk* by the Nazis.[20]

Finally, the radically anti-nostalgic, anti-sentimental vision of a Zionist future embraced by almost all Jewish DPs, regardless of their individual emigration goals, offered a sense of agency and future "normality" that mitigated the desire for retribution against Germans. There were acts of revenge, there was murderous violence, but for the most part people coexisted and interacted in relative harmony, disciplined by the protective and policing presence of the Allied occupation.

Relations between Germans and Jews became therefore even more complicated and tense after the establishment of the State of the Israel,

the easing of U.S. immigration restrictions, and the formation of the
Federal Republic between 1948 and 1950, when it became clear that a
small minority of those survivors in transit to new lives would in fact
become permanent residents of an only partially renovated post-Nazi
Germany. The U.S. Military Government's turn away from policies of
de-Nazification, justice, and restitution to cooperation with the former
enemy in the service of intensifying Cold War conflicts and the push
for German economic reconstruction and greater political autonomy
became ever more pronounced. Germans were chafing for more control
over their own affairs. Americans and Germans were growing ever more
impatient with the dependent Jewish refugee population, especially
given the social and economic pressures involved in integrating some
twelve million ethnic German expellees. Once the mass of Jewish DPs
had departed, Germans were even more likely to perceive those who
still remained not as victims of persecution but as "asocial" and "homeless" foreigners, "parasites" on West Germany's developing economy. In
1948, a DP leader sourly declared that "Jewish survivors in German DP
camps are an obstacle to Cold War reconciliation with Germany. ...
They are still in acute conflict with the nation which Allied occupation
policy wants to make into an ally."[21] Jewish DPs themselves were becoming more frustrated with their "waiting" life and increasingly anxious to
leave a more assertive West Germany.

Debates about the Future: To Stay or to Go

The truncated community of German Jews, tiny and considerably older
than the eastern European DPs, engaged in their own tormented debates about a Jewish future in Germany. By 1947, the tentative hopes
and occasional euphoria of the immediate postwar period had faded.
German Jews expressed more pessimism about German penitence and
willingness to engage the past than they had shortly after the war ended,
when memories of aid by "Aryan" friends and relatives that had enabled their survival were fresher. In the hard winter of 1946–47, Berlin
community leader Hans-Erich Fabian confessed that Germany had only
now become fully "*unheimlich*" (both eerie and no longer home) to him:
"We see that anti-Semitism in Germany today is becoming stronger by
the day, that wide circles of people have learned nothing on this score
and [worst of all] don't want to learn anything."[22] Not long thereafter he
too left, rather reluctantly, for the United States.

Jews living in occupied Germany were acutely aware that it was not the dead six million—already the established figure—who agitated resentful Germans, but the handful who were still present. Having been visible in Allied uniform, as de-Nazification and cultural officers, as interrogators, translators, and prosecutors, and maintaining their connections to the victors, Jews were perceived once again as much more numerous and powerful than they actually were. Familiar anti-Semitic stereotypes and *ressentiments* were openly voiced; Germans grumbled about the disproportionate number of Jewish lawyers and the unfair advantage they enjoyed over "Aryan" colleagues (temporarily) disqualified by their Nazi past. German Jews hanging on (at least for the moment) in Berlin, once the heart of a vibrant pre-Nazi community of over 160,000, yearned for more understanding, especially from fellow Jews, but they were entirely sympathetic to the many who refused to return or wanted to leave. Refugees knew all too well that the German Jewish world for which they might be nostalgic was irretrievably gone; the number of German Jews who actually re-migrated was extremely small, less than 4 percent (in contrast to a somewhat higher percentage among non-Jews, who might more properly be called "exiles"). Many who remained in the Federal Republic, whether they had survived within or outside the Reich, understood themselves as part of a (self-named) *Liquidationsgemeinde,* a "self-liquidating community," existing only to support those too old and disabled to leave or perhaps as a small beachhead for another future migration from the east. In April 1948, there were some 165,000 Jewish DPs left in Germany; by September their numbers had dwindled to 30,000.[23]

In July 1949, just as the Federal Republic was being established, a remarkable conference was convened in Heidelberg by Harry Greenstein, the last adviser on Jewish affairs to the U.S. Military Government. Representatives of both DP and German Jews, international Jewish organizations, the "other Germany" of anti-Nazi resistance, and the American occupiers gathered to take the measure of Jewish life in the new semi-sovereign Germany. They debated whether there was any justification for Jews to remain in Germany and about the nature of those justifications. Were they purely instrumental—that as long as Jews were there for whatever reason they must not be abandoned, and that Jews fleeing "from behind the iron curtain" were likely to continue to need a welcoming outpost in the west? Or were they existential and symbolic— that the departure of all Jews would grant Hitler a final victory?[24]

Ironically, it was left to the American high commissioner John Mc-Cloy, who had succeeded Military Government commander Lucius Clay when the Americans instituted civilian oversight of an independent Federal Republic, to make the most impassioned case for a Jewish future in Germany. Even if only some thirty thousand remained of the over five hundred thousand who had lived in Germany before 1933 and the several hundred thousand who had passed through after the war, that remnant, he insisted, had immense symbolic significance. The continued presence of Jews, he claimed, served as a kind of barometer of, and guarantee for, German moral rehabilitation. They served as a living reproach to the pervasive desire for normalization and closure of the guilt question, which wanted only to "forget the Auschwitzes and the Dachaus and the other concentration camps and think in terms of the new Germany we are trying to rebuild."

"To end Jewish life in Germany would be almost an acknowledgment of failure," McCloy argued. Presenting what would become his signature remark on the importance of the Jewish presence as a test of post-Nazi West German political maturity, McCloy stated, "What this community will be, how it forms itself, how it becomes a part and how it merges with the new Germany, will, I believe, be watched very closely and very carefully by the entire world. It will, in my judgment, be one of the real touchstones and the test of Germany's progress." It would, however, be the task of the Jews themselves to do the work of assimilation and integration, precisely a mission that the remaining DPs were utterly uninterested in undertaking. "The success of those that remain," the high commissioner insisted, "will to a large extent depend upon the extent to which that community becomes less of a community in itself and merges with the general community."

Eugen Kogon, a Buchenwald survivor and journalist, took a somewhat different and more credible tack to lobby for the same conclusion that Jews should not desert Germany. While still pleading for some measure of reconciliation, he expressed his deep disappointment that there had been "no horrified outcry" about Nazi atrocities and that, on the contrary, the very presence of the remnants had given rise to a new anti-Semitism, driven by resentment of Jews as the visible but unwanted reminders of German crimes, demanding some restitution. His position was forcefully challenged by Philipp Auerbach, a camp survivor from Hamburg who had, in 1946, taken on the unusual position of Bavarian state commissioner for racial, religious, and political persecutees. The campaign for financial reparations, Auerbach contended, was not, as so many, even ostensibly friendly, critics warned, "an unwarranted fixation with compensation"[25] or an incitement to anti-Semitism. It was rather the only means left by which to force responsibility on a "German people" who had "no sense of guilt and are not held culpable by others." Where Germans saw corruption and special favor as well as confirmation of old stereotypes about moneygrubbing Jews, Jews pressed the demand for minimal justice.

New Anti-Semitism, Postwar Scandals, and the "Hard Core"

With the relative normalization of the now semi-sovereign Federal Republic, the newly empowered German authorities and especially the police, long frustrated by their lack of authority over DP spaces, asserted more control. In a notorious incident in August 1949, police action exacerbated a melee, triggered by the publication in Munich's liberal *Süddeutsche Zeitung* of a letter to the editor responding to an editorial commenting favorably on McCloy's Heidelberg speech proclaiming that German attitudes toward Jews would be a "touchstone" of Germany's democratization. A week later, four letters to the editor, three of them supportive, were published, without any editorial comment. The fourth, signed by Adolf Bleibtreu (Adolf stay faithful) with an address listed as Palestrina Street, stated, "I am employed by the *Amis* and many of them have already said that they forgive us everything except for one thing and that is that we did not gas them all, for now America is blessed with them." When the paper appeared, several hundred (or thousand, depending on the source) Jewish DPs, who had quickly interpreted the letter as editorial opinion, marched on the newspaper's office, demanding that its American-approved publication license be withdrawn. In response, German police on horseback charged the crowd, which fought back with sticks and stones and set a police bus on fire. This riotous behavior provoked the arrival of more police reinforcements, swinging their clubs and reportedly shooting into the air. JDC officials and a U.S. Army chaplain managed to calm the crowd, but as in Oberrammingen, order was only finally restored when American MPs—still carrying authority—ordered the Munich police officers to leave the scene.[26]

These events clearly signaled the beginning of the end of Munich as an exceptional space in postwar Jewish and German life and reflected changing conditions as Germany regained partial sovereignty and DPs emigrated in ever larger numbers. A four-block area around the Möhlstrasse in the once fashionable Bogenhausen district had become the undisputed economic, political, and administrative center of the Jewish "refugee nation," in the middle of the Bavarian capital, housing a Jewish high school, all major Jewish and Zionist agencies, as well as UNRRA and American Military Government installations such as the Counter Intelligence Corps, which both hunted Nazis and surveilled Jewish DPs.

The Möhlstrasse, with its bazaar-like atmosphere and multiple temporary structures and street peddlers selling a plethora of luxury or scarce wares, was the commercial hub. A sea of Yiddish signs as well as cafés and bars with American names evoked the district's real and symbolic extraterritorial status. As a Yiddish writer observed, "Should we weep at bitter destiny that has anchored Jews to this land for a short time? But Jews must, live, move, and make a living." The street conjured, he mused, evoking biblical enemies of the Jewish people, "remembrance of a life that the Amalek-German destroyed and uprooted and Jews sense the spring, the Passover air on alien, hated soil," but "the Möhlstrasse also depends precisely on encounters and exchange with those very people of Amalek."[27]

In fact, at least 60 percent of the eager shoppers on the Möhlstrasse were Germans seeking the better quality and lower prices of the goods offered there. In November 1949, right at the start of the Christmas shopping season, police closed the technically illicit shops. They were allowed to reopen at the end of January 1950, but the peculiar lively liminal DP world—arguably the last remaining center of eastern European Jewish life—was shutting down.[28]

All these issues, highlighted by the tensions of the Oberrammingen case in 1946, the debates about a Jewish future at the Heidelberg Conference or among the few remaining German Jews, and the Möhlstrasse "riot," were not resolved and continued to be contested for many years to come. But they did lay the groundwork for an umbrella organization of Jewish communities in the new Germany, which would develop into the Central Council (*Zentralrat*) of Jews in Germany (who, recognizing both the diversity of their membership and the ruptures of recent history, did not call themselves German Jews). On Sunday, 17 December 1950, the Central Committee of Liberated Jews held its last meeting in Munich. The Jewish DP era was officially closed. By 1950, Jewish visitors were noting, with palpable regret and concern, "the almost complete normality" that had been restored to a rapidly prospering West Germany. Jews continued to bemoan the perceived failures of de-Nazification, the restoration of former Nazis to public office, and the infuriating general absence of "public conscience." Ironically, it often seemed that those who were least "guilty" were most willing to accept responsibility, while the great majority of Germans remained awash in self-pitying "moral obstinacy." They obdurately remembered their own victimization, while, as an embittered Jewish envoy reported in 1950, forgetting the crimes they claimed not to have noticed while they were happening.[29]

The resentment of Germans and exasperation of relief officials hardened with time. Germans became increasingly and unapologetically vocal about the "asocial" and criminal character of the remaining "hard core" of DPs unable or unwilling to emigrate, while still supposedly privileged by JDC "supplements." As "Jews," survivors functioned as a kind of living memorial and reproach, to be treated with an anxious respect, but in their everyday role as foreigners and former DPs, they were viewed as unscrupulous operators and a danger to the precariously reviving economy of postwar West Germany. All these problems were exacerbated by the explicit rejection of any reconstituted Jewish community in Germany by international Jewish organizations, on the one hand, and German resentment about the perceived material benefits and political protection accorded this "outsider" population, on the other hand. This dislike was often couched in unflattering comparisons between the "good" German Jews, who seemed to have mysteriously vanished, and the "bad" eastern European Jews, who had taken their place.[30]

Once the mass of Jewish DPs had departed, Germans were even more likely to perceive those still there not as victims of persecution but as "homeless" foreigners (*heimatlose Ausländer*), "parasites" on West Germany's developing economy. Familiar stereotypes about financial and real estate speculation, endangerment of youth and women in bars owned or managed by DPs, prostitution and black-market dealing, filth and disorder, became more common and openly acceptable. The first year of the Federal Republic saw a wave of cemetery desecrations. German police determined to safeguard the currency reform of 1948 routinely raided locales where Jewish "black marketeers" were thought to congregate. Requisitioned German housing was restored to the former tenants. German officials, partially freed from American disciplinary control, were now even more apt to deny that anti-Semitism motivated their actions, insisting that they were merely enforcing law and order. From the perspective of local Germans, many of whom had always perceived the Jewish camps as unjustly favored centers of crime and disorder, the "hard core" who had dug in at Föhrenwald, the very last camp to remain open, were now acting like "state pensioners," entitled to generous welfare, including free room and board, from both the government and the JDC. As the local historian bitingly remarked, for people who insisted that they were victims unable to work, they were surprisingly energetic in pressing their compensation claims.[31] In another particularly blatant resonant statement, and using vocabulary that would have been entirely familiar to anyone who had lived through the Third Reich, officials in Bamberg in southern Germany, anxious about any settlement of Jewish DPs near ethnic German refugees, preemptively declared in 1950, "We know that in certain circles our position against the DPs is seen as reviving anti-Semitism." Typically, they denied any anti-Jewish prejudice and insisted, "None of us are plagued by such thoughts, but the population is justifiably defending itself against people who feel comfortable in dirt and vermin and therefore constitute a dangerous site of contagion."[32] Indeed, there should be no doubt that the philo-Semitism or shamed silence that tabooized anti-Jewish acts or utterances often attributed to postwar Germany not only coexisted with, but was often overwhelmed by, a strong and entirely acceptable anti-Semitism. Even if it was clothed as resentment of and outrage over all manner of perceived shady dealings and social irresponsibility by especially eastern European Jews, and even if the explicit references to "race" had shifted to groups defined by skin color, especially African Americans, anti-Semitism was still clearly legible in a language of *Volk*, hygiene, xenophobia, and victimization that drew from both pre-Nazi and Nazi terminology and practice.[33]

These early confrontations around anti-Semitism and intense debates about the future of Jews in Germany culminated in 1951 with the sensational prosecution in Munich of Bavaria's most prominent survivor, state commissioner for persecutees Philipp Auerbach, who was aggressively pursuing reparations and recognition for all Jews in Germany. Auerbach, dubbed the "Caesar of *Wiedergutmachung* [reparations]" by the German press, was accused of corruption and fraud. He was convicted on lesser charges, including having illegitimately granted himself a "*Doktor*" title, and sentenced in August 1952 to a fine and two and a half years in prison. The presiding judge spoke disparagingly of Auerbach's "Aryan" wife and compared the Jewish defendant's fate in German camps with his own in Soviet captivity. Auerbach denounced the "terror sentence" of a new "Dreyfus case" and committed suicide. After four years of investigation, a commission of the Bavarian Parliament (*Landtag*) concluded that he should be "completely rehabilitated." His trial had become a stage on which postwar conflicts between Germans and Jews played out.[34] The DP camps closed in the early 1950s, the last, Föhrenwald, in February 1957, just about a year after the last German prisoners of war returned from the Soviet Union and two years after the Federal Republic had attained full sovereignty. The Jewish DP era, which had been such a significant but, in most historical accounts, strangely invisible part of postwar German history, was over. But the small and fragile communities (*Gemeinden*) which, led by the *Zentralrat*, took over Jewish life were substantially marked by the presence of those DPs who remained. Membership was divided between about 52 percent DP and 48 percent German Jews, although it was very unevenly distributed according to place (in Berlin, 71.4 percent German Jewish, in Bavaria only 6.3 percent in 1949).[35] Jews lived in West Germany, but for the most part, still with the (by now often symbolic) packed suitcases close at hand and many familial and emotional connections around the world and especially in Israel. The sense of transience that had facilitated everyday encounters among Jewish survivors and defeated Germans during the DP period continued to shape the lives of the minority of Jews who stayed.

The peculiar ambivalent, sometimes contradictory, orchestration of collective suspicion and individual contact, of suspicious distance and pragmatic coexistence, of participating in German life but denying any real attachment, established at a point when there were several hundred thousand Jewish survivors in Germany, continued into the early years of the Federal Republic. By 1952, about 70 percent of DPs had accepted German citizenship, albeit without full allegiance, becoming the peculiarly but tellingly named Jewish *Mitbürger* (co-citizens) of the Federal Republic, and a significant minority chose to remain stateless or maintain Israeli citizenship. In a response that continues to challenge multicultural relations in Germany today, certainly with its large Turkish minority, Germans, who tended to demand more unambiguous signs of commitment to the new state, saw Jews' multiple allegiances as a lack of loyalty and an unwillingness to integrate. Many former DPs, for their part, approached Germans with the proverbial "chip on the shoulder," quick to interpret haphazard slights—a misstep in the trolley or such—as expressions of anti-Semitism. The pattern was not so different for most "native" German Jews and indeed set the model for the next decades of postwar relations.

Postwar Jewish life in Germany was the unexpected consequence of the flight of eastern European Jewish survivors seeking protection from postwar anti-Semitism into the American zone and the precarious survival of some mostly intermarried or "partial" German Jews within the Reich. On 1 January 1959, Jewish communities in the Federal Republic counted 21,499 members, a significant number in congregations formed by former DPs in towns where there had never been a Jewish presence before the war.[36]

The "reemergence" was numerically tiny and fraught with conflict and ambivalence, yet it became a matter of international debate and negotiation and a centerpiece of West Germany's struggle for legitimacy in the international, especially Western, community. Indeed, arguably, the fate of Jewry in postwar West Germany was of more importance to the nation's international relations than to its own domestic politics, which was much more focused on economic reconstruction (the proverbial miracle of the 1950s) and the integration of millions of "expellees." At the same time, and as paradoxically as everything related to postwar Jewish life in Germany, the Jewish community in Germany was isolated, stigmatized by international Jewish groups as well as by the young state of Israel, which refused to recognize Germany or Jews who traveled and lived there.

In Germany itself, all Jews struggled with their future, debating endlessly whether to "stay or to go." DPs were more likely to insist their stay was temporary, but in reality both "German" and former DPs from Eastern Europe were conflicted about their residence in Germany. A significant if relatively small number of twelve to fifteen thousand DPs remained in Germany, generally those with business or intimate ties, including at least a thousand who had married German women.

In the west, these peculiar circumstances proved remarkably enduring, but in the east, which had never officially accepted DPs, the tiny Jewish community became even more marginal with the escape to the west of Jewish leaders—accused of "cosmopolitanism"—in 1953. This rupture cemented the position of the Federal Republic as the postwar German state in which Jewish life could, however uneasily, continue, until the fall of the Berlin Wall in 1989 and the collapse of the Soviet bloc brought, as had been improbably predicted by some Jews who cited the possibility as a justification for remaining in Germany, the next substantial influx of Jews from the "east." The reunification of Germany in 1990 once again fundamentally changed the situation and initiated a new, still evolving revival of Jewish life in a united Germany within the European community.

Atina Grossmann is professor of history in the Faculty of Humanities and Social Sciences at the Cooper Union in New York City. Her publications include *Reforming Sex: The German Movement for Birth Control and Abortion Reform, 1920–1950* (Oxford, 1995), and coedited volumes *Crimes of War: Guilt and Denial in the Twentieth Century* (New York, 2002) and *After the Nazi Racial State: Difference and Democracy in Germany and Europe* (Ann Arbor, 2009), as well as articles on gender and modernity in interwar Germany, history and memory in postwar Germany, and gender and human rights. Her book *Jews, Germans, and Allies: Close Encounters in Occupied Germany* (Princeton, 2007) was awarded the George L. Mosse Prize of the American Historical Association and the Fraenkel Prize in Contemporary History from the Wiener Library, London. Her current research focuses on "Remapping Survival: Jewish Refugees and Lost Memories of Displacement, Trauma, and Rescue in Soviet Central Asia, Iran, and India" as well as on the intersections of family and academic history.

Notes

1. Atina Grossmann, *Jews, Germans and Allies: Close Encounters in Occupied Germany* (Princeton, 2007).
2. Donald Niewyk, *The Jews in Weimar Germany* (New Brunswick, NJ, 2001); Michael Brenner, *The Renaissance of Jewish Culture in Weimar Germany* (New Haven, 1998).
3. Laura Jockusch and Tamar Lewinsky, "Paradise Lost? Postwar Memory of Polish Jewish Survival in the Soviet Union," *Holocaust and Genocide Studies* 24, no. 3 (2010): 373–99; Atina Grossmann, "Remapping Relief and Rescue: Flight, Displacement, and International Aid for Jewish Refugees during World War II," *New German Critique* 117 (Fall 2012): 61–79.
4. The largest single DP camp, Belsen-Höhne, was in the British zone, adjacent to the site of the former Bergen-Belsen concentration camp, but the great majority of Jewish DPs resided in the American zone, which, unlike the British, tolerated the influx of "infiltrees" from Eastern Europe.
5. On the biblical references to the term *She'erit Hapletah*, see, for example, Zeev W. Mankowitz, *Life between Memory and Hope: The Survivors of the Holocaust in Occupied Germany* (Cambridge, 2002), 2.
6. Displaced persons (DPs) were defined as all those who had been expelled, deported, or fled as a result of German wartime policies; ethnic Germans who fled or were expelled from the Soviet-occupied east were not included. Initially, Jews constituted a small percentage, but as repatriation proceeded, they became an increasingly large and visible part of the DP population.

7. Michael Berkowitz, *The Crime of My Very Existence: Nazism and the Myth of Jewish Criminality* (Berkeley, 2007), 145–219; Maria Höhn, *GIs and Fräuleins: The German-American Encounter in 1950s West Germany* (Chapel Hill, 2002), 198–222.

8. Avinoam J. Patt, *Finding Home and Homeland: Jewish Youth and Zionism in the Aftermath of the Holocaust* (Detroit, 2009); Philipp Grammes, "Sports in the DP Camps, 1945–1948," in *Emancipation through Muscles: Jews and Sports in Europe,* eds Michael Brenner and Gideon Reuveni (Lincoln, NE, 2006), 187–212; Jeremy Varon, *The New Life: Jewish Students of Postwar Germany* (Detroit, 2014).

9. Moses Moskowitz, "The Germans and the Jews: Postwar Report: The Enigma of German Irresponsibility," *Commentary* 2 (July 1946): 7–14; Hannah Arendt, "The Aftermath of Nazi Rule: Report from Germany," *Commentary* 10 (October 1950).

10. Kathryn Hulme, *The Wild Place* (Boston, 1953), 211–12; Grossmann, "Grams, Calories, and Food: Languages of Victimization, Entitlement, and Human Rights in Occupied Germany, 1945–1949," *Central European History* 44, no. 3 (2011): 118–48; and Laura J. Hilton, "The Black Market in History and Memory: German Perceptions of Victimhood from 1945 to 1948," *German History* 28, no. 4 (2010): 479–97.

11. Simon Schochet, *Feldafing* (Vancouver, 1983), 22–23, 131.

12. See, for example, Adam R. Seipp, *Strangers in the Wild Place: Refugees, Americans, and a German Town, 1945–1952* (Bloomington, IN, 2013).

13. On "shame" (rather than "guilt"), see Ulrike Weckel, *Beschämende Bilder: Deutsche Reaktionen auf alliierte Dokumentarfilme über befreite Konzentrationslager* (Stuttgart, 2012).

14. See Margarete Myers Feinstein, *Holocaust Survivors in Postwar Germany, 1945–1957* (New York, 2010), 68–106.

15. Account by Philip Bernstein, special adviser for Jewish affairs to U.S. Military Government, cited in Berkowitz, *The Crime of My Very Existence,* 180–81. There are slightly different versions and dates for this well-reported incident.

16. Transcript of Proceedings, Case Nr. 227, Intermediate Court, 27 May 1946, in YIVO, Leo W. Schwarz Papers, RG294.1, Folder 461, Microfilm Roll 38.

17. *Der Weg* 1, no. 1 (March 1, 1946).

18. Hotel Biltmore, New York, 1 October 1946, cited in Berkowitz, *The Crime of My Very Existence,* 195.

19. Koppel S. Pinson, "Jewish Life in Liberated Germany: A Study of the Jewish DPs," *Jewish Social Studies* 9, no. 2 (January 1947): 111–12.

20. Speech recorded in film *These Are the People.* See Grossmann, *Jews, Germans, and Allies,* 168–70.

21. Samuel Gringauz, "Our New German Policy and the DPs: Why Immediate Resettlement Is Imperative," *Commentary* 5 (1948): 508, 509.

22. *Der Weg* 2, no. 9 (28 February 1947). See also Hans-Erich Fabian, "Unheimliches Deutschland," *Der Weg* 2, no. 5 (31 January 1947), 1.

23. Michael Brenner, "Displaced Persons," in *The Holocaust Encyclopedia,* ed. Walter Laqueur (New Haven, 2001), 154.

24. All quotes from conference on "The Future of the Jews in Germany," Heidelberg, 31 July 1949. Minutes edited by Harry Greenstein, adviser on Jewish affairs, U.S. Military Government in Germany, 1 September 1949. See also Jay Geller, *Jews in Post-Holocaust Germany, 1945–1953* (New York, 2005), 72–77.

25. Ronald Webster, "American Relief and Jews in Germany, 1945–1960," *Leo Baeck Institute Yearbook* 38 (1993): 304.

26. 31 August 1949. Report from Mr. Harry Greenstein, adviser on Jewish affairs, to U.S. commander in Germany on riot of 10 August 1949. JDC file 499.

27. David Wohl in *Unzer Weg*, 31 March 1950.

28. See Kierra Crago-Schneider, "Antisemitism or Competing Interests? An Examination of German and American Perceptions of Jewish Displaced Persons Active on the Black Market in Munich's Möhlstrasse," *Yad Vashem Studies* 38, no.1 (2010): 167–94; Anna Holian, "The Ambivalent Exception: American Occupation Policy in Postwar Germany and the Formation of Jewish Refugee Spaces," *Journal of Refugee Studies* 25, no. 3 (2012): 463-68.

29. Dr B. Sagalowitz, "Report on Trip to Germany," April 1950, *Archives of the Holocaust*, vol. 9, 361–62, 368, 377–78.

30. See, for example, "Antisemitismus-1948," *Süddeutsche Zeitung*, 17 April 1948, blaming DPs' "asocial behavior" for anti-Semitism and favorably contrasting the "unobtrusive" profile of remaining German Jews.

31. Eugen Steppan, "Waldram: Anspruch auf Vergangenheit und Zukunft," in *Die Geschichte des Wolfratshauser Ortsteiles Waldram* (1982), 67–68, in Zentral Archiv der deutschen Juden, Heidelberg, file 033.5 (433.6).

32. *Neues Volksblatt*, 13 July 1950. See also *Fränkischer Tag*, 8 July 1950, filed in YIVO DPG 294.2/49/MK483/R5.

33. See Frank Stern, *The Whitewashing of the Yellow Badge: Antisemitism and Philosemitism in Postwar Germany* (New York, 1992). On the shifting language of race, see Heide Fehrenbach, *Race after Hitler: Black Occupation Children in Postwar Germany and America* (Princeton, 2005).

34. Elke Fröhlich, "Philipp Auerbach (1906–1952), 'Generalanwalt für Wiedergutmachung,'" in *Geschichte und Kultur der Juden in Bayern*, vol. 2, *Lebensläufe*, eds Manfred Treml and Wolf Weigand, Veröffentlichung zur Bayerischen Geschichte und Kultur 18 (Munich, 1988), 320. See also Constantin Goschler, "The Attitude towards Jews in Bavaria after the Second World War," *Leo Baeck Yearbook* 36 (1991): 443–58.

35. Harry Maor, "Über den Wiederaufbau der jüdischen Gemeinden in Deutschland seit 1945," Dissertation, University of Mainz, 1961, 19.

36. Ibid., 32.

Selected Bibliography

Berkowitz, Michael. *The Crime of My Very Existence: Nazism and the Myth of Jewish Criminality.* Berkeley, 2007.

Brenner, Michael, ed. *Geschichte der Juden in Deutschland von 1945 bis zur Gegenwart: Politik, Kultur und Gesellschaft.* Munich, 2012.

Fehrenbach, Heide. *Race after Hitler: Black Occupation Children in Postwar Germany and America.* Princeton, 2005.

Feinstein Myers, Margarete. *Holocaust Survivors in Postwar Germany, 1945–1957.* New York, 2010.

Geller, Jay. *Jews in Post-Holocaust Germany, 1945–1953.* New York, 2005.

Grossmann, Atina. *Jews, Germans and Allies: Close Encounters in Occupied Germany.* Princeton, 2007.

Höhn, Maria. *GIs and Fräuleins: The German-American Encounter in 1950s West Germany.* Chapel Hill, 2002.

Holian, Anna. *Between National Socialism and Soviet Communism Displaced Persons in Postwar Germany.* Ann Arbor, 2011.

Mankowitz, Zeev W. *Life between Memory and Hope: The Survivors of the Holocaust in Occupied Germany.* Cambridge, 2002.

Patt, Avinoam J. *Finding Home and Homeland: Jewish Youth and Zionism in the Aftermath of the Holocaust.* Detroit, 2009.

Seipp, Adam R. *Strangers in the Wild Place: Refugees, Americans, and a German Town, 1945–1952.* Bloomington, 2013.

Stern, Frank. *The Whitewashing of the Yellow Badge: Antisemitism and Philosemitism in Postwar Germany.* New York, 1992.

Weckel, Ulrike. *Beschämende Bilder: Deutsche Reaktionen auf alliierte Dokumentarfilme über befreite Konzentrationslager.* Stuttgart, 2012.

Appendix A
Proclamation of the Alliance against the Arrogance of Jewry
1912

The German spirit is outcast,
Victoriously it shall return at last.
Stinging whiplashes will teach you
To know German Strength anew.

The Alliance against the Arrogance of Jewry has been founded because the instances of such arrogance are increasing in number and because the effects on the German nation—its religious, economic, and political life—are immeasurably damaging and horrifying.

The Reichstag elections of 1912 have taken place under the sign of Jewry—that is, under the sign of open and clandestine republicanism and internationalism. "National is irrational" ... was and is the slogan that misled millions of Germans, blinded by the fraudulent Jewish catchwords of international culture and international progress. That the German nation is politically immature had to be demonstrated by democratic elections. Millions of Germans, confused and naive, followed those blinding phrases without suspecting that they served only to hide the chains with which Jewry wants to saddle our nation.

Jewry is international in the sense of Schopenhauer's phrase: "The fatherland of the Jews is other Jews." It is a net thrown over all the nations. Its mesh becomes all the narrower and stronger the more the national strength and determination of individual peoples diminish. ... We Germans don't reproach the Jews for being international in this sense. But [internationalism] seeks to weaken individual Germans as Germans and to destabilize the whole national organism economically and politically. This signifies arrogance on the part of a guest people. Against this and all its visible forms, it is the sacred duty of every German to fight with all his strength.

Jewry works systematically and in mighty associations in every area of German life in order to push out or dominate the Germans and to make Jewish influence decisive. This holds not only for the realm of politics and the economy but also for literature, art, theater, science, the whole educational system, the practice of law, and not the least in the workers' and women's movements.

Richard Wagner has told us: to be German means to do a thing for its own sake! The spirit of Jewry is the opposite: to be Jewish is to make a business out of everything. To want to make the Germans like this is an arrogance of the Jewish guest people, an injury and a danger of the most serious kind for our German nation.... Jews would like to penetrate into the ranks of the officers and reserve officers of our army—into our German army, the shield of the kingdom, the security of the fatherland, and all the best of its German character! ...

Whither we turn we meet the same machinations of Jewry, conscious of the goal and with unlimited money means, always aiming at dominance in any form. Its progress and effects are horrifying. National, intellectual, religious, moral, and physical decomposition of the Germans, the growing economic dependence of Germans upon Jews—these are the consequences and the purposes of such actions. To be sure, the ignorant remain untouched by all this; to the fainthearted, the horror of battle outweighs the abhorrence of subjection. Therefore, we want to make knowers out of the ignorant, to strengthen and encourage the timid. The German nation ought clearly to see the danger threatening its noblest possessions. It ought also learn that it only takes the will to vanquish such dangers.

This is the initial work that the Alliance against the Arrogance of Jewry wants to undertake.

The alliance forswears public agitation. It is directed not against the person and hopes, on the contrary, to avoid such embittering outbreaks. The alliance is thoroughly convinced that German affairs can be served only by German practicality. The immediate objective is dissemination of knowledge about Jewry, about its working methods, its organizations, and its purposes. In this activity the defense against the arrogance of Jewry is contained. The alliance does not want to and will not do injustice to the Jews, nor will it injure justifiable feelings. Our slogan is: protection of the German way of life, inwardly and outwardly, against Jewish *infiltration* and against the Jewish *work of decomposition*. Our struggle is not directed against the Jewish religion but against those characteristics of Jews that operate at the cost of the German nation.

It is high time that conscious Germans unite to inform and prove to their countrymen just how high the time is!

Source: Gottfried zur Beek [Ludwig Müller], *Die Geheimnisse der Weisen von Zion* (Charlottenburg, 1919), 45–47.

Translated by Richard S. Levy.

Appendix B
Reports from American Diplomat George S. Messersmith to the State Department (Excerpts)
1933

American Consulate General
Berlin, Germany, March 31, 1933

Subject: With further reference to the manifold aspects of the anti-Semitic movement in Germany

Strictly Confidential

The Honorable
The Secretary of State
Washington

[...]

The boycott proclamation and the advice which has been issued to-day to employers to discharge all Jewish employees are instances of a brutality and a directness of action which have not been excelled in the history of modern times since the declaration of unrestricted submarine warfare by Germany during the world war. It has been very properly observed that it is only the peculiar mentality and the extraordinary disregard of certain principles which would make it possible for the leaders of a people to promulgate, and for a people to accept such declarations as unrestricted submarine warfare and what is practically unrestricted persecution of a race. One must appreciate that reason is in reality absent from the majority of the leaders of the National-Socialist movement. They have no comprehension of the outside world and of its reactions. They have further than that a complete disregard of what the outside world thinks.

[...]

No. 1421

American Consulate General
Berlin, Germany, July 10, 1933

Subject: A summary of the recent Developments in the political, economic, social, and industrial situation in Germany

Important and Strictly Confidential

The Honorable
The Secretary of State
Washington
[…]
There has been a recrudescence within the last two weeks of the movement against the Jews, not in the nature of physical injury but in
accentuating the steps which will make the life of Jews in Germany
intolerable. According to the "Tempo" of July 7, thirty Jewish physicians were arrested that day by the secret police on the ground that they
were engaged in Marxistic propaganda in sending atrocity propaganda
abroad. It is quite clear that the arrests were due only to the opposition
and denunciation of physicians who wished to get these Jewish doctors
out of the way.
[…]

Berlin, Germany, November 23, 1933

Dear Mr. Phillips, [William Phillips, Undersecretary of State—eds]
[…]
In the Jewish situation there is no change whatever for the better. I am
reliably informed that in Hessen about three weeks ago a considerable
number of Jews were attacked and maltreated so that several hospitals
had many cases. Mr. Flinsch, a close friend of mine, who is the head of
the Association of Berlin Merchants and Industrialists, informed me that
three days ago he received instructions he was to throw out immediately the 900 Jewish members of the organization. Although a National-
Socialist himself, he flatly refused to do it and said, that if it was done,
someone else would have to do it. He went to Dr Schmitt [German
Minister of Economics—eds] and Schmitt told him to refuse. The only
encouraging feature is that Flinsch had the courage to say no and that
Schmitt is willing to back him up, but what will actually happen is yet
in the balance.
[…]

Source: University of Delaware Library, Special Collections, George S. Messersmith
Papers.

Appendix C
Police Precinct Report, Berlin
1938

108. R. H.T.

Berlin, 12 November 1938

Report

Subject: Conduct hostile to the state

Braun, Julius, sales representative, born 13 November 1866 in Berlinchen, residing Berlin 027, Blumenstrasse 31 was arrested on 10 November 1938 at around 9.55 by Police Inspector Lehmann. According to Lehmann, Braun was standing in the entrance of the Jewish eatery "Savoy" in Köpenicker Strasse 29, owned by the Jew Kaplan, warning the waiter of the establishment to close up, otherwise the windows would be smashed by an approaching formation.

Braun is Aryan.

Signed Lübke, Police Chief Constable

Source: Landesarchiv Berlin, A Pr. Br. Rep. 030, No. 21620, fol. 103 108, Police precinct report, 12 November 1938.

Translated by Alan E. Steinweis

Appendix D
Social Democratic Party (SoPaDe) Report on
the November 1938 Pogrom (Excerpts)
1938

[...]

Our reports can only provide a very limited picture of the events that have happened recently. Those in power vehemently claimed that the arson, looting, and abuse represented the spontaneous revenge of the people for the attack in Paris.

In contrast, it is quite clear that the economic looting of the Jews started months ago with the introduction of the requirement to declare Jewish property. The attack in Paris was only a suitable pretext to impose on the Jews a "fine" of one billion Reichsmarks. Without the attack, they would have found another pretext. At the same time, it is clear that the pogrom actions were carried out by SA, SS, NSKK, and HJ and that on the morning of 10 November the German people were as surprised by them as anyone outside of Germany. The fact that here and there the mob used the opportunity to plunder has nothing to do with a supposed "spontaneous rage of the German people."

[...]

Rhineland-Westphalia, 1st Report:

[...]

Many Jews were badly abused, some were beaten to death. Many Jews from Düsseldorf, and more generally many Jews from the Rhineland, were brought to Dachau. In some cases, the Jews fled. That was only possible because the people, even the police and some Nazis, helped them. To this very day, an Aryan is housing eleven Jews in his apartment in X. The Jews don't dare to leave, as they are afraid of continued abuse.

[...]

South-West Germany, 1st Report (Baden):

[...]

Despite the fact that the newspapers reported very little about these operations, the truth gradually filtered through, and the population learned that many Jews committed suicide, especially former doctors and lawyers. The population, both workers as well as bourgeois circles, received the news about the terror against the Jews with disapproval and disgust.

[…]

4th Report:
It was particularly sad seeing children joining in the looting. If anyone shows any excitement or enthusiasm for these actions, it is children and youths. They have no life experience and really see the Jews as criminals and villains, as this is what they are taught these days. Thus the youth considered it important and necessary to join in with the destruction of Jewish property. And because they had been told that everything had been stolen or dishonestly acquired, they did not see anything wrong with taking some pieces in the hope of pleasing their parents.

[…]

Danzig, 2nd Report:
On the main roads of Danzig (old town) on 11 November in the afternoon, I saw five Nazis disguised in scruffy old clothes with axes in their hands. They led a screaming horde of twenty children. Ten steps behind the Nazi scoundrels followed two officers of the Protective Police [Schutzpolizei]. The Nazis went into the small Jewish stores, which almost exclusively belong to Polish Jews, and smashed the entire interior—shop windows and doors had already been smashed the night before. From time to time the group also went into the private homes of Jews. The two policemen kept close to the Nazis and dispersed curious or angry onlookers. They even used rubber truncheons to beat the onlookers—men, women, and children. One could see that the policemen lashed out in blind rage; perhaps they felt a sense of shame. As the Nazis were smashing another store—the Protective Police were at some distance—a woman yelled from the other side of the road, "Constable, when are you going to stop these scandalous actions taking place right before your eyes? One has to be ashamed of this." The police officers did not do anything, but told her to move on. But the woman just stood there, and they did not touch her. In those terrible days all Jews were thrown out of the streetcars of Danzig. At different stops SS men got on and demanded that the Jews get off. Jews who were on the streetcars often were severely beaten by the Nazis. The same happened to Jews who wanted to enter a cinema—something that most of them have practically stopped doing a long time ago anyway. As a consequence of all of this a great many Jews don't dare to go out into the street anymore. They

stay at home and Christian acquaintances and friends go food shopping for them.

[…]

Source: *Deutschland-Berichte der Sozialdemokratischen Partei Deutschlands (Sopade) 1934–1940,* Fünfter Jahrgang, 1938, no. 11.

Translated by Susanna Schrafstetter.

Appendix E
Report from the Mayor of Amt Borgentreich
to the Gestapo in Bielefeld (Excerpt)
1938

Subject: Operation against the Jews on 10 November 1938
17 November 1938
In response to the memorandum of the Gestapo office in Bielefeld, dated 14 November 1938, we would like to report the following from the district of the Amt Borgentreich:

[...]

Large segments of the population did not understand the operation, or rather, they did not want to understand it. Some people felt sorry for the Jews. In particular, they felt sorry for them because their property was damaged and because male Jews were sent to concentration camps. To be sure, these sentiments were not shared by the entire population, but I would estimate that around here at least 60 percent of the population thought in this way. Upon questioning, some people said that it would have been good if all of these things had not been destroyed but rather given to the Winter Relief. Given that the account books of the Jewish store owners were confiscated, those segments of the population who still shopped in Jewish shops are now greatly worried. These individuals must now fear being publicly shamed, as their names have become known through the account books.

By the way, we occasionally hear that German debtors of Jews had been hoping that they would no longer have to fullfil their obligations to the Jews, as everything had been destroyed, presumably including the account books. Their disappointement is all the more palpable.

I don't think there will be any negative consequences, at least not in the long run. Today, hardly anyone is talking about the events of last week any more.

I would like to point out that in the community of Bühne the businessman and farmer Josef Grone said that these actions reminded one of the situation in Russia, and that all the goods should have been distributed to the population rather than be destroyed. He claims, however, that he did not know that the measures had been sanctioned by the government. The Gestapo office has been informed.

Source: Otto Dov Kulka and Eberhard Jäckel, eds, *Die Juden in den geheimen NS-Stimmungsberichten, 1933–1945* (Düsseldorf, 2004), document 368 (2624 on the CD-ROM).

Translated by Susanna Schrafstetter.

Appendix F
SD Reports on German Popular Opinion
during Word War II (Excerpts)
1943–44

Report from SD office in Schweinfurt
6 September 1943

Daily conversation in almost all parts of the population in the cities as well as in the countryside continues to focus on the air raid on Schweinfurt. In certain instances the people remain deeply shaken, especially those who were directly affected, who lost family members and all of their possessions. Morale among these people today is still depressed and not the rosiest. One can often hear the assertion that this was revenge for our actions against the Jews in November 1938. One only wishes and hopes that a second air raid does not come, but it is nevertheless generally expected.

Report from SD office in Würzburg
7 September 1943
[...]
With regard to the [Allied] bombing, one hears assertions that this is the revenge for our actions against the Jews in November 1938. It is also being contemplated whether the Jews will reclaim their homes after we lose the war. For this reason, people are noting the exclusion from the bombing of pronouncedly Jewish cities (Fürth, Frankfurt, etc.).

Report from SD office in Lohr
15 May 1944
[...]
From conversations in air raid bunkers it had become apparent that the severe bombardments are regarded as Jewish revenge, and one repeatedly hears, especially among the rural population, that the Jews should not have been bullied, then there would have been no air war.
[...]

Report from the SD office in Stuttgart
6 November 1944

[In response to the publication of a press report on German casualties]:
"What does the leadership intend to achieve by the publication of images like those in the *NS-Kurier* on Saturday? It should say to itself that, upon seeing these victims, every thinking person is reminded of the atrocities that we have committed on enemy territory, in fact in Germany as well. Have we not slaughtered Jews by the thousands? Don't soldiers repeatedly describe how the Jews were forced to dig their own graves? And what did we do with the Jews who were in the concentration camp in Alsace? Jews are human beings too. We've shown the enemy how they may treat us in the event of their victory." (Numerous voices from all sectors of the population.)

Source: Otto Dov Kulka and Eberhard Jäckel, eds, *Die Juden in den geheimen NS-Stimmungsberichten, 1933–1945* (Düsseldorf, 2004), CD-ROM documents 3647 (Schweinfurt), 3648 (Würzburg), 3718 (Lohr), and 3740 (Stuttgart).

Translated by Alan E. Steinweis.

Appendix G
Statement by Benno Schülein (Excerpt)
1946

Sworn Statement

[…]
When on 8 March 1943 [my deportation] became imminent, Herr [Rudolf] Kammerer helped me to escape. On the evening of 8 March he brought me to the shop of a friend of his in Orleansstrasse. There he provided me with food. On the following day, he brought me to some mutual friends of ours. We then agreed that in early June 43 I would come to his house in Denning. As agreed, he took me in, and I stayed there for about six weeks. During this entire time, he and his wife bore the burden of my presence and my nourishment. In the evenings we listened together to British radio stations and discussed the development of the situation. So I was always well informed about what was going on. Reasons of health then forced a change of hiding places, but Herr Kammerer told me that his house would be open to me at any time. On 3 January 1944 I returned to him. I encountered the same selfless reception. In early May 44 his brother August was denounced to the Gestapo for hiding me. Herr Rudolf Kammerer was therefore also summoned to the Gestapo and questioned. Herr Kammerer told me so when he returned home. The danger that his house would be searched as well was now very real.
[…]
Munich, 4 March 1946
B. Schülein

Source: Staatsarchiv München, Spruchkammern, K 833, Kammerer, Rudolf, Eidesstattliche Erklärung von Benno Schülein, 4 March 1946.

Translated by Susanna Schrafstetter

Appendix H
Statement by Dr Sophie Mayer (Excerpts)
1946

[This statement was submitted in connection with the de-Nazification procedure of police commissar Paul Mayer, to whom Sophie Mayer was not related. "Mayer" is a very common surname in Bavaria—eds]

Dr Sophie Mayer
General Practitioner
Munich 22, Kaulbachstr. 65

Sworn Statement

I am of fully Jewish descent by the definition of the Nuremberg Laws.

In November 1941, my father, my mother, my sister, and I were forced to move into a detention camp for Jews located in the Munich suburb of Berg am Laim.

On 10 July 1942, my mother learned (my father had died shortly before in the detention camp) that she would be on the next transport to the east. We immediately agreed that my sister and I would not allow ourselves to be separated from our mother and that we wanted to share our mother's fate.

When we wanted to say good-bye to old acquaintances, a woman called Lettner [correct: Lethnar—eds] and her daughter, they both declared that it would be out of the question that we would be sacrificed to those beasts. They suggested that we flee and seek shelter with their relative, the police commissar Paul Mayer in Lenggries. The enormous emotional pressure that we experienced led us to accept this offer of assistance from people whom we did not know. Given that there would not be enough space for the three of us in Lenggries, my mother and sister found another hiding place in the Bavarian Forest, and I went to live with Commissar Mayer by myself.

I was welcomed with exceptional warmth by Herr and Frau Mayer, who made their living room available to me, and who fed me on the basis of the ration cards that they had received for themselves and their ten-year-old son. It went without saying that I could not let myself be seen by anyone.

Herr and Frau Mayer took exceptionally good care of me. There was never a sign of impatience; never did they remind me of the danger in which I placed them. In the long period of time that we spent together, they repeatedly helped me overcome my despondency and melancholy. They always provided comfort and lifted up my spirits.

[...]

If today I reflect on the fact that this man was a member of the party and will be thrown into the same pot with those who wore the same party badge, I must say that this was not the case of a party comrade who did something good, but one of a good brave man who was forced to wear a party badge.

I hereby swear to the truth of this statement and I am fully aware that perjury is a crime.

Munich, 15 May 1946

Signature

(Dr Sophie Mayer)

Source: Staatsarchiv München, Spruchkammern, K 3643, Mayer, Paul, Eidesstattliche Erklärung von Dr Sophie Mayer, 15 May 1946.

Translated by Susanna Schrafstetter.

Appendix I
Moses Moskowitz, "The Germans and the Jews: Postwar Report" (Excerpts)
1946

Amidst the ruins of an ancient German city, the leader of a crew that was clearing away wreckage pointed to an inscription on a toppling wall near the site of the former Nazi party headquarters. "What does it read?" he asked. "Die Juden sind unser Unglück" (The Jews are our misfortune). After a moment's pause, he added: "This inscription is incomplete; it should read: Die Juden-Pogrome waren und sind unser Unglück" (The pogroms against Jews were and are our misfortune). That crew leader, who was supervising a crew of "party members," was an old Social Democrat. He believed that anti-Semitism was the beginning of Nazism, and that Auschwitz, Dachau, and Maidanek were the end of Germany.

So clear-cut a point of view is, however, quite exceptional. Not that anyone has found a single German today who tries to justify the mass murder of Jews, the burning of synagogues, the Ausschaltung of a Jewish friend, neighbor, or acquaintance. Indeed, there is hardly a German who doesn't express horror at the mention of concentration camps and crematoria. As a matter of fact, if we were to take every German at his word, the number of Nazis—if by Nazi we mean a conscious or convinced believer in Nazi doctrine—must have been exceedingly small. Most Germans produce one excuse or another to explain away their former association with the Nazi activities. Some will say it was coercion, pressure, blackmail, and superior force; others that it was misguidance, deception, or ignorance. And, after talking to hundreds of former Nazis, one comes to the conclusion that this disclaimer of Nazi belief and conviction is not deception prompted by fear or expediency. It is sincere—and in some ways this makes the phenomenon more frightening. There is a kind of passivity and indifference, a wholesale absence of any sense of responsibility.

A further fact underlines this. If the number of Germans who admit having approved of Jewish extermination is nil, the number who would agree that the pogroms were Germany's misfortune is not much larger. In the recitals of Nazi crimes now featured at public forums and party meetings in Germany, the six million Jewish dead in Europe do not loom large. The role of anti-Semitism in the rise of Nazism to power is rarely discussed in public, and German newspapers have shied away from the subject. To date no one (except the philosopher Jaspers) has arisen in Germany to exhort his people to repentance and expiation for the mass graves of Jews dotting half the European continent.

What accounts for this absence of a sense of guilt, of remorse, and a spirit of atonement? Six million Jews have been killed, and those who inspired and did the killing were Germans. Perhaps these Germans belong to a particular type that is not to be identified with the average run of Germans. Yet even so, the German people are in the position of a parent sheltering a wayward son who has terrorized his neighbors, and this parent has accepted the proceeds of his son's crimes. Sins of omission are sometimes as great as sins of commission, and the failure of the German people to protest against the mass execution of Jews implicates them in this, the most hideous of Nazi crimes. "Am I my brother's keeper?" is a Cain's excuse.

There is in addition a special kind of shamelessness. The Nazis represented anti-Semitism as an emanation of the German soul, racial Aryanism as an integral part of the German's personality. Yet came liberation, and Jewish parentage was at once at a premium in Germany. One corpuscle of Jewish blood was highly prized, while former associations with Jews were invoked as personal recommendations. The files of the Special Branch sections of Military Government are stuffed with documents submitted by Germans in support of their claims to political reliability. These almost invariably refer to past social and business relations with Jews.

Today the German woman who consorts freely with non-Jews also consorts with the Jewish soldier and officer. German women have been known to be on intimate terms with Jewish men who only a year ago were behind concentration-camp gates. Among these women are a number who held leading positions in the Bund der Deutschen Mädel, the Nazi organization for girls. One former group leader of the Bund was very earnest in her endeavors to join her Jewish "sweetheart" in the United States; and her Nazi father, who had been dismissed from office by Military Government, was very much concerned lest his compromised political record might interfere with his daughter's happiness. German men and women have sought and found employment with re-established Jewish professionals, while in hospitals and sanatoriums German nurses work side by side with their Jewish colleagues.

Again the question: Was it mere opportunism that, after their defeat, prompted the Germans to advertise their "Jewish blood" and their Jewish "friends and associations," in the belief that it would help them escape some of the consequences of de-Nazification? The sight of the emaciated Jews who then walked the streets of Germany and the no less pathetic sight of those who congregated in front of the guarded gates of bleak displaced-persons camps could not have inspired fear of Jewish might and power. The demeanor of the "liberated" Jews was not such as to give support to Goebbels' warning that the Allied admirals and generals were so many "agents of Jewish-Bolshevism."

Opportunism there undoubtedly was. But people who adhere to a tenet of faith that expresses their innermost feelings, and in the name of which six million human beings have been slaughtered, do not readily disavow their belief in a moment of adversity. The Germans have not, for example, abandoned their faith in German nationalism and in the resurrection of the German state.

[...]

One saw many German homes celebrating the return of one or more Jewish members of the family. In some cases it was a Jewish wife or husband, in others, a Jewish son-in-law or daughter-in-law. The celebrations were not strictly family affairs. Friends, neighbors, and acquaintances were invited and they came with gifts and presents. The return from abroad of the Jewish wife of a highly placed public official was made practically a gala occasion. Not all of the returnees readily adjusted themselves to their new environment. But in many cases they drifted back to their old circles of friends and acquaintances. A Jewish lawyer was swamped by his old clientele. A Jewish physician now enjoys a lucrative practice among his old neighbors.

One ventures some generalizations: Genetically the Germans are no more anti-Semitic than any other people in the world; anti-Semitism is not an hereditary quality. It is an ancient social disease that most virulently attacks people with the weakest political character, and the weakest spiritual and moral convictions. It thrives best in an atmosphere of lawlessness, sadism, and moral chaos. Had the German people been more mature politically, Nazism would never have come to power or assumed the form it did. Had they shown greater spiritual and moral stamina, millions of human beings would not have been sacrificed to their presumed glory and honor. Those Jews in Europe who escaped the concentration camps and crematoria owe their lives to Gentile neighbors who hid and protected them. But few indeed were the German homes that sheltered Jews. This was not because the German hated the Jew with all his heart and soul, and sought to deliver him into the hands of the executioner. It was because persecution was on the order of the day, and he did not have the moral conviction to oppose it. The German people's deadly sin was—and is today—aquiescence.

At the moment the order of the day is anti-Nazism. The German masses have abandoned Nazism with the same readiness with which they embraced it in 1933.

Certain conclusions seem warranted. The community of blood and soil, in whose name and for whose glory Hitler conquered Germany within and sought to conquer the world without, has been dissolved. [...] [T]he denunciations of Nazis, the refusal on the part of the average German to share responsibility for the events of 1933–1945, and his perennial cries against the deceit and betrayal practiced by his recent rulers, all indicate that Nazism as a political, social, and cultural philosophy is no permanent part of the make-up of the German masses.

Nor has racism, the Nazi form of anti-Semitism, sunk any more deeply into German consciousness than the equally Nazi blood-and-soil philosophy, with its national consciousness founded on "community of fate." After Nazi defeat, longinterrupted courtships between "racially incompatible" men and women were resumed and marriages that were not sanctioned by Nazi law were made. [...] The frequent sight of German girls walking arm in arm with our colored troops offers additional evidence that the racial theory of the Nazis has not survived their defeat. Indeed, an informal poll among approximately one hundred German men and women of all ages revealed that only nine had a clear notion of what the racial theory and the Nuremberg Laws were all about.

In the course of a year this writer interviewed hundreds of German men and women from all classes of German society. Few of them were free from anti-Jewish bias of one kind or another. But the number who betrayed the specific influence of Streicher's propaganda was not much larger. Many of those interviewed made distinctions between one Jew and another, between Jews from the East and West, North and South. None of them betrayed the personal, emotional animosity towards Jews that was to be found, for example, among Polish displaced persons.

There were no typical answers, and their replies could not be reduced to a tabular form, but some comments were more striking than others. A middle-aged tavern keeper remarked that Bismarck had been a greater statesman than Hitler. "Bismarck," he said, "first waged successful wars and then proclaimed the Empire. Hitler first proclaimed a thousand-year Reich and then waged a losing war. Bismarck fought only against one church and went to Canossa. Hitler fought heaven itself and went to hell. Bismarck founded a German nation and it prospered. Hitler founded an Aryan race and it perished. Bismarck fought in alliance with the Jews and won. Hitler fought against the Jews and lost."

The young manager of an industrial plant remarked, "I can understand why a man like Hitler, who dealt with absolutes, hated an Einstein, who dealt with relativities. I can also understand why he hated the Jewish shopkeepers whose prices were relative. But I cannot understand why he hated my Jewish friends and neighbors, who were absolutely good Germans."

[...]

Perhaps the most common mechanism by which the German masses avoid a sense of guilt for the fate of the first and most tragic victims of Nazism, the six million Jewish dead, is to convince themselves that they, too, have been victims of Nazism, and possibly in greater measure than any other people.

Our propaganda to the effect that the destruction of Hitler's regime was not only a necessary condition for the peace of the world, but was also a boon to the Germans themselves since it freed them from the threat of perpetual enslavement, must have made a deep impression on their minds. They came to regard themselves as another oppressed people deserving not blame but sympathy. How can they feel guilty of crimes committed by a criminal who "threatened" them, too? Unanimously they complain that they were deceived and betrayed.

Typical of this attitude is the comment made by an intelligent German business executive, formerly a member of the Nazi party but otherwise politically inactive. We discussed the events in Germany during the past twelve years and we spoke of the conditions that followed the last war, of the rise of Hitlerism, the character of the German people, anti-Semitism and the extermination of the Jews of Europe, the military occupation of Germany, etc. At the conclusion of our talk, he remarked, "Yes, we were all in the same boat. Who knows but that we, too, would have ended up in concentration camps and crematoria. Jews, Germans, Catholics, Protestants, Communists, Socialists, and Democrats, we were all oppressed and we all suffered. Look what happened to Germany! But for the Nazis, Germany would have remained a happy land."

Moreover, to confess a sense of guilt would simply imply the acceptance of the collective-guilt principle. The German masses recoil from this instinctively. In the early days of the occupation there were a few Germans who attempted to convince their compatriots that they could expect no salvation until they confessed the sins they themselves had committed or permitted others to commit in their name. These prophets won no ready listeners and were finally banished from the public forums. Today all the major political parties in Germany emphatically reject the collective-guilt theory. If they disclaim responsibility for the regime, they certainly will not accept responsibility for any of its individual acts.

When all is said and done, the most striking over-all impression is the absence in the German of any emotional reaction towards Jews, be it positive or negative. It was shocking at times to listen to people decrying the evils of Nazism, reciting the horrors of concentration camps, detailing the enormities committed in the torture chambers and crematoria, without expressing one word of sympathy for the victims. A former German army reporter, who witnessed many "offensives" against Jewish quarters in Poland, was unsparing in his denunciation of Nazi cruelty. But at no time did he betray any emotion or express any sympathy with the victims of that cruelty. "I was filled with disgust," he would say, "at the sight of strong armed men running after men, women, and children. Their cries and lamentations were worse than the crossfire of guns and mortars, than the din of exploding rockets. These people knew that they were meeting their doom." If the Germans had been emotionally antagonistic towards Jews, Nazism would not have had to expend so much intellectual effort to enlist the people in the anti-Semitic campaigns. But if they had had more warmth for their Jewish friends and neighbors, the Nazis would not have realized their anti-Jewish program so fully.

The Germans have talked themselves into innocence. We cannot, therefore, expect them to atone for a sin they do not admit having committed. Like human beings in general, the Germans, too, prefer to delete from their minds painful past experiences; because they now realize how cruel, senseless, and unprofitable the entire Nazi system was, they have convinced themselves they always thought so.

[...]

Just as the German masses feel no sense of guilt for the six million Jewish dead in Europe, so the great majority of the surviving Jews feel no particular vindictiveness towards the German people. The day the Landsberg concentration camps were uncovered in April 1945, an incident occurred that was difficult to explain at the time but which, in retrospect, has a symbolic significance. German prisoners of war were on hand to clear the barracks of the dead, to dig graves, burn infested clothes, and do menial labor of every kind. When they lined up for their evening meal, one of the Jewish inmates spotted a pair of shiny boots on the feet of a German soldier. He approached him and forced him to follow him into a vacated barracks. I decided to look.

The half-naked, skeleton-like Jew was stripping the soldier of his boots and in the process ceremoniously addressing him, half in Yiddish and half in German, as follows: "In reality, I should take not only your boots, but your life as well. You and your kind killed my wife and my children, my mother, my aunts and uncles, my cousins, and everybody who was dear to me. You killed all the Jews, burned all the synagogues, and trampled upon everything that was holy to us. Why don't I kill you? Because I only want your boots and not your life. God will take care of you and mete out the punishment you deserve. Who am I to sit in judgment?" The soldier remained seated throughout in stony silence. After the Jew tried on the boots and thought they fitted him, he asked the soldier to step into his worn-out wooden clogs. The soldier obeyed, but his face turned blue with agony.

"They are not very comfortable," the Jew remarked, and launched into another tirade. "In reality," he said, "you don't deserve even these wooden clogs. But what shall I do with you, let you go barefoot? I shall give you a piece of advice. If you want to be more comfortable, pad the inside with some cloth or cotton. Stand up and let me see how you walk. Good, you will get used to them. Now get back to the chow line." With what looked like a pat on the soldier's back, he escorted him to the field kitchen.

If the Jews had been given to vindictiveness, they would have had many opportunities to avenge themselves. But there has been no recorded incident of Jews who took the law into their own hands, unprovoked. Very few Jews regard German property as legitimate booty, even though many suspect that the clothes worn by German men, women, and children were once theirs. To be sure, they deeply resent the freedom enjoyed by those Germans whose rightful place is behind bars, and the comfortable quarters of others who belong in dungeons. But they are careful to distinguish between innocent and guilty, and to think clearly about the Germans as a political and human problem. Among Jewish displaced persons one can hear the most objective discussions on de-Nazification and the political trends of the different German political parties.

The attitude of the Jews towards Germans seems to be guided by an unshaken belief in humanity, a deep sense of justice, plus incurable optimism. A Jewish physician, who, together with his twenty-year-old son, survived six years of the most cruel tortures in Dachau and other concentration camps, once remarked that if it were proven that all the seventy-odd million Germans were capable of committing the crimes perpetrated against him and his thousands of fellow inmates, Jews and minorities in general were threatened everywhere. But he refused to condemn the entire human race by condemning so large a segment of it. In the interest of justice, he preferred to see the million or so Germans who engineered and executed the enormities against the human race hang, rather than to distribute the guilt among seventy million people and reduce their sentences proportionately. Like the Rabbi of Berdichev, the Jews in Germany, native or foreign, bend over backwards to find some goodness in the German so as to justify his existence on this earth.

Of course, German-Jewish postwar relations have not yet even begun to be tested in the crucible of experience. Comparatively few of the surviving German Jews have returned to their former homes and occupations. With the abolition of Nazi discriminatory legislation, they regained their former rights of German citizenship; but that is no particular privilege today, and its liabilities are great. Those who did return and re-establish themselves have found no particular difficulties because of their Jewish antecedents—perhaps because they have been "blessed" with German relatives. Half-Jews, quarter-Jews, and decimal-Jews are to be found among the higher state and municipal officials, in industry and in commerce. At least one of the highest German state officials in the American zone has close Jewish relations and his political position has not been impaired on that account. Indeed, one of the local leaders of the Christian Democratic Union, a school superintendent, is heavily mortgaged with close Jewish blood relations.

So far the Germans' principal contacts with Jews have been with displaced persons, former concentration-camp inmates, slave laborers, and infiltrees—and the Germans have met these people more as groups than as individuals. Their contacts have in a number of instances led to unfortunate results, to rioting and bloodshed. Are these incidents to be construed as meaning that the Germans are beginning to show their true colors again? No, the origin of these incidents is local in character and is part of the general displaced-persons situation in Germany. The Germans are deeply resentful of the latter's privileged status, their preferential treatment in respect to food and shelter, and certain freedoms and immunities they receive that are denied to the Germans. The Germans are bitter because they have in many cases been dispossessed of their houses and apartments, and they begrudge the displaced persons the extra rations they may receive from UNRRA, the Red Cross, and other public, quasi-public, and private organizations. They are also in mortal fear lest the burden of feeding the displaced persons soon be thrown upon the meager German larder. Besides, the lawlessness of certain groups of displaced persons, especially Poles—who have been terrorizing the German countryside, and against whom the Germans were totally powerless until recently because of restrictions on their police power—has immeasurably increased German hostility towards the displaced persons. And the relatively easy access of the displaced persons to black-market merchandise, which they in turn sell to Germans, certainly does not conduce to friendly relations.

The fact that the majority of the displaced persons were brought into Germany against their will, tortured in concentration camps, or compelled to work for a cause hostile to the most vital interests of their own countries, is lost upon the Germans. Such being the case, the tension between Germans and Jewish displaced persons is not necessarily to be attributed to a recrudescence of anti-Semitism—although the personal attitude of the individual German has no doubt been a contributing factor. To say the least, however, this tension on the German side does indicate a painful lack of sympathetic understanding for the most tragic victims of Nazism. After all, the cause of the tension lies in the Jews' more than justifiable resentment over their position in Germany. But the Germans are not prepared to abandon even a minimum of their comforts to make the lives of Jews more bearable.

[...]

The impact of German-Jewish relations is not limited to the several thousand Jews who have not irrevocably severed their ties with their native land. It is of interest to Jews everywhere and also perhaps to the world at large. If the Jews decide to abandon Germany forever and excommunicate it as they did Spain of old, it will be a terrible admission of the hopelessness of the Jewish position in the heart of Europe. The implication will be inevitable that all efforts to regenerate Germany from within are condemned to total failure, and that anti-Semitism is incurable. If the German Jews decide to remain and start life anew, their treatment by their neighbors will be the true measure of the German people's progress towards decency, progress, and democracy.

[...]

Source: Moses Moskowitz, "The Germans and the Jews: Postwar Report," *Commentary* 2 (July 1946), 7–14.

INDEX

surveillance by, 62–64, 66–67, 163
Glazik, Margot, 72
Gleiwitz, 99
Goebbels, Joseph, 65, 68
  and anti-Jewish actions in 1938, 65, 68
  and wartime propaganda, 89–90,93, 96–98, 172
Goering Hermann, 66, 96–98
Goethe, Johann Wolfgang von, 100
Göttingen, 1
Goldhagen, Daniel, 53
Gottlieb, Leo, 63
Greenstein, Harry, 143
Grone, Josef, 163
Grundmann, Margarete, 69

H., Stanislaus, 114–15, 118
Haag, Anna, 87
Haase, Hugo, 29
Handge, Otto, 63
Halle, 53
Hamburg, 50, 53, 94, 109, 121, 144
Hechingen, 45
Heidelberg, 49, 143, 146
Helldorff, Wolf-Heinrich Graf von, 62, 65
Heimtücke, see under malice cases
Hessen, 158
Himmler, Heinrich, 90, 93, 98, 100
Hirsch, Judith, 112, 122
Hitler, Adolf, 71, 132, 141, 143, 173–74
  and anti-Jewish policies, 42, 47, 65, 67, 111, 140
  Mein Kampf, 48–49, 99
  role of anti-Semitism in political rise of, 18, 20, 22–23, 32
Hitler Youth, 45, 62, 65, 67, 73, 160
Hoegner, Wilhelm 141
Holocaust survivors, 5, 11, 85, 131–32, 134, 137, 142
  restitution and financial compensation for, 133, 142, 144, 148
  see also DPs

Holzmann, Hugo, 121
Honacker, Samuel, 49

Israel, 133, 141, 149–50
Italy, 97

Jaspers, Karl, 171
Jacobs, Lilly, 88
Jacobson, Kurt, 72
Jenkins, Douglas, 48
Jews
  attacks against Jewish businesses, 8, 61–62, 65
  census of Jews serving in WW I, 28
  and conversion, 20, 21–22
  deportation of, 4–6, 9–10, 12, 52, 71–74, 86, 91–95, 100, 107–10, 112–14, 117, 119, 167
  East European (*Ostjuden*), 11, 28, 136, 138
  emigration of, 4, 21–22, 111, 133, 136, 138, 141, 145, 147 (*see also* DPs)
  Geltungsjuden, 121
  German Jews after 1945, 142
  ghettoization in Jew Houses, 70, 112–13, 119
  in hiding in Germany, 10, 72, 74, 107–11, 113–22, 131–32, 167–68
  intermarriage, 5, 20, 21–22, 70, 113, 131, 140
  Jewish searchers (*Fahnder, Greifer*), 120
  violence against, 4, 6, 8, 12, 18, 24, 29–31, 46, 49–50, 52, 61–65, 67, 73–74, 111
  "White Jews," 50
  see also "non-Aryan Christians," partial Jews
Johst, Hanns, 90
Jünger, Ernst, 90

Kaletztko, Franz, 65
Kammerer, August, 167